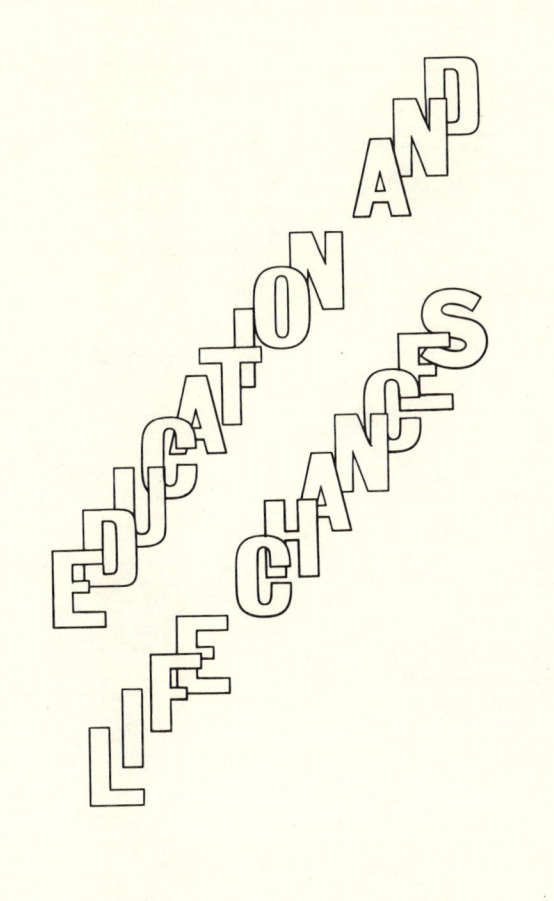

EDUCATION AND LIFE CHANCES

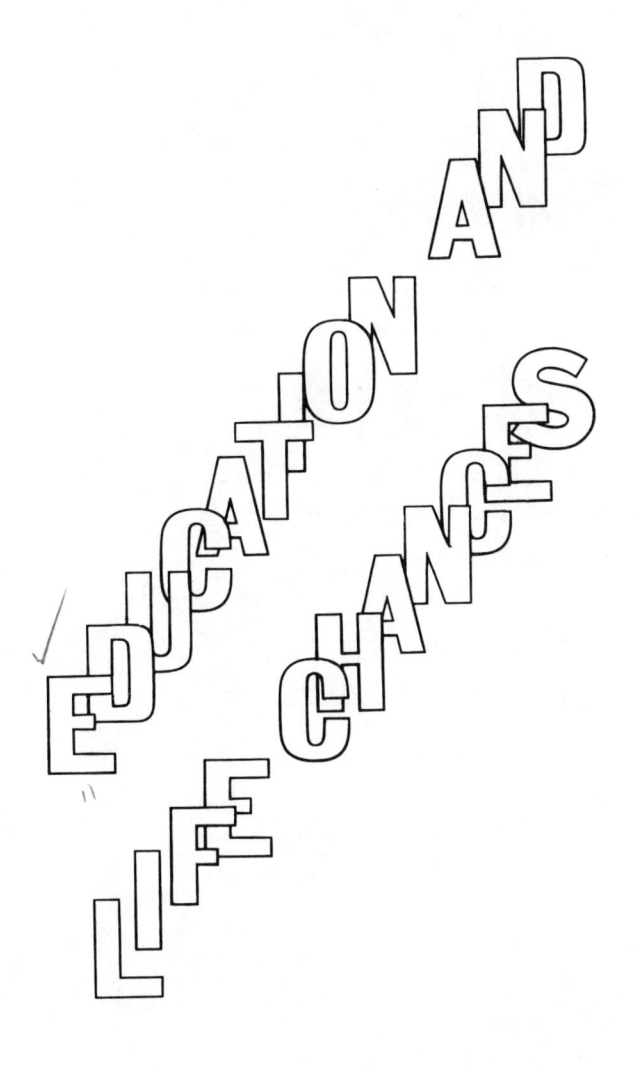

EDUCATION AND LIFE CHANCES

Reprint Series No. 12
Harvard Educational Review

Copyright © 1977 by President and Fellows of Harvard College.
All rights reserved. No part of this publication may be reproduced or transmitted in any form or by any means, electronic or mechanical, including photocopy, recording, or any information storage and retrieval systems, without permission in writing from the publisher.

Library of Congress Card Number 77-88030. ISBN 0-916690-14-8.
Printed by Capital City Press, Montpelier, Vermont 05602. Cover design by Cynthia Brady.

Harvard Educational Review
Longfellow Hall, 13 Appian Way
Cambridge, Massachusetts 02138

EDUCATION AND LIFE CHANCES

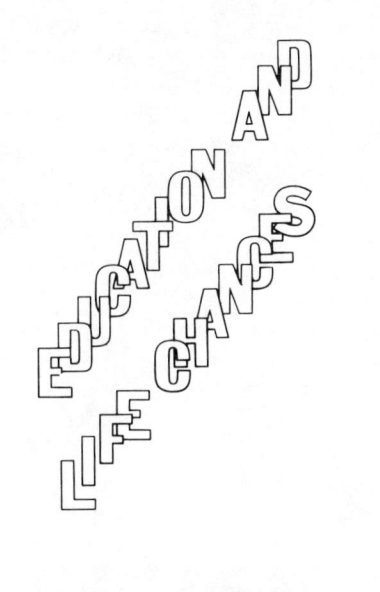

PAUL J. DiMAGGIO
vii Introduction

CHRISTOPHER S. JENCKS
MARSHA D. BROWN
1   Effects of High Schools on Their Students

JEROME KARABEL
53 Community Colleges and Social Stratification

FREDERICK ERICKSON
95 Gatekeeping and the Melting Pot: Interaction in Counseling Encounters

RANDALL COLLINS
123 Some Comparative Principles of Educational Stratification

THOMAS J. LA BELLE
ROBERT E. VERHINE
151 Nonformal Education and Occupational Stratification: Implications for Latin America

W. NORTON GRUBB
MARVIN LAZERSON
183 Rally 'Round the Workplace: Continuities and Fallacies in Career Education

207 NOTES ON CONTRIBUTORS

Introduction

Political debate in the United States has focused increasingly upon the issue of distributive justice. Questions of who gets what, how much, and why have dominated discourse in academic and social-policy circles to a degree unprecedented in modern history. Throughout these discussions the role of the schools has been a constant preoccupation, so much so that, for social scientists at least, the subjects of education and social inequality have become intimately entwined.

The relevance of schooling to the life chances of individuals has long been appreciated. Pitirim Sorokin (1927), the pioneer American student of social mobility, posited the relationship in this way:

> The institutions for training and education, whatever their concrete forms may be, have always been channels of vertical social circulation. In societies where "the schools" are accessible to all members, the school system represents a "social elevator" moving from the very bottom of a society to its top. In societies where the schools generally, or the privileged kind of schools, are accessible only to its higher strata, the school system represents an elevator moving only within the upper floors of a social building and transporting up and down only the dwellers of these upper stories. (p. 169)

In the first blush of optimism, as secondary education became universal and mass higher education first appeared on the horizon, most commentators saw the problem as one of crowding as many children as possible into the elevator and pressing the button for the highest floor. The less capable might grow restive and get off prematurely, but the talented would make it to the top.

By the mid-sixties, however, it became clear that the educational system was not functioning as it should. Despite an infusion of federal aid to the schools, children of the poor and minorities continued to drop out, and children of the well-to-do kept proceeding to college at rates inexplicable on the basis of aspirations or test scores alone. For the past fifteen years or so, social scientists, sharing a general commitment to increasing equality, have expended a great deal of energy attempting to get inside the mechanism of the "school elevator," to understand how it works, and to fiddle with its pulleys and gears. Wielding notepads, videotape cameras, and computer programs, they have returned from their explorations giving very different accounts of roughly similar situations. For example, the more cheerful suggest that education effectively "mediates" the relationship between family background and occupational success (Hauser, 1969; Heyns, 1974). These researchers argue that children with prosperous parents have almost always had better life chances than children from working-class families; but, by allocating rewards partially on the basis of such factors as ability and ambition, schools at least have made the connection less direct. The more skeptical point to the continuing impact of family background on attainment, even after test scores are controlled. These skeptics argue that the educational system serves to reward the rich and penalize the poor in a manner that tricks students into thinking that they have received more or less what they deserve (Bourdieu, 1973; Bowles & Gintis, 1976). Some researchers have even gone into the schools to delineate the processes by which class-biased channeling occurs (Cicourel & Kitsuse, 1963; Rist, 1970). Still others have observed that education may not do much of anything, since knowledge of a person's educational attainment predicts eventual income only marginally better than knowledge of cognitive test scores and parents' socioeconomic status (Jencks et al., 1972). Thus, for example, being born Black no longer has the depressing effect on one's educational attainment it once did, but Blacks still fare less well than equally educated whites in competition for occupational success and financial reward (Hauser & Featherman, 1976). In this view, we can reduce educational inequality by changing the schools; but, to reduce occupational and income inequality, we must change the world (Boudon, 1974; Jencks et al., 1972).

The incompatibility of such divergent interpretations of similar findings has encouraged researchers to look still more closely at the factors that cause variation in school (and life) success and at the processes by which students are selected for reward and failure. The articles in *Education and Life Chances,* all reprinted from the *Harvard Educational Review,* are outstanding examples of recent work on these factors and processes. Taken together these articles highlight the subtlety and complexity of the relationship between education and life chances and suggest both the relevance of separate research traditions to one another and some new directions for further research. Their publication in one volume should be welcomed by educators, social scientists, and teachers of courses in a variety of fields.

In light of this recent work, Sorokin's image of schools as elevators still seems apt. The schools remain institutions that sort and select students, transporting them from their socioeconomic origins to occupational destinations. Much current work suggests the importance of what goes on during the beginning of the ascent in elementary schools for shaping students' attitudes toward school and toward themselves. Jencks and Brown's research on high schools, for example, indicates that students' aspirations and relative test scores are largely fixed by ninth grade. Thus, although high-school differences are inconsequential, elementary-school variation may be important:

> It follows that if the relative size of students' gains varied as much from one elementary school to another as from one high school to another, elementary-school quality would explain far more of the total variance in fourth-grade scores than high-school quality explains in twelfth-grade scores. (p. 293)

In "Gatekeeping and the Melting Pot," reprinted here, Frederick Erickson closely examines an interaction in a specific and fateful school process—the junior-college academic and career-counseling interview. His findings indicate that the outcomes of such encounters are influenced by the degree of ease experienced by participants; this in turn is related, in part, to the ethnic and cultural backgrounds of counselors and students. If, as Erickson demonstrates, the ease of encounter can influence the outcomes of interactions between relatively mature, well-socialized junior-college students and their counselors, how much more strongly must interactional factors affect young children in their first experiences in a formal organization outside the home? Recent work (Bernstein, 1975; Leiter, 1974; McDermott, 1975, 1977; Mehan, 1974; Phillips, 1972) has illustrated how the potent differences between home and early school as well as the institutionalized demands upon teachers' time and patience combine to label students and to produce tension and miscommunication in the classroom.

Such variables as aspiration, industry, and even intelligence, which appear by high school to be relatively inflexible attributes, explaining significant portions of later success, may be formed in interaction with teachers and peers in the early years of schooling. Thus, the conventional distinction between ascriptive (read unfair) determinants of success like race, sex, and parental socioeconomic status and achieved (fair) determinants like grades, test scores, and ambitions (Parsons, 1959) may well be a false one. If, as McDermott (1975, 1977) has demonstrated, school failure is achieved by students and teachers acting together under organizational constraints, more attention must be paid to what happens to whole persons in classrooms and less to the relative weights of attribute variables kept analytically distinct.

Blau and Duncan (1967), Jencks and his colleagues, and the Wisconsin school (Sewell & Hauser, 1975; Sewell, Hauser & Featherman, 1976) have made (and continue to make) vital contributions to public-policy discussion and academic discourse by testing the assumptions of social critics and establishing statistical descriptions of the status-attainment process with which any divergent interpretations must be consistent. But the time is ripe to explicate their findings with research into school processes. Such an inquiry may ultimately do less to clarify the results of survey research than to shift the focus of debate to a different set of questions and a more subtle set of grounded variables. If this should occur, students of school processes must not lose sight of the impact of race and social class on school success. Rather, they must seek to explain the conditions that generate unequal outcomes for students of different backgrounds and to suggest, as Erickson does, ways in which schools can be changed to accommodate and acknowledge the "leakage of ethnicity and other particularistic factors" without which "face-to-face interaction simply could not proceed" (p. 67).

Intimations of such a reorientation have already begun to emerge from empirical work. In their contribution to this volume, "Effects of High Schools on their Students," Christopher Jencks and Marsha Brown definitively demonstrate the absence of consistent effects of differences among high schools on cognitive-test scores and on educational as well as occupational attainment. As they conclude,

> For those who want to alter not only symbols and feelings but individual outcomes, the data suggest a shift in emphasis from differences among high schools to differences within high schools. Most of the variation in adult characteristics arises

among individuals who attend the same high school. Our data do not tell us whether schools can reduce such variation, much less how they can do so, but the data do show that progress on this front is potentially far more important than progress in reducing differences between schools. (p. 324)

Although research on one aspect of high-school life—the effects of tracking—has produced divergent results (Alexander & McDill, 1976; Heyns, 1974), a great deal more work remains to be done.

The examination of school processes should not be restricted to elementary and secondary education. The advent of mass higher education in the 1970s has increased the importance of colleges and universities in tracking and allocating students into different occupations. The school elevator has been transporting more and more students to academe's higher floors but, as they debark, graduates encounter hustling crowds and few jobs. A few hastily return to the elevator and press the button marked "Professional Training"; many more take their places among the white-collar proletariat. But, increasingly, the glut of college graduates has been perceived as a danger to the economic system (Coleman et al., 1974; Useem & Miller, 1975). In response, higher education has been pressed to assume the sorting function once performed by high schools when the secondary-school diploma was the most common terminal degree. In "Community Colleges and Social Stratification," reprinted here, Jerome Karabel contends that, in an age of mass higher education, the community college, far from extending equal educational opportunity, serves as a class-based tracking mechanism to cool out ambitious working-class youth. Elsewhere, Karabel and Astin (1975) note systematic differences in the socioeconomic backgrounds of students in differentially selective and prestigious four-year colleges and suggest that tracking among four-year colleges and universities influences students' eventual success. As Collins (1971) and others have argued, schools serve an important function for employers by granting educational credentials that designate some young people as employable. To the extent that mass higher education dilutes the efficiency of this process, employers must find alternative criteria for hiring. It is therefore essential for researchers to assess the effects of formal and informal college tracking on occupational attainment and to evaluate the impact of higher education's expansion upon hiring decisions and the structure of the labor market.

Two articles in this collection clarify the significance of education as a certifying institution for the life chances of students and the more general embeddedness of schools in the total economic structure. In "Rally 'Round the Workplace: Continuities and Fallacies in Career Education," W. Norton Grubb and Marvin Lazerson place the career-education movement in historical perspective and argue that schools are wholly unsuited to remedy ills intrinsic to the workplace and the economy. Similarly, Thomas LaBelle and Robert Verhine, in "Nonformal Education and Occupational Stratification: Implications for Latin America," warn that if, as evidence indicates, schooling helps people get jobs largely by giving them marketable diplomas rather than by imparting skills, education in nonformal settings can do little to encourage occupational mobility among the poor.

Finally, in a period in which the educational system has come under continual challenge, it is necessary to keep in mind that changes in the form and dimensions of schooling—educational expansion, for example—are not preordained but represent responses to changes in relationships among groups in society. Bernstein (1975), Bourdieu (1973), and Bowles and Gintis (1976) have all written perceptively on the relationship between schooling and the economy. But these and other theorists must take to heart the fact that a variety of political actors attempt to influence different parts of the educational system and that educational change reflects compromises among a range of aspirations and demands, with different interests predominant at different times. Randall Collins addresses precisely this issue in "Some Comparative Principles of Educational Stratification," reprinted in this collection. Collins's essay is an impressive effort, in the Weberian tradition of comparative historical analysis, to enunciate a multidimensional theory of growth and change in educational systems. Drawing on materials ranging in time from ancient Greece to contemporary America, Collins argues that educational systems develop and evolve in response to three kinds of educational demands: the desires of individuals for technical skills needed to earn a living; the requirements of large bureaucracies for efficient and reliable workers; and the demands of dominant status groups for schools that will permit them to monopolize and promulgate their elite cultures. The nature of a society's educational system—the mix of apprenticeship or informal training, bureaucratic institutions for mass education, and elite schools and universities—is thus determined by the struggles of individuals, organizations, and status groups in the educational marketplace.

Seen from this perspective, the persistent relationship Jencks and his colleagues have noted between socioeconomic status and educational attainment may stem from the efforts of the well-to-do to use their resources to equip their children with the technical skills, bureaucratically negotiable credentials, and cultural capital that schooling provides; Erickson's gatekeepers can be seen as acting unwittingly to reward conformity to the cultural style of their own status groups; and backers of community colleges may include both bureaucrats seeking to rationalize credentialing procedures for lower-white-collar positions and working-class youth aspiring to modest upward mobility. Never mind that such youth may not receive the returns from education they expect (Freeman, 1976), nor that industrialists investing in education may not find their employees any more productive or dependable than before (Berg, 1971). The objective consequences of social structures must be distinguished from their subjective purposes, but the latter may be as important as the former in causing educational change.

Schools have always been a focus of Americans' concerns with justice and social inequality. Their association in the public mind with the promise of personal mobility has persisted since the nineteenth century (Cohen & Rosenberg, in press), and there seems to be little social science can do to induce people to turn their attentions elsewhere. Ultimately, then, Sorokin's metaphor was accurate: the educational system—complex, enigmatic, and imperfect as it is—is the principal visible social elevator in American society and promises to remain so for the foreseeable future. As long as this is the case, social scientists will be bound to observe its ascents, note the positions and frequency of its stops, measure the changes in its freight, and interpret its motions to the world.

PAUL J. DiMAGGIO

References

Alexander, K., & McDill, E. Selection and allocation within schools: Some causes and consequences of curriculum placement. *American Sociological Review,* 1976, 41, 963–980.
Berg, I. *Education and jobs: The great training robbery.* Boston: Beacon Press, 1971.
Bernstein, B. *Class, codes and control. Volume 3: Towards a theory of educational transmissions.* Boston: Routledge & Kegan Paul, 1975.
Blau, P., & Duncan, O. D. *The American Occupational Structure.* New York: Wiley, 1967.
Boudon, R. *Education, opportunity and social inequality.* New York: Wiley, 1974.
Bourdieu, P. Cultural reproduction and social reproduction. In R. Brown (Ed.), *Knowledge, education and cultural change.* London: Tavistock Publications, 1973.
Bowles, S., & Gintis, H. *Schooling in capitalist America.* New York: Basic Books, 1976.
Cicourel, A., & Kitsuse, J. *The educational decision-makers.* Indianapolis: Bobbs-Merrill, 1963.
Cohen, D., & Rosenberg, B. Fantasies and functions: Schooling in capitalist America. *History of Education Quarterly,* in press.
Coleman, J., Bremner, R. H., Clark, B. R., Davis, J. B., Eichorn, D. H., Griliches, Z., Kett, J. F., & Ryder, N. B. *Youth: Transition to adulthood* (Report of the Panel on Youth of the President's Science Advisory Committee). Chicago: University of Chicago Press, 1974.
Collins, R. Functional and conflict theories of stratification. *American Sociological Review,* 1971, 36, 1002–1019.
Duncan, O. D., Featherman, D., & Duncan, B. *Socioeconomic background and achievement.* New York: Academic Press, 1975.
Freeman, R. B. *The overeducated American.* New York: Academic Press, 1976.
Hauser, R. Schools and the stratification process. *American Journal of Sociology,* 1969, 74, 587–611.
Hauser, R., & Featherman, D. Equality of schooling: Trends and prospects. *Sociology of Education,* 1976, 49, 99–120.
Heyns, B. Social selection and stratification within schools. *American Journal of Sociology,* 1974, 79, 1434–1451.
Jencks, C., Acland. H., Bane, M. J., Cohen, D., Gintis, H., Heyns, B., & Michelson, S. *Inequality: A reassesment of the effect of family and schooling in America.* New York: Basic Books, 1972.
Karabel, J., & Astin, A. Social class, academic ability and college "quality." *Social Forces,* 1975, 53, 381–398.
Leiter, K. C. W. Ad hocing in the schools: A study of placement practices in the kindergartens of two schools. In Cicourel, A., Jennings, K. H., Jennings, S. H. M., Leiter, K. C. W., MacKay, R., Mehan, H., & Roth, D. R., *Language use and school performance.* New York: Academic Press, 1974.
McDermott, R. P. Achieving school failure: An anthropological approach to illiteracy and social stratification. In G. D. Spindler, (Ed.), *Education and cultural process.* New York: Holt, Rinehart, & Winston, 1975.
McDermott, R. P. Social relations as contexts for learning in school. *Harvard Educational Review,* 1977, 47, 198–213.
Mehan, H. Accomplishing classrooms lessons. In Cicourel, A., Jennings, K. H., Jennings, S. H. M., Leiter, K. C. W., MacKay, R., Mehan, H., & Roth, D. R. *Language use and school performance.* New York: Academic Press, 1974.

Parsons, T. The school class as a social system: Some of its functions in American society. *Harvard Educational Review,* 1959, **29,** 297–318.

Phillips, S. Participant structures and communicative competence: Warm Springs children in community and classroom. In Cazden, C., John, V., & Hymes, D. (Eds.), *The functions of language in the classroom.* New York: Teachers College Press, 1972.

Rist, R. Student social class and teacher expectations: The self-fulfilling prophecy in ghetto education. *Harvard Educational Review,* 1970, **40,** 411–459.

Sewell, W. H., & Hauser, R. M. *Education, occupation, and earnings: Achievement in the early career.* New York: Academic Press, 1975.

Sewell, W. H., Hauser, R. M., & Featherman, D. (Eds.). *Schooling and achievement in American society.* New York: Academic Press, 1976.

Sorokin, P. *Social and cultural mobility.* New York: Free Press, 1957.

Useem, M., & Miller, S. M. Privilege and domination: The role of the upper class in American higher education. *Social Science Information,* 1975, **14,** 115–145.

Effects of High Schools on Their Students

CHRISTOPHER S. JENCKS
Harvard University

MARSHA D. BROWN
University of California, Los Angeles

Few people doubt that there are good and bad high schools, or that high-school quality is related in some way to high-school characteristics. Yet findings from studies of high-school effectiveness have not been consistent. Using data from Project Talent, Christopher Jencks and Marsha Brown show that earlier findings have been inconsistent because comprehensive high schools rarely have consistent effects on test scores, eventual educational attainment, or occupational status. Moreover, the authors find few relationships between high-school characteristics and any measure of high-school effectiveness. From these findings, they argue that, at least for whites, changes in high-school characteristics like teacher experience, class size, and social composition are unlikely to change high-school effectiveness, and that holding schools accountable for one outcome is unlikely to guarantee effectiveness on another. They also argue that the equalization of high-school quality would do little to reduce inequality among young adults, and that high schools should therefore concentrate on the elimination of intramural inequities.

* The research reported here was conducted at the Harvard Center for Educational Policy Research and was supported by the Carnegie Corporation of New York. We are indebted to Project Talent and to James McPartland for the data we analyzed, and to Charles Bidwell, Robert Hauser,

Virtually all educators and laymen believe that a school affects its students' intellectual and social development, and that "good" schools have more favorable effects than "poor" schools. But neither educators nor laymen agree on what constitutes a good school. There is consensus that more resources are better than fewer, but not that any particular resource affects any particular outcome. There is also some consensus that advantaged classmates are preferable to disadvantaged classmates, but it is not clear what specific effects classmates have.

Since 1965 hundreds of social scientists, including ourselves, have investigated these issues. Almost all of us have used the same basic method. We have measured schools' effects by surveying students who attended schools with different characteristics. Usually we have concentrated on students' test scores, but sometimes we have looked at students' attitudes, their plans for further education, their actual educational attainment, their occupational plans, their actual occupational attainment, or their earnings. Using regression analysis, we have then tried to determine whether there was any systematic relationship between the characteristics of the schools and the characteristics of their alumni.

Suppose, for example, that we wanted to know whether an increase in per-pupil expenditure raises students' test scores. Using Y to denote a student's test score, X_1 to denote his school's per-pupil expenditure, B_0 to denote the score of a hypothetical student whose school spends nothing whatever, B_1 to denote the average effect of a one-dollar increase in expenditure, and e to denote the influence of all unmeasured factors, we can write a simple equation:

$$Y = B_0 + B_1 X_1 + e$$

If we have survey data on students whose schools spent different amounts (have different values of X_1), and if we know each student's test score (Y), we can estimate the value of B_1 (the effect of a one-dollar increase in expenditure). If B_1 is positive, we can say that test scores rise with expenditure. If we also compute the sampling error of B_1, we can calculate the likelihood of getting the observed result by chance.

Unfortunately, if the other factors that affect test scores are correlated with school expenditure, i.e., if X_1 and e are correlated, B_1 will provide a biased estimate of the effect of school expenditure on test scores. In order to avoid this problem, we must measure every other factor that is likely both to affect test scores and to

---

Robert Klitgaard, Marion Shaycoft, and the staff of the Center for the Study of Public Policy for critical comments on earlier drafts of this article. Needless to say, none of these organizations or individuals is responsible for what we have written.

be correlated with expenditure. If we have done this, we can write a more general equation:

$$Y = B_0 + B_1X_1 + B_2X_2 + B_3X_3 + \cdots + B_nX_n + e$$

where X_1 is per-pupil expenditure (or any other school characteristic) and X_2, $X_3, \ldots, X_n$ are all the other factors that correlate with X_1 and influence Y. If we have included all such factors, the unmeasured factors that contribute to e will be uncorrelated with X_1. The value computed for B_1 will then provide an unbiased estimate of the effect of expenditure on test performance. (This simplified presentation ignores a variety of problems which we will consider later, such as nonlinearity, interactions, and reciprocal causation.)

Probably a hundred studies in the past decade have used this general method to analyze schools' effects.[1] Reviewing these studies produces two contradictory impressions. On the one hand, almost every study has identified one or more school characteristics that appeared to have a nonrandom effect on test scores or plans. On the other hand, the school characteristics that have appeared significant in one study have not been particularly likely to appear significant in other studies. Findings of this type suggest that the studies in question must use methods that differ in critical respects, and in fact they do.

(1) Different studies use different outcome measures. Some concentrate on the number of high-school students who hope or plan to attend college. Others concentrate on one or two arbitrarily selected cognitive tests. Only a handful of studies have investigated several outcomes simultaneously.[2]

(2) Different studies use different measures of students' characteristics when they enter a given school. Many studies control only parental status. Some studies also control test scores and curriculum assignment. Virtually no study has controlled initial motivation or aspirations.

(3) Different studies cover different cities and states. Although school characteristics are not likely to have genuinely different effects in different cities or states, there are many situations in which their effects would appear to differ.

[1] The most comprehensive review is in Appendix A of Harvey Averch, Stephen Carroll, Theodore Donaldson, Herbert Kiesling, and John Pincus, *How Effective is Schooling? A Critical Review and Synthesis of Research Findings* (Englewood Cliffs, N.J.: Educational Technology Publications, 1974). A few additional studies are cited in Christopher Jencks, Marshall Smith, Henry Acland, Mary Jo Bane, David Cohen, Herbert Gintis, Barbara Heyns, and Stephan Michelson, *Inequality: A Reassessment of the Effects of Family and Schooling in America* (New York: Basic Books, 1972).
[2] See especially Robert M. Hauser, "Schools and the Stratification Process," *American Journal of Sociology*, 74 (1969), 587–611.

(4) Different studies have used different statistical methods to assess the impact of school characteristics and to control for the effects of initial differences among students entering different schools. Some investigators have looked only at the effects of those school characteristics they were actually able to measure, ignoring the possible effects of unmeasured school characteristics. Other investigators have concentrated on the contribution of school characteristics to variance in one or another outcome, without trying to determine how large an effect a change in a given school characteristic might have on the average outcome.

The research reported in this paper tries to deal with each of these problems.

(1) Our data include ten different measures of the outcomes of schooling: six cognitive tests, two measures of educational status after leaving high school, a measure of occupational status five years after leaving high school, and a measure of occupational plans five years after high school.

(2) Our data on the initial characteristics of students entering different high schools include not only measures of parental status and ninth-grade scores on our six cognitive tests, but school grades, curriculum assignment, and educational plans—how much education each student expected to get.

(3) Our sample of schools is national and reasonably representative. The sample of students located after they left school is not representative, but this does not appear to bias our results.

(4) We use a series of related statistical methods to analyze our data. First, we investigate how much of the variance in individual outcomes could possibly be explained by disparities in high-school quality, both measured and unmeasured. Second, we investigate the extent to which high schools that appear to confer an advantage in one area also confer advantages in other areas. Finally, having examined the size and consistency of high schools' overall effects, we examine the effects of specific school characteristics that might be expected to influence each outcome.

We present our analysis in eight sections. Section 1 describes our data, which come from Project Talent. Section 2 examines the effects of students' ninth-grade characteristics on their test scores in twelfth grade, and estimates the contribution of high-school quality to variation in such scores. Section 3 investigates the effects of ninth-grade characteristics on educational status one year after high school, and estimates the contribution of high-school quality to the variance in educational status at this point. Section 4 uses educational attainment five years after high school to check the validity of inferences based on educational status one year after high school. Section 5 examines the possible effects of high-school quality on students' occupational status and career plans five years out of high school. Section 6 examines the extent to which schools that raise scores on one test raise scores on other tests as well, and the extent to which schools that raise test scores also raise educational and occupational status. Section 7 examines some specific school characteristics that might be expected to affect our ten outcomes. Finally, Section 8 discusses the policy implications of our data.

1. Data

Project Talent is a longitudinal study of individuals who were enrolled in grades nine through twelve in March, 1960. The sample design was meant to include roughly 5 percent of all Americans who met these criteria. To achieve this, Talent selected a stratified probability sample of 1,063 public and private senior high schools. When a high school enrolled no ninth graders, Talent also sampled the junior high schools from which the senior high school drew its ninth graders. Ninety-three percent of the sample schools agreed to participate.[3] In theory, all students in each participating school took two days of cognitive tests and answered an extensive questionnaire about their families, plans, and attitudes. Talent also sent followup questionnaires to all the members of its 1960 sample both 15 and 63 months after their class finished high school.

This paper deals only with a subsample of 98 comprehensive public high schools covered by the initial Talent survey. We selected these 98 schools because Talent retested all twelfth graders in these schools in the spring of 1963, using the same tests it had given to ninth graders in 1960.[4] This yielded a large sample of individuals who had been enrolled in the same school for three years and who had been both pretested and posttested. Talent followed up these students again in the fall of 1964 and in the fall of 1968.

Our analyses will concentrate on 17 variables.

Sex is coded 1 for females and 0 for males. We eliminated students who did not answer this question from all analyses. Since 0.6 percent of a sample of students who were reinterviewed in 1972 reported a different sex than they had in 1960, the implied reliability of Sex is 0.988.

---

[3] John C. Flanagan, *The American High School Student* (Pittsburgh: Project Talent, 1964).

[4] In 1963, Talent tested twelfth graders in 118 of its original high schools. Seventeen of these were vocational schools, which we eliminated. The remaining 101 schools were representative of comprehensive high schools in the United States, except that Talent eliminated schools in New York City, Chicago, Los Angeles, Philadelphia, and Detroit. Two of the 101 schools had defective data and one enrolled only American Indians. We eliminated them.

Race is coded 1 if the student said he was black, 0 if he said anything else. Project Talent did not collect this information until the five-year followup, which had a 32 percent response rate. This means that racial data are not available for most of those in the ninth-grade, twelfth-grade, or one-year-followup samples.

SES is a composite measure created by the Talent staff. It is based on father's occupation, father's education, mother's education, family income, books in the home, appliances in the home, TV sets and radios in the home, the value of the home, and whether the student had his or her own room. Students provided this information in ninth grade; when they did not answer a given item, Talent estimated their SES using the items they did answer. We used the correlation between the responses of 1,200 pairs of siblings to estimate the reliability of the composite and obtained a value of 0.785.

Siblings is the number of brothers and sisters the student reported in 1960. The correlation between siblings' responses to this item is 0.895.

Curriculum is coded 1 for all students who said they were in a college preparatory curriculum and 0 for all others. Neither the reliability nor the validity of students' answers is known. If one takes student reports at face value, about one-fifth of all students change curricula between ninth and twelfth grades, with almost as much movement into the college curriculum as out of it. We doubt that transferring is actually this common. We therefore suspect that students' answers to this question depend on their college plans as well as their formal curriculum assignment, if any.

Plans is derived from a question which asked students to name the level of school or college they planned to complete. We do not know the reliability of students' statements about Plans. In ninth grade, only 74 percent answered the question. By twelfth grade, 95 percent did so. The correlation between ninth- and twelfth-grade Plans for those who answered at both times was 0.61.

Grades is the student's average self-reported grade in academic subjects for the fall semester of ninth grade. We scored responses from 1 ("mostly D's and below") to 6 ("all A's"). The reliability of responses is unknown.

Test scores were obtained in both ninth and twelfth grades. We use a (9) to indicate ninth-grade scores and a (12) to indicate twelfth-grade scores. We will look at six different tests and two composites. Two of the tests supposedly measure *Vocabulary* and *Social Studies Information*. The other four tests supposedly measure *Reading Comprehension, Abstract Reasoning, Arithmetic Reasoning,* and *Arithmetic Computation*. We will combine students' ninth-grade scores on Vocabulary and Social Studies Information to create a composite called *Total*

Information. For certain purposes we will augment this composite with scores on Reading Comprehension and Arithmetic Reasoning to create a measure called *Composite Achievement.*

All students took all six tests in ninth grade. In twelfth grade, the tests were divided into six overlapping batteries. Only Abstract Reasoning was included in all six batteries. The other five tests were readministered in only 45 to 49 schools each. Because no individual took all six tests in twelfth grade, we cannot compute Composite Achievement for twelfth graders.

Education(14) is the number of years of schooling we expected the average student to complete in light of his or her educational status fifteen months after high school. Students who were not in school were assigned the highest grade they had completed at the time of the followup. Students who were still in school were assigned 13 if they were in a business or vocational program, 14 if they were in a two-year college, and 15 if they were in a four-year college. These projections proved quite accurate for all groups except those in four-year colleges, who should have been assigned about 15.64 years. Correcting this error would have raised the standard deviation of Education(14) from 1.41 to 1.50 years. *Education(18)* is scored in the same general way as Education(14), but using data supplied five years and three months after high school.

Occupation is the estimated Duncan score of the respondent's occupation at the time of the five-year followup.[5] *Career Plans* is scored in the same way as Occupation. We eliminated those who planned to be housewives. We included those who were currently housewives but who planned to become something else. We know neither the reliability nor the validity of Career Plans.

2. Determinants of Twelfth-Grade Test Scores

The Retest Sample

We had no racial data on 68 percent of our initial ninth-grade sample. This posed a potential problem, since analyses of the Equality of Educational Opportunity Survey had suggested that there were significant interactions between race and the other determinants of test scores.[6]

---

[5] Otis Dudley Duncan, "A Socioeconomic Index for All Occupations," in *Occupations and Social Status*, ed. Albert J. Reiss (New York: Free Press, 1961). Since Talent's occupational categories differed from the coding used by the U.S. Bureau of the Census, we had to make several approximations in assigning Duncan scores to Talent categories.

[6] For data on this point see James S. Coleman, Ernest Q. Campbell, Carol J. Hobson, James McPartland, Alexander M. Mood, Frederic D. Weinfeld, and Robert L. York, *Equality of Educational*

In order to circumvent this difficulty we decided to eliminate the seven high schools in which the principal reported that more than 25 percent of the students were black. A few of the remaining 91 schools may have been as much as 25 percent black. However, only 1 percent of the students who returned five-year-followup data from these 91 schools said they were black. Whites were 2 to 3 times more likely than Blacks to return five-year followup data. This implies that only 2 to 3 percent of the ninth graders in these schools were black. For all practical purposes, then, we are dealing with a white sample. The sampling procedure and school participation rate are such that we expect these 91 schools to be quite representative of the nation's predominantly white comprehensive public high schools in 1960.

Our 91 junior and senior high schools probably enrolled close to 12,000 ninth graders in 1960. Talent tested 11,022. We estimate that 15 percent of these 11,022 students dropped out between ninth and twelfth grades, about 15 percent transferred to another high school or repeated a grade, and perhaps 8 percent were still enrolled but absent on the day the twelfth grade was retested in 1963.[7] Thus about 62 percent, or 7,000 students, were retested in 1963. Of these, 4,938 supplied complete data on all the relevant items in ninth grade. These students constitute our "retest" sample. Since about half the retest sample took each specific test, the sample for any particular test includes 2,400 to 2,500 students.

Taken as a group, the absentees and transfers appear to have been much like the rest of the ninth-grade sample. Those who failed to provide complete data in ninth grade and those who dropped out between ninth and twelfth grade tended to come from low-SES homes, to have low test scores, and to have less ambitious ninth-grade plans than their classmates. The retest sample is thus more advantaged

---

Opportunity (Washington, D.C.: Office of Education, U. S. Department of Health, Education, and Welfare, 1966), and Marshall S. Smith, "Equality of Educational Opportunity: The Basic Findings Reconsidered," in *On Equality of Educational Opportunity*, ed. Frederick Mosteller and Daniel P. Moynihan (New York: Random House, 1972). But also see Christopher Jencks, "The Coleman Report and the Conventional Wisdom," in the Mosteller and Moynihan volume.

[7] We do not know the exact number of students enrolled in ninth grade but not tested. We assumed that 6 percent of enrolled students were absent on survey days, and that another 2 percent were present but not tested. We estimated the number of transfers by assuming that all students tested in twelfth grade but not in ninth grade were either absent in ninth grade or had transferred in since ninth grade. We then assumed that out-transfers equalled in-transfers. We assumed that the excess of tested ninth graders over tested twelfth graders was due to dropouts. The resulting estimates agree reasonably well with other national samples. On dropout rates, see U.S. Bureau of the Census, "Educational Attainment: March 1968," *Current Population Reports*, Ser. P-60, table 1. On transfer rates, see A. Stafford Metz, *Pupil Mobility in Public Elementary and Secondary Schools During the 1968–1969 School Year* (Washington, D.C.: National Center for Educational Statistics, 1971). On average daily attendance, see Coleman et al.

than the full ninth-grade sample. It is also slightly more advantaged than a representative twelfth-grade sample, since it excludes those who omitted relevant items. However, the upward bias in the means for the retest sample does not appreciably alter either standard deviations or correlation coefficients. The regression results for the retest sample should therefore approximate those for a representative sample of seniors enrolled in predominantly white comprehensive public high schools in 1963.

Methods

We define high-school quality as any set of school characteristics that affects the average student's rate of growth between ninth and twelfth grades. This definition means that we cannot say in advance whether "quality" is a function of the resources that school administrators worry about: adequate salaries, small classes, experienced teachers, well-equipped science laboratories, and the like. We cannot even be sure that high-school quality is related to *any* set of measurable school characteristics. We can, however, try to predict what would happen to each student in our sample if he or she attended the "typical" school in the sample. We can then compare each student's predicted score to his or her actual score. Any discrepancy must be due either to measurement errors or to experiences between ninth and twelfth grades. We can then ask whether the apparent effects of experiences between ninth and twelfth grades vary systematically from school to school. If they do, we can impute the systematic portion of this variation to disparities in school quality.

Although we use this general strategy throughout the article, we implement it in different ways in different sections. In this and the next section we will use a technique that is computationally similar to the analysis of covariance.[8] In Sections 4 and 5 we will use a slightly different method, in which we enter a dummy variable for every school in our regression equations.[9] The covariance analyses in this section proceed as follows:

(1) We calculate each student's deviation from his or her school's mean on each of the variables listed above.

(2) We regress students' twelfth-grade deviation scores for each test on all their

---

[8] For a formal presentation of this approach, see Robert M. Hauser, *Socioeconomic Background and Educational Performance* (Washington, D.C.: American Sociological Association, 1971).

[9] The reason for this change is historical. When we began our work, we did not have a versatile computer program capable of estimating a regression equation with 100 variables. We therefore used the more laborious "covariance" method. Once such a program became available, we used it instead. But we did not redo the 18 months of work we had already completed.

deviation scores for various ninth-grade characteristics. This is equivalent to running regression equations within each school and averaging the results, though the implicit averaging procedure is rather complex. The coefficients of individual ninth-grade traits in this average "within-school" regression equation cannot be biased by correlations between ninth-grade traits and high-school quality, since the coefficients in effect derive from comparing students enrolled in the same school.

(3) We use the within-school coefficients from step 2 to predict each school's twelfth-grade mean on each test. This tells us how well the students in any given school could be expected to do if they attended the average school.

(4) We subtract each school's predicted mean from its actual mean to obtain the school's "mean residual." This mean residual provides a crude measure of the average advantage or disadvantage associated with having attended any particular school. We then calculate the variance of the mean residuals for all schools. This provides a crude measure of the range of schools' effects relative to the typical school, whose "effect" is defined as zero.

(5) We calculate the expected contribution of experiences between ninth and twelfth grades and of random errors in measuring both ninth- and twelfth-grade scores to the mean residual, if these factors did not differ systematically from school to school.

(6) We subtract this expected "random" variance from the total variance of the mean residuals to estimate their "true" variance.

The true variance of the mean residuals estimates the cumulative impact of three factors: (a) systematic but unmeasured differences between the students entering different high schools, (b) differences between the communities in which students live, and (c) differences in high-school quality. If factors (a) and (b) are negligible, the true variance of the mean residuals provides an unbiased estimate of the contribution of high-school quality to variation in individuals' twelfth-grade scores. If factors (a) and (b) are not negligible, the estimated true variance of the mean residuals probably overestimates the effects of high-school quality.

Effects of Ninth-Grade Traits on Twelfth-Grade Test Scores

Table 1 presents some descriptive information about the six basic tests and about the Total Information composite. The twelfth-grade means are consistently higher than the ninth-grade means. Surprisingly, only one of the standard deviations increases between ninth and twelfth grades. Four out of six decline. This is not because of attrition between ninth and twelfth grades; the ninth-grade data cover the same individuals as the twelfth-grade data. The reduction occurs because gains between ninth and twelfth grades all have large negative correlations with initial ninth-grade scores. Correcting for measurement error reduces but does not eliminate these correlations, which range from −0.32 to −0.54. This suggests that there may have been ceiling effects on these six tests. Yet very few twelfth graders got every item or every item but one correct. The average reliability was, moreover, as high for twelfth-grade as for ninth-grade scores. Any ceiling effects must, then, have been of a somewhat unusual kind. Whereas "easy" items on these tests must have been such that almost everyone who did not know them in ninth grade learned them by twelfth grade, the "hard" items must have been such that even clever students were not likely to master them between ninth and twelfth grades.

For the five basic tests on which we have the required data, the gains range from 0.545 to 0.778 standard deviation (line 10 of table 1). A moment's reflection will suggest that if the average gain between ninth and twelfth grades is only two-thirds of a standard deviation, school-to-school variations around this average would have to be quite dramatic for school quality to explain much of the variance in twelfth-grade performance. Consider, for example, a student who scored two standard deviations above the mean when he entered high school. This would put him in the 97th percentile. If he were in an unusually bad school and learned nothing whatever for three years, his twelfth-grade score would still be about 1.33 standard deviations above the mean, or in the 90th percentile. Now compare this student to another who entered high school scoring at the 15th percentile. Even if he gained twice as much as the average high-school student over the next three years, he would still only score at the 36th percentile in twelfth grade. Such gains and losses would obviously not be trivial for the individuals involved. Yet even with such dramatic differences in gain scores, twelfth-grade performance would depend largely on what each student knew when he entered high school, not on how much he gained during high school.

A school's average gain is also inversely related to its average initial score. (Arithmetic Reasoning is an exception to this rule.) This does not seem to be due to ceiling effects, since no school has a mean ninth-grade score close to the ceiling for any test. The most obvious explanation is that the easier items on the Talent tests cover material taught in all schools, while the harder items are not taught anywhere. If this were the case, schools with low initial means would rise substantially, since they would teach items many of their ninth graders had missed; schools with high initial means would rise less, since they would teach items many of their ninth graders already knew.

TABLE 1

Statistics on Six Basic Talent Tests and on Total Information for all Students with Complete Ninth-Grade and Twelfth-Grade Data in 91 Predominantly White High Schools

	Information Tests			Skills Tests			
	Vocab-ulary	Social Studies Infor-mation	Total Infor-mation	Reading Compre-hension	Abstract Reasoning	Arith-metic Reason-ing	Arith-metic Compu-tation
1. Talent designation	R-102	R-105	None	R-250	R-290	R-311	F-410
2. Number of items	21	24	45	48	15	16	72
3. Grade-9 mean	11.89	14.45	26.34	29.36	8.90	8.16	29.97
4. Grade-12 mean	14.45	17.29	31.74	35.28	10.25	10.01	37.73
5. Mean gain between grades 9 and 12	2.56	2.84	5.40	5.92	1.35	1.85	7.76
6. Grade-9 S.D.	3.76	4.92	8.00	9.83	2.88	3.24	17.75
7. Grade-12 S.D.	3.76	4.64	7.79	9.35	2.69	3.55	17.58
8. Grade-9 reliability	.767[a]	.834[a]	.886[b]	.922[a]	.740[a]	.718[a]	NA[c]
9. Grade-12 reliability	.776[a]	.817[a]	.883[b]	.919[a]	.724[a]	.765[a]	NA[c]
10. Ratio of gain between grades 9 and 12 to true grade-9 S.D.	.778	.632	.716	.627	.545	.674	NA
11. Observed S.D. of grade-9 school means	1.32	1.90	3.21	2.58	.799	.85	3.68
12. Observed S.D. of grade-12 school means	1.22	1.50	2.81	2.64	.751	1.11	5.30
13. Observed S.D. of mean school gains between grades 9 and 12	.58	.990	1.11	1.78	.493	.52	4.87
14. Percent of observed grade-9 variance between schools	12.3	14.9	16.1	6.9	7.7	6.9	4.3
15. Percent of observed grade-12 variance between schools	10.6	10.5	13.0	8.0	7.8	9.8	9.1
16. Percent of true grade-9 variance between schools[d]	15.3	17.5	17.9	7.3	9.8	8.9	NA
17. Percent of true grade-12 variance between schools	12.9	12.4	14.5	8.5	10.1	12.2	NA
18. Correlation of grade-9 and grade-12 school means	.899	.857	.941	.792	.799	.896	.459

TABLE 1 (Continued)

	Information Tests			Skills Tests			
	Vocab-ulary	Social Studies Infor-mation	Total Infor-mation	Reading Compre-hension	Abstract Reasoning	Arith-metic Reason-ing	Arith-metic Compu-tation
19. Correlation grade-9 and grade-12 individual deviations from school means	.729	.753	.818	.717	.542	.615	.399
20. Number of individuals with complete grade-9 data and retest data	2,536	2,536	2,536	2,470	4,938	2,565	2,565
21. Number of schools in retest sample	49	49	49	45	91	48	48

Notes

[a] Calculated by Shaycoft (see text footnote 16) separately for males and females in 101 retest schools using split-half formula. Value shown here is mean of male and female values.

[b] Calculated by adding the error variances for Vocabulary and Social Studies Information implied by Shaycoft's reliability estimate, dividing by the total observed variance of the composite, and subtracting from 1.

[c] Not calculated by Shaycoft. Reliability was probably low. This was a speeded test.

[d] Estimated as $(s_{\bar{9}}^2 - s_{\bar{e}9}^2)/(s_9^2 - s_{e9}^2)$, where $s_{\bar{9}}^2$ is the variance of school means in ninth grade, $s_{\bar{e}9}^2$ is the error variance of the means, s_9^2 is the variance of individual scores, and s_{e9}^2 is the error variance of individual scores. We assume $s_{e9}^2 = (1 - r_{9,9})s_9^2$, where $r_{9,9}$ is the ninth-grade reliability. We also assume that $s_{\bar{e}9}^2 = s_{e9}^2/N$, where N is the mean number of pupils per school.

Line 15 of table 1 indicates that between 7.8 and 13.0 percent of the observed variance in twelfth-grade test scores falls between schools. This somewhat understates the true variability of twelfth-grade means, however, since most of the error variance is within schools. Line 17 shows that after correction for measurement error, between 8.5 and 14.5 percent of the true variance in twelfth-grade scores is between schools.[10] Our task is to say how much of this between-schools variance in twelfth-grade scores is attributable to school quality.

Within-School Effects of Ninth-Grade Traits on Twelfth-Grade Test Scores

If we define school quality as the set of factors that produces differences between initially similar students in different schools, one obvious way to hold quality constant is to examine the determinants of twelfth-grade test scores within a single

---

[10] These estimates are roughly consistent with Coleman et al.'s estimates of between-schools variance for Northern and Southern white twelfth graders covered by the Equality of Educational Opportunity Survey. Our estimates are not weighted and not corrected for degrees of freedom, so strict comparability with the EEOS should not be expected.

school. In order to get reliable estimates, we examined variations within all 91 high schools simultaneously. We did this by calculating the school mean for each ninth-grade trait and each twelfth-grade trait. Then we subtracted the school mean from each individual's score on each variable. The difference represented the student's deviation from his or her school mean. Then we regressed students' twelfth-grade test score deviations on their ninth-grade deviations. The resulting coefficients are the weighted means of the within-school regression coefficients for all 91 schools.[11] Table 2 shows the standardized coefficients from these regression equations.

The best single predictor of a student's score on a twelfth-grade test is his or her score on the analogous ninth-grade test, but several other ninth-grade tests also enter each equation. The other ninth-grade tests enter these equations partly because no one ninth-grade test is perfectly reliable. But they continue to enter even when the observed correlations are inflated to correct for unreliability. This means that a student's cognitive skill in any given area in twelfth grade depends not only on ninth-grade skill in the same area, but also on some kind of generalized learning capacity that can only be measured using a broad array of tests. This finding is neither novel nor surprising, but neither is it trivial. It means that educational evaluations made on the basis of a single pretest, however reliable that pretest might be, are likely to underestimate the extent to which variations in the posttest depend on initial ability. Such evaluations are therefore likely to overestimate the effects of other traits or experiences, such as SES or school quality.

The only other ninth-grade trait that seems to have appreciable effects on our

[11] We assumed that the effects of ninth-grade characteristics were additive. In order to test for non-additive relationships, we created eight dichotomous variables: Sex, Curriculum, Region (North/South), Urbanism (urban/rural), Ninth-grade Test Score (above the mean/below the mean), SES (above 100/below 100), Grades (above the mean/below the mean), and Plans (college/no college). We then created 28 dummy variables, each of which represented having a high score on two of these eight dichotomies simultaneously (e.g., both being assigned to the college curriculum and having high ninth-grade scores). These 28 dummy variables increased the corrected R^2 for the twelfth grade by less than 0.001. This increase was not statistically significant. Although this is not a definitive test for all possible interactions, it should suffice to detect most large interactions.

In light of this we did not check for interactions between the school an individual attended and his or her measured traits, i.e., for school-to-school variations in the coefficients of the 91 within-school equations for each test. Such interactions would not have much impact on our estimates of a school's additive effects, but they would be interesting in their own right if they followed a systematic pattern.

Furthermore, we did not make a systematic study of nonlinearity in the relationship between ninth-grade traits and twelfth-grade scores. If there are any nonlinearities, they will inflate the residuals for individuals. If they recur systematically from school to school, they will lead to an over-estimation of the role of school quality.

TABLE 2
Standardized Within-School Regressions of Twelfth-Grade Test Scores on Ninth-Grade Characteristics for Students with Complete Data in 91 Predominantly White High Schools

Dependent Variable (Twelfth-Grade Score)	(1) Vocabulary	(2) Social Studies Information	(3) Reading Comprehension	(4) Abstract Reasoning	(5) Arithmetic Reasoning	(6) Arithmetic Computation	(7) Sex	(8) SES	(9) Siblings	(10) Plans	(11) Curriculum	(12) Grades	(13) R^2
1. Vocabulary	0.376	0.141	0.238	—	0.089	—	−0.054	[−0.002]	−0.038	0.048	[0.011]	0.032	0.620
2. Social Studies Information	0.081	0.514	0.148	—	0.049	—	−0.097	[0.008]	−0.025	[0.020]	0.056	0.033	0.616
3. Total Information	0.565		0.199	—	0.071	—	−0.082	[0.002]	[−0.032]	[0.038]	[0.038]	[0.037]	0.706
4. Reading Comprehension	0.145	0.131	0.436	0.044	0.079	[0.023]	0.088	[−0.016]	[−0.002]	0.074	[0.012]	[0.001]	0.569
5. Abstract Reasoning	[0.033]	0.049	0.082	0.373	0.136	0.041	−0.036	0.026	[0.016]	0.041	[0.000]	[0.018]	0.360
6. Arithmetic Reasoning	0.108	0.087	0.118	0.139	0.330	0.061	−0.088	[0.020]	[0.005]	[0.022]	0.040	[0.023]	0.493
7. Arithmetic Computation	[−0.007]	0.055	0.034	0.068	0.081	0.324	[0.015]	[−0.008]	[0.002]	[0.002]	[0.043]	[0.041]	0.202
8. Mean of rows 1–2 and 4–7	0.123	0.163	0.176	0.156	0.127	0.112	−0.029	0.004	0.007	0.035	0.027	0.025	—

Coefficients in brackets are not significantly different from zero at the 0.05 level.

six tests during the high-school years is Sex. Since Sex is dichotomous with a mean of about 0.50, its standard deviation is also 0.50, and males differ from females by two standard deviations. Table 2 therefore implies that on the Reading Comprehension test twelfth-grade girls score about a sixth of a standard deviation above twelfth-grade boys who had comparable scores in the ninth grade. For Social Studies Information and Arithmetic Reasoning, the pattern is reversed, with twelfth-grade boys ending up a sixth of a standard deviation ahead of initially similar girls. The average effect of Sex is close to zero (see row 8), but the variations around this average are clearly significant.

The standardized coefficients of SES and Siblings average less than 0.01 for our six basic tests. This implies that home environment exerts no direct influence on cognitive development after ninth grade, though it obviously exerts an indirect influence by dint of having influenced ninth-grade test scores.

The coefficient of Curriculum is consistently positive, occasionally significant, but never large. Its average value is 0.027. This has important methodological implications. In order to get unbiased estimates of the coefficients of ninth-grade traits, we must hold constant the quality of the educational environment between the ninth and twelfth grades. We have eliminated the effects of environmental differences between schools by subtracting out school means. But students may encounter different educational environments even if they are in the same school. Indeed, tracking is a deliberate effort to provide some students with a more intellectually demanding environment than others. If these environments have important effects, and if these effects are not measured, the coefficients of ninth-grade test scores will be biased. The fact that curriculum assignment has very little impact on test scores suggests that this problem is less serious than we initially assumed. We therefore believe that the observed within-school coefficients of the ninth-grade tests provide relatively unbiased estimates of the coefficients when students encounter identical educational environments.

Effect of High-School Quality

If we use the unstandardized coefficients corresponding to the equations in table 2, we can predict how each student would perform on each twelfth-grade test if he or she attended the average high school. If we make such predictions for each student and then average them for an entire school, we can predict how well the students in that school would do if their school had the same impact as the average school. If the school's observed mean on a given twelfth-grade test exceeds its predicted mean, we can infer that the school did a better than average job. If the school's observed mean is lower than its predicted mean, we can infer that the school did a worse than average job. The difference between the observed and predicted means, which we label the "mean residual," thus estimates the average effect on the student body of having attended that particular high school rather than the average high school. Note that the mean residuals do *not* estimate the effect of having attended a particular high school as against having dropped out. Rather, they measure the effect of having attended one school rather than another. Their overall mean is therefore zero. The statistic of interest is the standard deviation, which measures the dispersion of scores due to attending one high school rather than another.

Line 1 of table 3 shows the observed standard deviation of the mean residual for each test. These standard deviations measure not only the effects of disparities in high-school quality but also the effects of random error. The within-school equations in table 2 leave between 30 and 80 percent of the within-school variance in twelfth-grade scores unexplained. An appreciable fraction of this unexplained variance is attributable to imprecise measurement of students' ninth-grade traits.[12] Another fraction is due to misspecifying the effects of these traits on twelfth-grade scores, i.e., assuming that these effects are linear and additive. Still another fraction is due to not measuring all the experiences that influence test scores between ninth and twelfth grades. The rest is due to random error in measuring twelfth-grade scores. All these errors in predicting individual scores inevitably imply errors in predicting school means as well. The question is how large such errors are likely to be.

Let us assume that none of these sources of error for individuals differs systematically from school to school. If that were true, and if schools were infinitely large, the errors would average out to zero for each school. But in schools of finite size, errors do not always average out to zero in any given year. We can estimate the magnitude of these random annual fluctuations fairly accurately once we know how big the average school is. Line 2 of table 3 estimates the standard deviation of the mean residuals after the variance due to random fluctuations is eliminated.

---

[12] Observed ninth-grade traits never explain as much of the variance in observed twelfth-grade scores as would a "true" ninth-grade score on the same test. (Compare the values of R^2 in table 2 with the values obtained from table 1 by squaring line 19 and dividing by line 8.) This is not an entirely satisfactory comparison, however, since the ninth- and twelfth-grade tests were not alternative forms of the same test but literally identical. The test-retest correlation for two administrations of the same test can, and often does, exceed the internal reliability, which is logically equivalent to using alternative forms. See Shaycoft, "The Coefficient of Internal Precision," American Institutes of Research, Palo Alto, Calif., 1968, offset.

TABLE 3
Mean Residuals and Mean Gains for Twelfth-Grade Test Scores in 91 Talent High Schools

	Information Tests			Skills Tests			
	Vocabulary	Social Studies Information	Total Information	Reading Comprehension	Abstract Reasoning	Arithmetic Reasoning	Arithmetic Computation
1. Observed S.D. of mean residuals	.46	.86	.92	1.84	.49	.59	4.93
2. Estimated "true" S.D. of mean residuals[a]	.33	.72	.71	1.65	.39	.48	4.43
3. Variance of "true" residuals/variance of "true" grade-12 scores[b]	.010	.029	.009	.034	.029	.024	NA
4. Estimated gain if average student is in average school[c]	2.56	2.84	5.40	5.92	1.35	1.85	7.76
5. Estimated gain if average student is in one of best 18 schools[d]	3.02	3.85	6.39	8.23	1.88	2.52	13.96
6. Estimated gain if average student is in one of worst 18 schools[d]	2.10	1.83	4.41	3.61	0.82	1.18	1.56
7. Ratio of gain in top 18 schools to gain in bottom 18[e]	1.44	2.10	1.45	2.28	2.29	2.14	8.95

Notes

[a] Calculated as $\sqrt{s_{\overline{r}O}^2 - s_O^2(1 - R_O^2)/N}$, where $s_{\overline{r}O}^2$ is the variance of the observed mean residual, from line 1; s_O^2 is the variance of the observed scores, from line 7 of table 1; R_O^2 is the percent of variance in the observed scores explained by ninth-grade traits, from column 13 of table 2; and N is the average number of pupils per school, from rows 20 and 21 of table 1.
[b] Calculated as $s_{\overline{r}T}^2/s_O^2 r_{OO}$, where $s_{\overline{r}T}^2$ is the variance of the true mean residuals from line 2, s_O^2 is the variance of observed scores, and r_{OO} is the reliability of observed scores from line 9 of table 1.
[c] Same as line 5 in table 1.
[d] Lines 5 and 6 assume that the distribution of true mean residuals is normal, and hence that schools above the 80th percentile or below the 20th percentile average 1.4 standard deviations from the mean. The assumption of normality is based on the approximate normality of the observed mean residuals, along with the fact that the errors in these observed means are presumed to be random.
[e] Line 5 divided by line 6.

One can think of these "true" standard deviations as the standard deviations that would be obtained if a high school's quality remained the same and its mean residuals were averaged over an infinitely long period of time.[13]

Unfortunately, the factors that lead to errors in predicting an individual's twelfth-grade score probably vary systematically from school to school. There may well have been systematic differences between schools with respect to both ninth- and twelfth-grade testing conditions, for example. This appears particularly likely for the Arithmetic Computation test, which was supposed to be speeded. Misspecification of the equations in table 2 would usually have the same effect. Systematic errors of this type are likely to inflate the standard deviations in line 2, leading to overestimation of the effects of high-school quality. This is not *necessarily* true, however. If the unmeasured factors that contributed to rapid cognitive growth between grades nine and twelve had a very strong negative correlation with high-school quality, they could work to reduce the variance of the mean residual instead of inflating it. Then we would underestimate the effects of school quality.

In order to get some idea of the likely sign of this correlation, we calculated the correlation between schools' mean residuals and the measured ninth-grade characteristics of individuals that influenced their twelfth-grade scores. These correlations were positive for the four skills tests. They were negative for the two information tests. They were statistically insignificant for all six tests. We therefore concluded that the observed correlations were probably due to sampling error, and that the true correlations for a larger sample of schools would be close to zero. By analogy, we inferred that the correlations between school quality and unmeasured ninth-grade traits were also close to zero. If this line of reasoning is correct, the standard deviations in line 2 must overestimate the effects of school quality.[14] We doubt that the bias is large, however, and we will ignore it in subsequent computations.

---

[13] The ratio of the standard deviation in line 2 to the standard deviation in line 1 estimates the correlation between the mean residual for a single year and the "true" mean residual averaged over many years, assuming the latter is stable. The square of this ratio is comparable to a reliability coefficient. In priniple, it predicts the correlation between mean residuals in sequential years.

[14] We can think of schools' mean twelfth-grade test scores (T) as the sum of four components: a predicted score (P) based on measured ninth-grade traits, an adjustment (e) due to random errors in measuring either ninth- or twelfth-grade traits, an adjustment (E) due to systematic errors in measuring either ninth- or twelfth-grade traits, and an adjustment (S) due to the effects of school and community characteristics. The mean residual (R) is the observed mean minus the predicted mean, $T - P$. Since $T = P + e + E + S$, it follows that $R = e + E + S$, and that $s_R^2 = s_e^2 + s_E^2 + s_S^2 + 2s_e s_E r_{e,E} + 2s_e s_S r_{e,S} + 2s_E s_S r_{E,S}$. But since e is random, $r_{e,E} = r_{e,S} = 0$. Then $s_R^2 - s_e^2 = s_E^2 + s_S^2 +$

Line 3 of table 3 estimates the probable contribution of disparities in high-school quality to the total variance of twelfth-grade test scores. Variations in high-school quality explain between 0.9 and 3.4 percent of the twelfth-grade variance. Line 4 gives the estimated gain between ninth and twelfth grade on each test in the average school. Line 5 estimates the true gain in the 18 most effective schools (i.e., the top fifth of the sample), while line 6 estimates the true gain in the 18 least effective schools.

Line 7 shows the ratio of estimated gains in the 18 most effective schools to gains in the 18 least effective schools. Ignoring the deviant case of Arithmetic Computation, where we suspect systematic errors in test administration, it seems clear that students gain about twice as much in the "best" schools as in the "worst." The reason high-school quality explains so little of the variance in the twelfth-grade scores is not, as Jencks et al.[15] and others have asserted, that all high schools have about the same effect on cognitive development. Rather, the reason is that high schools have relatively small effects on cognitive development, at least compared to the enormous variation among entering students. Thus, if students start high school at the 50th percentile on Arithmetic Reasoning, and attend one of the 18 worst high schools, they can expect to gain $1.85 - 1.18 = 0.67$ points less than if they had attended the average school. From table 1, we can calculate the true twelfth-grade standard deviation for individuals to be $(3.55)(\sqrt{0.765}) = 3.10$. So these students will score $0.67/3.10 = 0.216$ standard deviations below the mean in twelfth grade. This will put them at the 41st percentile. If they attend one of the 18 best high schools, they will gain more than twice as much as they would in one of the 18 worst, and will end up at the 58th percentile. These calculations suggest that even substantial variations in high-school quality produce only modest changes in a student's percentile rank between ninth and twelfth grades.

All the foregoing calculations involve averaging schools' effects on all sorts of students. Certain groups of students may, however, be particularly susceptible to variations in high-school quality. To test this possibility we split the sample into those who were above and below the mean on each of six traits: ninth-grade Total Information, ninth-grade Grades, ninth-grade Curriculum, ninth-grade Plans, SES,

---

$2s_{E}s_{S}r_{E,S}$. The estimated standard deviation in line 2 is $\sqrt{s_R^2 - s_e^2} = \sqrt{s_E^2 + s_S^2 + 2s_{E}s_{S}r_{E,S}}$. Thus if $r_{E,S} \geq 0$, the value in line 2 will be upwardly biased by an amount equal to $s_E^2 + 2s_{E}s_{S}r_{E,S}$. It can even be upwardly biased when $r_{E,S} < 0$, so long as $s_E^2 + 2s_{E}s_{S}r_{E,S} > 0$. The bias will be downward only if $s_E^2 + 2s_{E}r_{E,S} < 0$.

[15] Jencks et al., *Inequality*.

and Sex. We then calculated the mean residual for each of these twelve groups in each school. The standard deviations of the mean residuals for those who were above the mean on SES, Plans, Curriculum, and Sex did not differ consistently from the standard deviations for those who were below the mean. This suggests that none of these groups is unusually sensitive to variations in high-school quality. But the standard deviations for students with low ninth-grade Information scores or low Grades consistently exceeded those for students with high ninth-grade Information scores and Grades. This could mean that students with low ninth-grade scores are unusually sensitive to disparities in high-school quality. The evidence is hardly conclusive, however, since low-scoring ninth graders may have more variable twelfth-grade scores than high-scoring ninth graders even when both groups attend the same school. Since the standard deviation of the mean residuals for low-scoring ninth graders was only 1.33 times that for high-scoring ninth graders, we did not pursue the question.

High schools' effects might be larger if we looked at tests covering material that is part of the formal curriculum. Shaycoft's analysis of the Talent retest data shows, for example, that virtually no ninth grader knew any advanced high-school math, that some twelfth graders knew some advanced math, and that twelfth-grade Advanced Math scores, unlike scores on other tests, were related to having taken specific math courses.[16]

Our conclusions might also have been quite different if we had had comparable data for elementary schools. Students learn so much between first and fourth grades that educators almost never use the same tests to assess them at both times. This makes it hard to say exactly how much they gain. But using the logic of the Stanford-Binet, a first grader with the "mental age" of the average fourth grader has an IQ of about $(9/6)(100) = 150$ and ranks about three standard deviations above the mean for all first graders. This implies that the average student gains about three standard deviations between first and fourth grades, compared to 0.65 standard deviations between ninth and twelfth grades. It follows that if the relative size of students' gains varied as much from one elementary school to another as from one high school to another, elementary-school quality would explain far more of the total variance in fourth-grade scores than high-school quality explains in twelfth-grade scores.

---

[16] Marion F. Shaycoft, *The High School Years: Growth in Cognitive Skills* (Pittsburgh: American Institutes of Research and Project Talent, University of Pittsburgh, 1967).

3. Determinants of Educational Status One Year After High School

In the fall of 1964 Talent sent a followup questionnaire to all students who had been tested as ninth graders in 1960. Respondents who had stayed in school and progressed at the normal rate were thus entering their sophomore year in college. The response rate for students from our 91 predominantly white high schools was 56 percent. We eliminated 30 percent of these respondents because they had failed to answer one or more ninth-grade items—usually the item about their educational plans. Our one-year followup sample thus consisted of 4,315 students with complete ninth-grade data and one-year followup data, or 39 percent of the initial sample. We estimate that 85 to 95 percent of these students spent their entire high-school careers in one of our 91 schools, while 5 to 15 percent transferred to another high school at some point after the ninth-grade survey. Unfortunately, we could not identify these transfer students. The means for our one-year followup sample exceed the means for the initial ninth-grade sample, but the standard deviations and correlations are quite close to those for the ninth-grade sample. Regression results should therefore be relatively unbiased.

Within-School Effects of Ninth-Grade Traits on Education(14)

We used the same procedure to estimate high schools' effects on educational status one year after graduation that we used to estimate their effects on twelfth-grade test scores. First, we subtracted the school mean from each student's score on each variable. Then we regressed each student's Education(14) deviation score on his or her deviation scores for Total Information, Reading Comprehension, Arithmetic Reasoning, SES, Siblings, Sex, Plans, Grades, and Curriculum. This yielded the average within-school relationships shown in table 4. Line 1 of table 4 shows the average within-school correlation of Education(14) with each ninth-grade trait. Line 2 shows the standardized coefficients when all ninth-grade variables are used simultaneously to predict Education(14). The best single predictor of educational status one year after high school is educational Plans at the start of high school. But Education(14) is also influenced by other ninth-grade traits, notably test scores and SES. This means that students' chances of realizing their ninth-grade plans are significantly affected by their SES and by their test scores in ninth grade. Of the three tests shown in table 4, Total Information is the best predictor of educational status one year after high school, Reading Comprehension is the second best, and Arithmetic Reasoning is third. (Abstract Reasoning and Arithmetic Computation had small and statistically insignificant effects on Education(14) once the other tests were controlled, so we deleted them from the equation.)

The modest coefficient for Grades should not be taken as definitive. Grades were reported for the first semester of ninth grade. These reports correlated only 0.492 with twelfth-grade reports of average grades over the three previous years. The latter predict Education(14) far better than the former.

The small coefficient of ninth-grade curriculum should also be interpreted cautiously. Students report considerable movement both into and out of the academic curriculum between ninth and twelfth grades. Twelfth-grade curriculum assignment is much more strongly related to subsequent educational attainment than ninth-grade assignment.

The regression equation in table 4 leaves 58.6 percent of the within-school variance in Education(14) unexplained. We explored three possible reasons for this unexplained variance. First, we adjusted the observed correlations to eliminate the effects of measurement error in the four ninth-grade test scores, SES, and Siblings. These adjustments explained only another 1.4 percent of the within-school variance. Second, we looked for interactions among the measured variables by including 28 dummy variables representing all the two-way interactions among 8 independent variables. These interactions raised R^2 by 0.004 after correction for degrees of freedom. Neither of these increases seemed large enough to be of substantive interest. We therefore decided not to complicate our subsequent analyses by adjusting for measurement error or including interactions. Finally, we examined the effects of 107 other student characteristics measured in ninth grade. Four of these traits were significant at the 0.01 level. Ninth graders who planned to get vocational training after high school ended up with slightly less education than our coding of ninth-grade Plans implied they should, but the discrepancy did not seem large enough to justify adding another variable to our equation. Ninth graders whose fathers were active in a church, a civic organization, or the PTA also got less education than their other traits implied they should. Since none of these three effects was large, and since none made intuitive sense, we decided to ignore these variables in subsequent analyses.[17]

---

[17] We used the dummy variables listed in footnote 11 to test for interactions. The 107 additional ninth-grade traits came from questions 47–52, 54–56, 60–63, 106–114, 118, 137–157, 168, 173, 176, 190, 191, 198, 201, 205, 208, 211, 212, 219, 220, 222–225, 230, 231, 239, 297–303, and 305 of Talent's Student Information Blank which is reprinted in *The Project Talent Data Blank: A Handbook* (Palo Alto, Calif.: American Institutes of Research, 1972).

TABLE 4
Within-School Relationship of Education(14) to Ninth-Grade Characteristics of 4,315 Students in 91 Predominantly White High Schools

	Sex	SES	Siblings	Total Information	Reading Comprehension	Arithmetic Reasoning	Grades	Curriculum	Plans[a]	Standard Error	R^2
1. Observed correlation	−.134	.424	−.167	.481	.427	.368	.296	.445	.533		
2. Standardized regression coefficient	−.076	.178	−.031	.108	.107	.051	.085	.112	.246	.766	.414
3. Unstandardized regression coefficient	−.207	.0276	−.0212	.0199	.0154	.0217	.110	.319	.236	1.026	.414
4. Reliability	.988	.785	.895	.886	.922	.718	NA	NA	NA		
5. Estimated true correlation with Education(14)	−.136	.479	−.187	.511	.445	.434	NA	NA	NA		.430[b]

All coefficients are significant at the 0.05 level.
[a]Plans were coded 0 to 6 in these analyses.
[b]Calculated from a matrix in which the observed correlations involving test scores, SES, and Siblings were divided by the square root of their reliabilities, while other correlations were left unchanged.

Effects of High-School Quality on Education(14)

The standard deviation of Education(14) is 1.41 years. The standard deviation of school means is 0.45 year, indicating that $(0.45)^2/(1.41)^2 = 10.1$ percent of the variance in Education(14) is between schools. In order to assess the contribution of high-school quality to the between-schools variance, we estimated each school's mean residual for Education(14), using the same procedures we had used to estimate mean twelfth-grade test score residuals.[18] The standard deviation of schools' mean residuals was 0.26 year, indicating that 3.4 percent of the variance in Education(14) was attributable to the combined effects of unmeasured differences among students entering different schools, random differences in the high-school experience of students in different schools, random errors in measuring Education(14), variations in high-school quality, and variations in community characteristics. After allowance was made for random differences among high schools with respect to the unmeasured determinants of Education(14), the estimated "true" standard deviation of the mean residuals fell to 0.21 year. This implies that 2.2 percent of the total variance in Education(14) was attributable to systematic unmeasured differences among the students entering different schools, differences in high-school quality, and community characteristics. It also implies that if we rank high schools in terms of their effects on school and college attendance, students who attend the most effective fifth of all high schools end up getting an average of 0.6 more years of school or college than they would if they had attended a school that ranked among the least effective fifth.

4. Determinants of Educational Status Five Years after High School

Students' educational futures are far from settled 15 months after their class finishes high school. In order to check the validity of conclusions drawn from the one-year

---

[18] We used the unstandardized regression coefficients from line 3 of table 4 to predict each individual's total Education(14) score (not his or her deviation from the school mean). We then averaged these predictions for each school. We did not include the individual's Curriculum when predicting Education(14), since the percentage of students in the college curriculum could depend on school policy as well as on the characteristics of entering students. Purists might reasonably argue that we should also have excluded those student characteristics that might have been influenced by Curriculum, especially Grades and Plans. We initially retained Grades and Plans because we assumed that they influenced Curriculum far more than Curriculum influenced them. We subsequently discovered that the inclusion of Grades and Plans actually increased the variance of the mean residuals, rather than decreasing it. The change in the variance of the mean residual was statistically insignificant, however, so including these two variables has no important effect on our conclusions.

followup data we examined five-year followup data as well. Since the five-year followup asked students to report their race, we extended our analysis to include the seven predominantly black high schools and introduced Race as an independent variable. Since we had a more powerful program for estimating regression equations when we conducted these analyses, we also used a somewhat different statistical method, which we will describe below.

Unfortunately, the response rate in the five-year followup was even less satisfactory than the response in the one-year followup. Of the 11,137 ninth graders tested in our 98 schools in 1960, 7,361 answered all the relevant ninth-grade items. Of those with complete ninth-grade data, 4,360 returned one-year followup data, 2,434 returned five-year followup data, and 2,042 returned both one-year and five-year data. The analyses which follow deal with the 95 schools that had two or more respondents with both one- and five-year followup data. The nonrespondents were disproportionately likely to come from low-SES homes, to have low ninth-grade test scores, to be high-school dropouts, and to be black. Indeed, we concluded that the Blacks in our sample were so unrepresentative that we will not discuss the apparent effects of Race in any detail. In other respects, however, our reduced sample appears remarkably similar to the larger initial sample. When we compared the standard deviations and correlations of ninth-grade characteristics for the initial sample and the subsample with five-year followup data, we found no important differences. As a further check, we looked at a subsample of about 250 initial nonrespondents whom Talent had searched for by telephone. Talent obtained data from 167 of these initial nonrespondents. They had lower means than regular mail respondents on almost all variables, but their standard deviations and correlations did not differ significantly from those of the other respondents. We therefore concluded that sample attrition should not appreciably bias our regression results.

Changes in Educational Status Between Ages 19 and 23

Table 5 presents the regression equations for predicting Education(14) and Education(18). These equations differ in three respects from the Education(14) equation in table 4. First, they cover a smaller sample. Second, we replaced the four separate tests in table 4 with a single Composite Achievement score. This lowered R^2 by 0.002. Third, instead of controlling the effects of high-school quality by subtracting the mean from every student's score on every variable, we entered a dummy variable for each school in the regression equation. This innovation requires some explanation.

TABLE 5
Regression Equations for Education(14) or Education(18): Students with Complete Data from 95 Talent High Schools

Dependent Variable		Sex	Race	SES	Siblings	Composite Achievement (9)	Grades	Curriculum	Plans[a]	Education(14)	School Dummies	Standard Error	R^2	R_c^2 [b]	N [c]
1. Education (14)	B [d]	−.178	[.298]	.0268	−.0429	.0629	.0964	.364	.187		No	1.014	.425	.423	2042
	(S.E.)	(.047)	(.206)	(.0028)	(.0124)	(.0086)	(.0222)	(.059)	(.015)						
	beta[e]	−.066	.025	.193	−.061	.150	.078	.134	.291						
2. Education (18)	B	−.431	[.356]	.0322	.0828	.141	.264	.417	.216		No	1.550	.411	.409	2042
	(S.E.)	(.071)	(.316)	(.0420)	(.0189)	(.013)	(.034)	(.090)	(.022)						
	beta	−.106	.019	.153	−.078	.222	.142	.102	.223						
3. Education (18)	B	−.296	[.130]	.0119	−.050	.0931	.191	[.141]	.0745	.758	No	1.346	.556	.554	2042
	(S.E.)	(.062)	(.275)	(.0037)	(.017)	(.012)	(.030)	(.079)	(.0200)	(.029)					
	beta	−.073	.007	.057	−.047	.147	.103	.035	.077	.502					
4. Education (14)	B	−.157	[−.260]	.0264	−.0404	.0700	.0860	.397	.179		Yes	.993	.474	.447	2042
	(S.E.)	(.047)	(.276)	(.0030)	(.0127)	(.0090)	(.0245)	(.062)	(.015)						
	beta	−.058	−.021	.190	−.057	.167	.070	.147	.280						
5. Education (18)	B	−.448	[.119]	.0316	.0827	.138	.264	.458	.215		Yes	1.546	.441	.411	2042
	(S.E.)	(.073)	(.430)	(.0460)	(.0198)	(.014)	(.038)	(.096)	(.023)						
	beta	−.110	.006	.150	−.078	.217	.142	.112	.222						
6. Education (18)	B	−.328	[.318]	.0114	.0518	.0839	.198	[.154]	.0778	.767	Yes	1.346	.576	.554	2042
	(S.E.)	(.069)	(.375)	(.0041)	(.0172)	(.0124)	(.033)	(.085)	(.0210)	(.031)					
	beta	−.080	.017	.054	−.048	.132	.106	.038	.080	.508					
7. Education (18)	B	−.475	.775	.0574		.250					No	1.659	.354	.353	3317
	(S.E.)	(.058)	(.161)	(.0032)		(.010)									
	beta	−.115	.070	.278		.416									
8. Education (18)	B	−.479	[−.130]	.0570		.253					Yes	1.650	.379	.360	3317
	(S.E.)	(.059)	(.311)	(.0035)		(.010)									
	beta	−.116	.012	.275		.421									

Notes
[a] Note that coding of Plans is in years and so differs from table 4.
[b] The formula is $R_c^2 = 1 - s_e^2/s_t^2$, where s_e is the standard deviation of the residuals and s_t is the observed standard deviation of the dependent variable. Unlike the value of R^2, the value of s_e reported in conventional regression programs is corrected for degrees of freedom and is supposed to estimate the standard deviation of the residuals in an infinitely large sample. Hence its utility in estimating R_c^2.
[c] The N's for equations 1 through 6 differ from those for equations 7 and 8 because the latter equations did not exclude students who failed to report Plans, Grades, Curriculum, Siblings, or Education(14).
[d] Unstandardized coefficient. Coefficients in brackets are not significantly different from zero at the 0.05 level.
[e] Standardized coefficient.

Equations 1 to 3 in table 5 show the coefficients of students' ninth-grade characteristics without the school dummies in the equation. Insofar as any ninth-grade characteristic is correlated with high-school quality, its coefficient in these equations will be biased. To correct for this, equations 4 to 6 include dummy variables for each school. (Actually, we omitted one arbitrarily selected school, since its effects were already captured by the regression constant.) Since the school dummies can account for all the between-schools variance, the coefficients of the student characteristics in equations 4 to 6 are based entirely on the within-school relationship between these characteristics and educational attainment. This means that if table 5 covered the same sample and included the same variables as table 4, the unstandardized coefficients (B's) in equation 4 of table 5 would be exactly equal to the unstandardized coefficients in line 3 of table 4. As it is, comparing the two equations shows that reducing the sample size from 4,315 to 2,042 does not alter the coefficients appreciably, though it does increase their standard errors.

The coefficient of any given school's dummy variable in equations 4 to 6 represents the discrepancy between its observed mean on the dependent variable and the mean one would predict if one knew the characteristics of its ninth graders and used the within-school coefficient to estimate each characteristic's likely effect on the students' eventual educational attainment. This is logically identical to the procedure used to calculate a school's "mean residual" in the two previous sections. The standard deviation of the coefficients of the dummy variables is therefore equal to the standard deviation of the mean residuals defined earlier. If we want to estimate the contribution of disparities in high-school quality, community characteristics, and measurement error to variation in schools' mean educational attainment, we need only compute the standard deviation of these coefficients.

If there were no correlation between the school dummies and the ninth-grade student characteristics, adding the school dummies to equations 1 to 3 would increase the explained variance by an amount exactly equal to the variance of the dummies' coefficients. If there is a correlation, the variance of the coefficients will be larger than the increase in the explained variance.[19] The actual correlation be-

---

[19] Suppose we create a new variable, S, equal to the coefficient of each school's dummy variable in an equation that also includes some measure of students' initial characteristics (I), and a random error term (e). The equation for predicting educational attainment (U) is then $U = B_S S + B_I I + e$. By construction, however, the coefficient of S, B_S, must be 1. Not only that, but the variance of S must be equal to the variance of the school dummies (weighted by the number of individuals in each school). The explained variance in U is equal to $s_S^2 + B_I r_{SI} s_S s_I + B_I^2 s_I^2$. Now suppose we estimate a reduced-form equation that omits S. The reduced-form coefficient of I will be $\overline{B_I +}$

tween the individual characteristics that influence Education(14) and the mean residuals is 0.006. This makes the increase in R^2 when we add the high-school dummies an essentially unbiased estimate of the proportion of variance attributable to disparities in high-school quality, community characteristics, and measurement errors.

The high-school dummies raise R^2 for Education(14) from 0.425 (in equation 1 of table 5) to 0.474 (in equation 4). This increase is due to random as well as systematic differences between schools. Such random differences would disappear, however, if each school were infinitely large. Estimates of R^2 for infinitely large samples are shown under the heading "R_c^2" in table 5. Whereas adding the 95 school dummies increased R^2 by 0.049, it increases R_c^2 by 0.024. Section 3 showed that after eliminating fluctuations due to unreliability, the variance of the mean Education(14) residuals was 2.2 percent of tthe total variance. The agreement between these two results supports our assertion that sample attrition does not bias our estimates of the effects of high-school quality.

Now let us compare the determinants of Education(14) to the determinants of Education(18). Comparing the standardized coefficients (beta's) of ninth-grade traits in equation 1 to those in equation 2, we see that the relative importance of Sex, test scores, and Grades is slightly greater five years out, while the relative importance of SES and ninth-grade Plans has diminished slightly. The overall value of R^2 is therefore very similar. Since Education(18) has a larger standard deviation than Education(14), the unstandardized coefficients (B's) and the standard errors (S.E.'s) increase for all characteristics.

Equation 3 predicts educational status five years after high school, controlling educational status one year after high school. The coefficients of the ninth-grade traits thus measure the impact of these traits on changes in educational status between the one-year followup and the five-year followup. Ninth-grade Curriculum is the only variable that becomes statistically insignificant. All the other traits measured in ninth grade have a continuing effect on educational status, even after high-school graduation.

$B_S B_{S,I}$, where $B_{S,I}$ is the regression coefficient of I in an equation predicting S. $B_{S,I}$ is therefore equal to $r_{S,I} s_S / s_I$. As before, $B_S = 1$. The reduced-form coefficient is therefore $B_I + r_{S,I} s_S / s_I$, and the variance explained by the reduced-form equation is $(B_I + r_{S,I} s_S / s_I)^2 s_I^2 = B_I^2 s_I^2 + r_{S,I}^2 s_S^2 + 2 B_I r_I s_S r_{S,I}$. The increase in the explained variance when we move from the reduced-form to the full equation is thus $(1 - r_{S,I}^2) s_S^2$. If we use the increase in explained variance to estimate the variance of the school dummies (s_S^2), our estimate will be biased downward by a percentage equal to $r_{S,I}^2$.

Equation 6 is identical to equation 3 except that it includes the dummy variables representing the unique effects of having attended each high school. Including these variable raises R^2 from 0.556 to 0.576, but it does not raise R_c^2 at all. This implies that changes in educational status between the one-year followup and the five-year followup do not depend on the quality of the high school a student attended.

Nonetheless, we might well expect high-school quality to have *some* persistent effect on educational status five years after high school, simply because it affects status one year after high school. Since the high-school dummies raise R_c^2 for Education(14) by 0.024, and since Education(14) explains 49 percent of the variance in Education(18), we expected the high-school dummies to raise R_c^2 for Education(18) by about $(0.49)(0.024) = 0.012$. In fact, however, comparison of equations 2 and 5 shows that adding the school dummies raises R_c^2 by only 0.002. This increase is not statistically significant. Its modest size suggests that while high-school quality may affect educational status one year after graduation, these effects are peculiary transitory.

One possible objection to this conclusion is that equations 1 to 6 in table 5 control the effects of ninth-grade Curriculum, Grades, and Plans. These attributes may have been affected by high-school policy in the first half of ninth grade. Equation 7 presents the coefficients when we control only Sex, Race, SES, and Composite Achievement. Equation 8 adds the high-school dummies to this reduced-form equation. The dummies now increase R_c^2 by 0.007, which is statistically significant. Unfortunately, we cannot say how much of the between-schools variance in Grades, Curriculum, and Plans in the spring of ninth grade is due to variations in high-school policy and how much is due to differences that existed before students entered ninth grade. At most, however, high-school quality explains 0.7 percent of the total variance in eventual educational attainment.

If all effects of ninth-grade traits and high-school quality were additive, as we assume in table 5 and all other equations in this article, then the variation among "advantaged" subsamples—males, or those having high SES, test scores, or aspirations—should be the same as among "disadvantaged" subsamples. This is not the case. The variance is larger for "advantaged" groups. We therefore ran separate regression equations to see whether there were significant differences between the determinants of Education(18) for males and females, high- and low-SES students, high- and low-ability students, or college and non-college tracks. There were none. We also calculated separate equations within each of the 70 schools with more than ten alumni reporting Education(18). These equations did not differ significantly. Finally, we investigated the possibility that some schools produced more equal outcomes than others. Again, the differences were statistically insignificant. We concluded that high schools' effects on students' educational attainments were adequately measured by the additive equations in table 5. This does not mean that all the determinants of educational attainment have additive effects, but only that the ones we measured do. The larger standard deviations for advantaged students thus remain a puzzle. They may derive from differential response rates.

To see what effect interannual fluctuation might have, we also analyzed a sample of eleventh graders enrolled in these same schools in 1960. When we reestimated equation 7 of table 5 using eleventh-grade data, the results were virtually identical to those for ninth graders. The mean residuals for eleventh graders correlated 0.39 with the mean residuals for ninth graders, implying that 39 percent of the unexplained between-schools variance is stable over time. When both sets of results are taken together, they support our earlier conclusion that disparities in high-school quality explain about 2 percent of the variance in educational status one year after high school and 1 percent of the variance in educational status five years after high school.

5. Effects of High-School Quality on Occupational Status and Career Plans at Age 23

Talent's five-year followup was conducted when the average respondent was 22 or 23. Only 790 men and 832 women from our 98 schools reported paid civilian occupations. We ranked these occupations using Duncan's scale, which is based on the education and income of males in a given occupation.[20] Although this yields a reasonable rank order for both male and female respondents' occupations, it does not provide a satisfactory basis for comparing the status of females with that of males. Nor does it provide a basis for assessing the absolute distance between female occupations. Such comparisons would require both theoretical and empirical work beyond the scope of this article. We will therefore analyze males and females separately.

Disadvantaged men often failed to return questionnaires; advantaged men were often still in college or graduate school. The range of test scores, educational attainment, and occupational status is therefore lower than in older and more representative samples. These restrictions, along with the youth of the sample,

---

[20] Duncan, "A Socioeconomic Index."

make the observed correlations lower than they would be in an older or more representative sample.

The women who reported paid occupations appear even less representative than the men. These women were drawn from the upper end of the SES, test score, and education distributions. Seventy-nine percent said they were teachers, nurses, or secretaries.

Because of our reservations about the representativeness of those who reported current employment, we also examined respondents' statements about their career plans. Eighty percent of the males and 42 percent of the females answered the question about career plans, including some individuals who were still in school or in the military, and some who were currently housewives. The correlation between Occupation and Career Plans for those reporting both items was 0.684 for males and 0.847 for females. Individuals who reported Career Plans were well above national norms on education, and they planned to enter occupations that averaged well above national norms in status.

Table 6 shows the regression equations for both Occupation and Career Plans. We are not certain how seriously to take differences between the male and female equations. Still, the fact that academic ability has substantially more effect on male than female occupational status seems consistent with common observation. The fact that academic ability has more effect on women's career plans than on their current occupations is also suggestive. Whether able women will be able to fulfill their plans is an open question.

Except for the effects of academic ability on women, the equations for current Occupation and for Career Plans are remarkably similar. We interpret both current Occupation and Career Plans as fallible predictors of occupational status in maturity. We do not know how fallible either indicator will turn out to be.

In order to estimate the effect of attending one high school rather than another, we can compare the four equations in table 6 that include the school dummies to the four equations that exclude them. The school dummies raise R_c^2 by 0.024 to 0.048, depending on the equation. These increases are statistically significant in three cases out of four. We therefore conclude that either (a) unmeasured differences among the students entering different schools affect students' occupations in nonrandom ways, or (b) the schools themselves have different effects, or (c) the communities in which the schools are located provide different occupational opportunities for local youngsters. Unfortunately, our data do not allow us to distinguish between the effects of high schools and the effects of local job opportunities.

TABLE 6
Regression Equations for Occupation and Career Plans: Males and Females with Complete Data in Talent High Schools

Dependent Variable (Sample)		Coefficients (and Standard Errors) of Independent Variables						
		Race	SES	Composite Achievement(9)	School Dummies	R^2	Standard Error	R_c^2
Occupation (790 males)	B	[7.43]	.319	2.201	No	.168	19.420	.165
	(S.E.)	(4.75)	(.078)	(.234)				
	beta	.052	.147	.337				
	B	[2.43]	.257	2.144	[Yes]	.285	19.132	.189
	(S.E.)	(8.71)	(.085)	(.252)				
	beta	.017	.118	.329				
Career Plans (1,263 males)[1]	B	[3.89]	.394	2.198	No	.197	19.417	.195
	(S.E.)	(3.88)	(.063)	(.184)				
	beta	.026	.177	.341				
	B	[−7.03]	.290	2.171	Yes	.300	18.837	.243
	(S.E.)	(6.68)	(.068)	(.192)				
	beta	−.047	.131	.337				
Occupation (832 females)	B	[1.03]	.311	.886	No	.118	12.512	.115
	(S.E.)	(2.39)	(.051)	(.149)				
	beta	.015	.211	.213				
	B	[3.46]	.366	.964	Yes	.254	12.196	.159
	(S.E.)	(3.61)	(.057)	(.155)				
	beta	.049	.248	.232				
Career Plans (706 females)	B	9.51	.279	1.520	No	.172	13.743	.169
	(S.E.)	(2.41)	(.059)	(.178)				
	beta	.149	.181	.346				
	B	10.48	.284	1.569	Yes	.312	13.413	.208
	(S.E.)	(5.36)	(.065)	(.190)				
	beta	.165	.184	.357				

Coefficients in brackets are not significantly different from zero at the 0.05 level. Insignificant school dummies are denoted by [Yes].

We next sought to identify mechanisms by which school quality might influence Occupation and Career Plans. One conventional assumption has been that a good high school can improve students' occupational prospects by raising their cognitive skills. But individual changes in test scores between ninth and twelfth grades were not significantly correlated with eventual occupational status. We therefore abandoned the hypothesis that high schools influence occupational status by influencing test scores.

A second theory holds that a good high school can improve students' occupational prospects by encouraging them to finish high school and attend college. Table 7 tests this theory. It presents a set of regression equations identical to those in table 6, except that they include Education(18) as an independent variable. The high-school dummies raise R_c^2 by an average of 0.022 in these equations, as compared to 0.039 when Education(18) is not controlled. This suggests that the effects of high-school quality on educational attainment may explain 1 to 2 percent of the variance in Occupation and Career Plans. The reader should recall, however, that high-school quality explained less than 2 percent of the variance in Education(18) in our larger sample. This means that the influence of high-school quality on Education(18) could not plausibly explain more than 1 percent of the variance in Occupation in the larger sample. We clearly need a much larger sample to get a precise estimate of the contribution of high-school quality to variation in occupational status.

How are we to explain the 2.2 percent increase in R_c^2 that is independent of Education? One possibility is that there are important unmeasured differences among the students entering different high schools, and that these differences affect Occupation and Career Plans. Another possibility is that high schools produce important unmeasured differences among their graduates. A third possibility is that the graduates of different high schools confront different labor markets, and that this creates differences in both current Occupation and Career Plans for individuals who do not differ in any other significant respect.

6. The Meaning of "High-School Quality"

The four preceding sections have estimated the effects of "high-school quality" on six twelfth-grade test scores, on educational status one and five years after expected high-school graduation, and on occupational status and career plans five years after graduation. Our repeated use of the term "high-school quality" to describe the school characteristics that maximize these different outcomes may have con-

TABLE 7
Regression Equations for Occupation and Career Plans with Education Controlled: Males and Females with Complete Data in Talent High Schools

Dependent Variable (Sample)		Race	SES	Composite Achievement (9)	Education (18)	School Dummies	R^2	Standard Error	R_c^2
Occupation (790 males)	B	[4.68]	[.066]	1.168	5.783	No	.342	17.281	.339
	(S.E.)	(4.23)	(.071)	(.220)	(.401)				
	beta	.033	.031	.179	.475				
	B	[8.76]	[.021]	1.062	5.888	Yes	.437	16.996	.360
	(S.E.)	(7.75)	(.078)	(.238)	(.431)				
	beta	.062	.010	.163	.484				
Career Plans (1,263 males)	B	[.91]	.133	1.075	4.539	No	.328	17.767	.326
	(S.E.)	(3.56)	(.060)	(.183)	(.290)				
	beta	.006	.060	.167	.438				
	B	[−3.55]	[.053]	1.101	4.340	Yes	.407	17.338	.358
	(S.E.)	(6.16)	(.064)	(.191)	(.298)				
	beta	.024	.024	.171	.419				
Occupation (832 females)	B	[−1.14]	[.036]	[−.019]	4.360	No	.352	10.735	.349
	(S.E.)	(2.06)	(.047)	(.138)	(.253)				
	beta	−.016	.024	.005	.582				
	B	[2.97]	[.068]	[.071]	4.125	[Yes]	.430	10.670	.356
	(S.E.)	(3.16)	(.054)	(.148)	(.274)				
	beta	.042	.046	.017	.551				
Career Plans (706 females)	B	6.39	[.061]	.709	3.678	No	.327	12.400	.323
	(S.E.)	(2.19)	(.056)	(.172)	(.289)				
	beta	.100	.040	.161	.472				
	B	[8.57]	[.061]	.762	3.540	Yes	.438	12.133	.352
	(S.E.)	(4.85)	(.062)	(.185)	(.302)				
	beta	.135	.039	.173	.454				

Coefficients in brackets are not significantly different from zero at the 0.05 level. Insignificant school dummies are denoted by [Yes].

veyed the impression that "quality" is a one-dimensional phenomenon. This is not true. Table 8 shows the correlations among the mean residuals for thirteen different outcomes. The correlations are generally low and often insignificant. This means that the high-school characteristics that boost performance in one area are not especially likely to boost performance in other areas.

The fifteen correlations among the mean residuals for the six basic tests are shown in the top six rows of table 8. Four of the ten positive correlations are significantly different from zero. None of the five negative correlations is significantly different from zero. The correlations among the residuals for the six basic tests average only +0.17. This suggests that high-school quality is multi-dimensional, even with respect to test scores. This same pattern holds if we restrict our attention to the four tests that showed an independent relationship to subsequent educational attainment and occupational status—namely, Vocabulary, Social Studies Information, Reading Comprehension, and Arithmetic Reasoning. Thus the data suggest that if we had to construct a one-dimensional index of high-school quality, it would explain only about 17 percent of the variance in schools' mean residuals on a wide range of tests.[21] Since the mean residuals explain an average of 2.5 percent of the variance in individual twelfth-grade scores (see tables 1 and 3), the implication is that a one-dimensional index of high-school quality could explain only (0.17)(2.5) = 0.43 percent of the variance in individual performance on the typical test.

A one-dimensional notion of high-school quality would, of course, explain more of the variance in overall academic achievement than in performance on any specific test. Suppose we think of performance on specific tests as determined partly by general academic achievement and partly by specialized skills. If we define general academic achievement as the first principal component of our six tests, it explains 48 percent of the variance in these tests. Specialized skills and measurement error explain the rest, in roughly equal proportions. If the first principal component of high-school quality explains 0.43 percent of the variance in the typical test, and if the first principal component of individual achievement explains 48 percent of the variance in these same tests, we can infer that a one-dimensional conception of high-school quality could explain about 0.43/48 = 0.9 percent of the variance in general academic achievement.

Now let us turn to the correlations between the mean test-score residuals and the mean residuals for Education, Occupation, and Career Plans. These correla-

---

[21] The first principal component explains 25 percent of the variance in the mean residuals for the six basic tests in our battery, but the value would fall toward the mean correlation (0.17 in this sample) if we increased the number of tests.

TABLE 8
Correlations between Schools' Mean Residuals for Different Outcomes (with School N's in Parentheses)

	Vocab-ulary	Social Studies Infor-mation	Reading Compre-hension	Abstract Reason-ing	Arith-metic Reason-ing	Arith-metic Compu-tation	Total Infor-mation	Edu-cation (14)	Edu-cation (18)	Occu-pation (males)	Occu-pation (females)	Career Plans (males)	Career Plans (females)
Vocabulary	1.000 (49)												
Social Studies Information	.226 (49)	1.000 (49)											
Reading Comprehension	-.014 (18)	.515* (18)	1.000 (45)										
Abstract Reasoning	.388* (49)	.152 (49)	.421* (45)	1.000 (91)									
Arithmetic Reasoning	-.101 (16)	-.029 (16)	.279 (17)	-.174 (48)	1.000 (48)								
Arithmetic Computation	.165 (16)	.387 (16)	.259 (17)	-.230 (48)	.341* (48)	1.000 (48)							
Total Information	.652* (49)	.884* (49)	.380 (18)	.307* (49)	.040 (16)	.375 (16)	1.000 (49)						
Education (14)	.045 (49)	.065 (49)	.218 (45)	.065 (91)	-.214 (48)	.094 (48)	.022 (49)	1.000 (91)					
Education (18)	-.011 (49)	.151 (49)	.144 (45)	-.025 (91)	-.163 (48)	.028 (48)	.110 (91)	.468* (91)	1.000 (95)				
Occupation (males)	-.100 (48)	-.112 (48)	.129 (45)	-.084 (89)	-.105 (47)	.055 (47)	-.141 (48)	.023 (89)	.326* (91)	1.000 (91)			
Occupation (females)	.031 (48)	.422* (48)	.281 (45)	.070 (90)	.006 (48)	.117 (48)	.336* (48)	.276* (90)	.394* (91)	.020 (92)	1.000 (92)		
Career Plans (males)	.013 (48)	.056 (48)	.059 (45)	-.038 (89)	-.356* (47)	-.186 (47)	.043 (48)	.011 (89)	.406* (91)	.573* (91)	.012 (91)	1.000 (92)	
Career Plans (females)	.009 (48)	.130 (48)	.001 (45)	.025 (89)	-.063 (47)	-.247 (47)	.109 (48)	.229* (89)	.284* (91)	.122 (91)	.447* (91)	.077 (91)	1.000 (91)

*Significantly different from zero at the 0.05 level. Degrees of freedom estimated from number of schools. This overestimates significance levels, since schools were unequally weighted (by the number of ninth graders tested in 1960).

tions average 0.006, and the variations around this mean are within the range expected by chance. This suggests that schools which raise test scores unusually rapidly between ninth and twelfth grades are not particularly likely to help their students get a lot of further education or enter a high-status occupation. This implication was so contrary to our expectations that we decided to check it at the individual level. We found that we could predict Education(14), Education(18), Occupation, and Career Plans as accurately from ninth-grade scores as from twelfth-grade scores on the same test. It follows that test-score changes between ninth and twelfth grades have no effect on individual life chances. It also follows that if our real interest is in what happens to students after they graduate, it is a waste of time and money to assess high schools' "productivity" or "effectiveness" by trying to measure their impact on standardized tests of basic cognitive skills. This might not be true, of course, if such evaluations used tests covering more advanced skills. Nor is it necessarily true of elementary schools, although such evidence as we have on elementary schools is similar to the evidence in table 8.[22]

The correlation between the mean residuals for Education(14) and Education(18) is 0.468. More relevant, the regression coefficient of the Education(14) residuals when predicting the Education(18) residuals is only 0.62, indicating that a school that appeared to have boosted its students' average educational attainment by one year at the time of the one-year followup turned out to produce a gain of only 0.62 year four years later.[23] This may be partly due to random error in the Education(14) residuals, which are not based on exactly the same individuals as the Education(18) residuals. But the difference is also consistent with our suggestion in Section 4 that the effects of high schools on educational status one year after graduation may be peculiarly transitory.

The mean residuals for Occupation and Career Plans have an average correlation of 0.135 with the mean residuals for Education(14) and 0.353 with the mean residuals for Education(18). The positive correlation between the Education(18) residuals and the Occupation and Career Plans residuals is consistent with our earlier finding that controlling Education(18) appreciably reduced the unexplained between-schools variance in Occupation and Career Plans.

The mean residuals for Occupation and Career Plans correlate 0.573 for males and 0.447 for females. This is reassuring, since the individual residuals correlate about 0.40, and we expect a similar correlation between mean residuals by chance alone. The correlations between mean residuals for males and females average

[22] Jencks et al., *Inequality*, pp. 147-48.
[23] At the individual level the regression coefficient is 1.02.

0.048. This means one of two things. If high-school characteristics have any direct effect on occupational status or career plans, the characteristics that influence males must be completely different from those that influence females. Alternatively, local job opportunities for young men and women may be uncorrelated. Unfortunately, we cannot test this latter hypothesis adequately with the data in hand.

On the basis of these analyses, we conclude that sweeping generalizations about "good" and "bad" high schools are bound to be misleading. Among these white comprehensive public high schools, the estimated effectiveness of a given high school will vary dramatically according to the measure of success one chooses to emphasize. Very few schools rank high on all of the measures used in this investigation, and very few rank low on all of them. High schools that are unusually effective in boosting student performance on one standardized test are only marginally more effective than average in boosting performance on other tests. Those that are notably effective in boosting test scores across the board are no more effective than average in getting their students to finish high school, attend college, graduate from college, or enter high-status occupations. High schools that are unusually effective in increasing the amount of education a student gets are also appreciably more effective than average in boosting a student's eventual occupational status. However, high schools that are unusually successful in getting males into high-status occupations are no more successful than average in getting females into high-status occupations, and vice versa.

7. Determinants of High Schools' Effectiveness

Up to this point our analyses have focused on two questions: how much variation is there in schools' effectiveness, and how often do schools that are effective in one area prove effective in other areas as well? We will now consider whether several specific high-school characteristics are related to schools' effectiveness. In order to do this, we will treat a school's mean residual as an estimate of its effect on each measured outcome. Then we will ask whether schools' measured characteristics affect their mean residuals for various outcomes.

Determinants of Effectiveness for 98 Talent High Schools

We will investigate the effects of eight high-school characteristics that have often been thought to influence students' subsequent life chances. Principals estimated their schools' annual expenditure per pupil, mean starting salary for inexperienced teachers, percentage of teachers holding masters' degrees, teachers' average years of experience in the profession, and average class size. In addition, we computed Mean SES, Mean Plans, and Mean Information (Vocabulary plus Social Studies Information) for all ninth graders in each school. Since Mean SES and Mean Plans correlate 0.707, and Mean Information correlates 0.536 with Mean Plans and 0.796 with Mean SES, it will not be easy to distinguish the effects of these social-composition variables in our relatively small sample of schools.

Table 9 shows the means and standard deviations of these eight high-school characteristics for our 98 schools. It also shows their correlations with ten of our thirteen measures of schools' effectiveness. (Table 8 showed the intercorrelations among the measures of effectiveness and the number of schools for which we computed each measure.) We have omitted the correlations involving Total Information because its two components (Vocabulary and Social Studies Information) do not seem to behave in the same way. We have also omitted the correlations involving Abstract Reasoning and Arithmetic Computation because these two tests do not seem to provide any information about an individual's cognitive skills that is not provided by other tests.

The mean residuals for Vocabulary, Social Studies Information, Reading Comprehension, and Arithmetic Reasoning measure schools' "cognitive impact." When we correlated these four mean residuals with our eight measured school characteristics, two of the 32 values were more than twice their standard errors. This could easily occur by chance, so even the "significant" correlations may be due to random sampling error. Class size is the only school characteristic whose correlations have the same sign for all four measures of cognitive impact, and these correlations are too small to be either statistically or substantively significant. The most parsimonious explanation for these results is that the eight school characteristics measured in this study have no consistent effect on cognitive growth between ninth and twelfth grades, and that the observed relationships are all random. This is clearly at odds with the conclusion of Coleman et al. that a high school's socioeconomic composition affects its students' twelfth-grade scores.[24] We believe that conclusion to be an erroneous by-product of their inability to control individuals' ninth-grade scores. We will return to this point below.

We have two measures of high schools' effectiveness in boosting their students' educational attainment. Education(14) is based on almost twice as many cases as Education(18). But if schools' initial effects are peculiarly transitory, as Section 4

[24] Coleman et al., *Equality of Educational Opportunity*.

TABLE 9
Means, Standard Deviations, and Correlations of Selected School Characteristics with Ten Measures of School Effectiveness in 98 Talent High Schools

	High-School Characteristics							
	Mean SES	Mean Plans	Mean Information	Expenditures	Starting Salary	Percent Masters	Teacher Experience	Class Size
Mean	98.2	3.95	25.19	380	3958	53.9	12.0	28.4
S.D.	4.5	0.44	3.20	176	646	27.0	3.3	3.8
Correlation with Mean Residual for:								
Vocabulary	.303*	.162	.201	.038	.217	.188	.285	−.057
Social Studies Information	−.166	−.070	−.035	.047	.017	−.319*	−.038	−.081
Reading Comprehension	−.186	−.181	−.258	−.244	−.140	−.257	−.117	−.044
Arithmetic Reasoning	.171	.116	.188	−.132	−.200	−.182	.019	−.037
Education(14)	−.056	.034	−.228*	−.192	−.127	.032	.071	.215*
Education(18)	−.141	.247*	−.268**	−.148	−.306**	.020	.146	.198
Occupation (males)	.152	.345**	.041	−.114	−.159	.317**	.304**	.348**
Career Plans (males)	.159	.331**	.033	.054	−.051	.264*	.314**	.163
Occupation (females)	.192	.063	−.200	−.131	−.247*	−.179	−.069	.130
Career Plans (females)	−.041	.139	.017	−.050	−.037	−.006	−.105	.285**

As in table 8, all means, standard deviations, and correlations are weighted by the total ninth-grade N. The means and standard deviations therefore differ slightly from those in tables 1–7, which are based only on individuals who supplied data at two points in time. Significance is tested using school N's (see table 8).
*Significantly different from zero at the 0.05 level.
**Significantly different from zero at the 0.01 level.

suggested, Education(14) may overstate the ultimate effects of high schools on students' educational attainment. We will therefore give the two measures equal weight. Five of the 16 correlations between these two measures and our eight school characteristics are significantly different from zero at the 0.05 level. Two are significant at the 0.01 level. These are too many significant correlations to attribute to chance. All the correlations involving Education(14) have the same sign as the analogous correlations involving Education(18). These results suggest that our eight high-school characteristics have a nonrandom relationship to a school's effectiveness in boosting students' educational attainment.

We have two measures of a school's impact on male occupational success and two measures of its impact on female occupational success. For males, seven of the 16 correlations are significant at the 0.05 level, and six are significant at the 0.01 level. As with educational attainment, we conclude that our eight school characteristics have a systematic relationship to the occupational attainment of male alumni, even after these men's ninth-grade traits have been controlled. For females, the evidence is not so clear. Two of the 16 correlations involving female occupational status and career plans are statistically significant at the 0.05 level, and one is significant at the 0.01 level. These results do not provide conclusive evidence that high-school characteristics have a nonrandom relationship to female occupational attainment.

Multivariate analyses yield a somewhat clearer picture of the relationship between a school's social composition and its impact on individual students. Table 10 shows the regression coefficients of Mean SES, Mean Plans, and Mean Information when we use all three simultaneously to predict a school's impact on individual educational and occupational attainment.[25] The coefficient of Mean Plans is positive in every equation and statistically significant in every equation but one. The coefficient of Mean Information is negative in every equation but one, and it is statistically significant in the two education equations. The coefficient of Mean SES is consistently and significantly negative in the female occupational equations. It is sometimes positive, sometimes negative, and never statistically significant in the equations for educational attainment, male occupational status, and male career plans.

These results must be interpreted cautiously. Mean Plans has a much smaller coefficient in the equation predicting Education(14) than in the other equations. This is the only equation in which a school's effect was estimated after controlling individual students' ninth-grade Plans. It is therefore the only equation in which one can clearly distinguish the effects of classmates' Plans from the effects of the individual's own Plans. In all the other equations, Mean Plans is at least partly a proxy for individual Plans. The coefficient of Mean Plans in these equations is therefore biased upward to some unknown extent. The coefficient of Mean Plans

[25] We also estimated the effects of Mean SES, Mean Plans, and Mean Information on cognitive growth. Like the zero-order correlations, the results were essentially random.

TABLE 10
Regressions of Selected Measures of Effectiveness on Three Measures of Social Composition in 98 Talent High Schools

		(1)	(2)	(3)	(4)	(5)	(6)
		\multicolumn{3}{c}{Coefficient of Independent Variable[a]}			Proportion of Individual Variance
Dependent Variable		Mean SES	Mean Plans	Mean Information	R^2	R^2 Corrected for Unreliability[b]	Explained by Social Composition[c]
Education(14)	beta	.249	.121	−.491*	.102	.208	.0035
residuals	B	.014	.072	−.040*			
Education(18)	beta	−.317	.672*	−.375*	.311	1.111	.0089
residuals	B	−.024	.537*	−.041*			
Occupation (male)	beta	−.030	.465*	−.184	.148	.721	.0168
residuals	B	−.048	7.60*	−.412			
Career Plans (male)	beta	.037	.425*	−.224	.139	.298	.0090
residuals	B	.057	6.75*	−.487			
Occupation (female)	beta	−.389*	.391*	−.100	.119	.368	.0326
residuals	B	−.471*	4.90*	−.172			
Career Plans (female)	beta	−.411*	.343*	.161	.067	.240	.0110
residuals	B	−.554*	4.79*	.307			

*Significant at the 0.05 level. All significance tests use the number of schools to estimate degrees of freedom. As in tables 8 and 9, this is a liberal standard.
[a]Columns 1–4 are computed from correlations in tables 8 and 9.
[b]Column 4/reliability. Reliability for Education(14) residuals is taken from Section 3 as $0.21^2/0.26^2 = 0.652$. Reliability for Education(18) is taken from rows 7 and 8 of table 5 as $(R_{cD}^2 - R_c^2)/(R_D^2 - R^2)$, where R_{cD}^2 is the value of R_c^2 with school dummies included, R_c^2 is the value of R_c^2 without the school dummies, R_D^2 is the observed value of R^2 with the school dummies included, and R^2 is the observed value without the school dummies. The reliability is thus $(.360 - .352)/(.379 - .354) = 0.28$. Reliabilities for Occupation and Career Plans are derived from table 6 using the same method as for Education(18). This procedure is inexact, since the variance of the school coefficients actually exceeds $R_D^2 - R^2$, for reasons discussed in footnote 14.
[c]Estimated as $s_s^2 R^2/s_i^2$, where s_s^2 is the variance of the mean residuals or of the coefficients of the school dummies, R^2 is taken from column 4, and s_i^2 is the individual variance.

in the Education(14) equation may be biased downward, however, since Mean Plans may have affected individual Plans by the spring of ninth grade when the Talent survey was conducted. In the absence of data on Plans in eighth grade, there is no fully satisfactory way to resolve this dilemma.

A second problem is that with a relatively small sample of both schools and individuals, and with very high intercorrelations among the three measures of potential peer-group influence, all three coefficients have very large standard errors. Our confidence in our findings therefore depends in large part on the fact that a study by Meyer and one by Alexander and Eckland obtained essentially similar results with much larger samples.[26] Both these studies found that if a student attended high school with classmates who had high aspirations but only average test scores, he got more education than one would expect based on his other characteristics. If he attended school with classmates who had high scores but only average aspirations, he got less education than one would otherwise expect.

Our next question is: how much of the variance in schools' effects remains unexplained once we have taken account of their social composition? Except for the Education(18) equation, the values of R^2 in column 4 of table 10 are extremely modest, ranging from 0.067 to 0.148. Even for Education(18), R^2 is only 0.311. These estimates are quite misleading, however, since most of the unexplained variance is due to random errors in estimating schools' mean residuals. Column 5 shows the expected value of R^2 if these errors were eliminated. These values are considerably more impressive. Indeed, the value for Education(18) exceeds unity. This suggests that the random component of the Education(18) residuals happens to be correlated with socioeconomic composition in this particular sample.

Our final question is: how much of the variance in individual outcomes can be imputed to variations in high schools' social composition? Our estimates are shown in column 6 of table 10. Social composition explains less than 1 percent of the individual variance in Education(14) and Education(18). It explains from 0.90 to 3.26 percent of the individual variance in the various measures of occupational status.

We next investigate the effects of the other five school characteristics with social composition controlled. The coefficient of each school characteristic is shown in table 11. We have not presented the full regression equation, since the coefficients of Mean SES, Mean Plans, and Mean Information are not appreciably altered by controlling one other school characteristic. Nor have we presented equations with all school characteristics controlled simultaneously, since the causal connections among these school characteristics are ambiguous and the equation is therefore difficult to interpret.

[26] John W. Meyer, "High School Effects on College Intentions," *American Journal of Sociology*, 76 (1970), 59–60; Karl Alexander and Bruce K. Eckland, *Effects of Education and Social Mobility of High School Sophomores Fifteen Years Later (1955–1970)* (Washington, D.C.: National Institute of Education, 1973).

TABLE 11
Regression of Six Mean Residuals on Each of Five School Characteristics, Controlling Mean SES, Mean Plans, and Mean Information, in 98 Talent High Schools

		Expenditures	Starting Salary	Percent Masters	Teacher Experience	Class Size
Dependent Variable		\multicolumn{5}{c}{Regression Coefficient of Independent Variable with School Composition Controlled}
Mean residual for Education(14)	beta	−.151	−.079	.072	.059	.205*
	B	−.0002	−.00003	.0007	.0047	.0143*
Mean residual for Education(18)	beta	.052	−.056	.082	.100	.099
	B	.0001	−.00003	.0011	.0106	.0092
Mean residual for male Occupation	beta	−.124	−.158	.296*	.232*	.288*
	B	−.0050	−.0017	.0783*	.0539*	.5475*
Mean residual for male Career Plans	beta	.087	−.001	.223*	.246*	.101
	B	.0034	−.0000	.0574*	.5194*	.1866
Mean residual for female Occupation	beta	.022	−.065	−.134	−.078	.074
	B	.0007	−.0006	−.0273	−.1302	.1081
Mean residual for female Career Plans	beta	.010	.124	−.001	−.136	.245*
	B	.0003	.0012	−.0002	−.2526	.3983*

*Significant at the 0.05 level. All significance tests use the number of schools to estimate degrees of freedom. Data are weighted as in table 8.

Per-student expenditure has a small and statistically insignificant effect on both educational and occupational attainment. This suggests that expenditure does not appreciably affect students' life chances.[27] Teachers' starting salaries also have small and statistically insignificant effects on educational and occupational attainment. This suggests either that starting salaries have little impact on the quality of the teachers a school attracts or that the quality of the teachers has little impact

[27] Our results differ in this respect from those reported by Thomas Ribich and James Murphy, "The Economic Returns to Increased Educational Spending," *Journal of Human Resources*, 10 (1975), 56–77. They analyzed 8,902 Project Talent males from over 800 schools who returned five-year-followup data, in contrast to our 3,317 males and females from 98 schools who reported Education(18). They regressed Education(18) on Race, Region, SES, ninth-grade Composite Achievement, Mean SES, and district per-pupil Expenditures. They found that both Mean SES and Expenditures had coefficients significantly greater than zero.

We explored several technical explanations for this discrepancy, including different model or variable specifications and Ribich's and Murphy's exclusion of females. None seemed to account for the difference. The most plausible suggestion that remained was that in our 98 schools, through the luck of the draw, Expenditures had unusually low effects on educational attainment. Even this suggestion is not entirely satisfactory, however, since our more extensive EEOS sample results agreed with our Talent results. Consequently, the discrepancy between Ribich's and Murphy's results and ours remains perplexing.

on the students' life chances. The percentage of experienced teachers and teachers with masters' degrees has little effect on educational attainment or on female occupational attainment, but it seems to boost male occupational status and career plans to a statistically significant extent.

Large classes appear to have positive effects on all measures. These effects are statistically significant in three cases out of six. Their direction is precisely the opposite of what teachers and administrators assume. We could find no satisfactory explanation for this finding. Whatever the explanation, the finding should serve as a warning against taking the other coefficients in table 11 too seriously.

Determinants of Effectiveness in EEOS High Schools

Because our sample included relatively few high schools, we decided to check our conclusions using a much larger sample from the 1965 Equality of Educational Opportunity Survey. The EEOS sample includes the 630 high schools that returned ninth- and twelfth-grade test scores and student questionnaires, teacher questionnaires, and a principal questionnaire. The variables used in our analysis are Mean Twelfth-Grade Achievement (the first principal component of a school's mean score on five tests), Mean Ninth-Grade Achievement, Mean Twelfth-Grade SES, Mean Ninth-Grade Plans, Mean Educational Attainment (estimated from the principal's report of the percentage of ninth graders who finish twelfth grade and the percentage of twelfth graders who attend college), and 160 high-school characteristics measured in the teacher and principal questionnaires.[28]

Mean Ninth-Grade Achievement and Mean Twelfth-Grade SES explained 92 percent of the variance in Mean Twelfth-Grade Achievement. The unexplained between-schools variance in Twelfth-Grade Achievement was 2.0 percent of the individual variance. We estimated that the comparable figure for Talent would have been 0.9 percent. One reason for the discrepancy may be that our EEOS analysis had to use the mean scores of students who were in ninth grade in 1965 as a proxy for the initial scores of students who were in twelfth grade in 1965. This introduced an unknown amount of error, since there are random interannual fluctuations in mean ninth-grade scores, and since not all ninth graders reach twelfth grade.

---

[28] For detailed descriptions of the data, see Coleman et al., *Equality of Educational Opportunity*, and Christopher Jencks, "The Quality of the Data Collected by the Equality of Educational Opportunity Survey," in Mosteller and Moynihan. The school variables in the present analysis were almost all identical to those investigated by Jencks in "The Coleman Report and the Conventional Wisdom."

The EEOS data imply that 14 percent of the variance in educational status one year after high school is between schools.[29] Mean Twelfth-Grade SES, Mean Ninth-Grade Achievement, and Mean Ninth-Grade Plans explain 42 percent of the between-schools variance in educational attainment. This implies that (0.14) (1 − 0.42) = 8 percent of the total variance in educational attainment one year after high school is unexplained and between schools. In the Talent sample, only 10 percent of the variance in attainment one year after high school is between schools, and only 3.4 percent is unexplained once we control ninth-grade SES, Plans, and Achievement. The difference between Talent and EEOS is in the expected direction, since our estimate of EEOS students' initial characteristics contains considerable random error, and EEOS principals' reports of their students' educational attainment probably include substantial errors.

We tested the effect of adding each of the 160 high-school characteristics to the basic equation described above. Several school characteristics had coefficients that were more than twice their standard error, but this test of statistical significance cannot be taken at face value when one is screening 160 variables. In the equations predicting Mean Twelfth-Grade Achievement, for example, ten of the 160 coefficients were more than twice their standard error. This could happen by chance in one sample out of four. Three coefficients were more than 2.5 times their standard error. This would happen by chance in one sample out of eight. In the equations predicting Mean Educational Attainment, only two of the 160 school characteristics had coefficients that were more than 2.5 times their standard errors, which is exactly what one would expect by chance. Even more striking was the fact that school characteristics had intuitively "wrong" signs as often as they had "right" ones. There was no consistency between signs in the EEOS and Talent equations. We therefore conclude that the 160 school characteristics measured by the EEOS had no consistent effect either on changes in Mean Achievement between ninth and twelfth grades or on Mean Educational Attainment.

[29] The EEOS does not provide individual data on educational attainment. In order to estimate the individual variance, we treated the principal's estimate of the percentage of tenth graders finishing twelfth grade and the percentage of the twelfth graders entering college as the school means of dichotomous variables scored 1 if the student continues his education, 0 if he does not. The variance for individuals can then be estimated from their mean (X) as $s_X^2 = X(1 - X)$. Dividing the observed variance of the principals' responses by the implied variance of the individual responses yields the 0.14 ratio in the text.

8. Policy Implications

Our data are relevant to at least four possible policy objectives: (1) increasing schools' *effectiveness*, i.e., increasing students' mean test scores, mean educational attainment, and mean occupational status; (2) making schools *accountable*, i.e., determining whether schools have enhanced some politically determined set of outcomes; (3) reducing *inequality of opportunity*, i.e., reducing the effects of race, sex, parental SES, or other factors on any given outcome; and (4) reducing *inequality of condition*, i.e., reducing the dispersion of any given outcome relative to its mean.

Effectiveness

Some high schools are more effective than others in raising test scores. Nevertheless, the gains are never large relative to the variance of initial scores, and schools that boost performance on one test are not especially likely to boost performance on other tests. Moreover, high-school characteristics such as social composition, per-pupil expenditure, teacher training, teacher experience, and class size have no consistent impact on cognitive growth between ninth and twelfth grades. These findings imply that if we want to boost student performance, we will need drastically new methods. Our data tell us nothing about what methods might be most effective. They tell us only that more money, more graduate courses for teachers, smaller classes, socioeconomic desegregation, and other traditional remedies are unlikely to have much effect. We cannot say anything about the effects of racial desegregation, since we excluded schools with more than 25 percent black enrollment from our retest sample.[30]

Similarly, some high schools are more effective than others in boosting a student's eventual educational attainment. This effect has virtually nothing to do with a school's effect on cognitive growth between ninth and twelfth grades. However, a high school's effect on individual educational attainment does depend on its social composition, but not in any simple way. Mean Plans has a positive impact on individual attainment, whereas Mean Information has a negative effect and Mean SES has no consistent effect once Plans and Information are controlled.

---

[30] See Christopher Jencks and Marsha Brown, "The Effects of Desegregation on Student Achievement: Some New Evidence from the Equality of Educational Opportunity Survey," *Sociology of Education*, 48 (1975), 126–40, for a reanalysis of the EEOS data on the effect of racial composition on test performance. The effects appear trivial at the high-school level, though not at the elementary level.

Social composition explains considerably less than 1 percent of the variance in individual attainment. No other measured high-school characteristic plays a consistently significant role in determining a student's educational attainment. One characteristic—class size—has a statistically significant coefficient in both the Talent and EEOS analyses, but it has different signs in the two studies. These results suggest that if we want to boost the average student's eventual educational attainment, neither socioeconomic desegregation nor infusion of traditional resources is likely to help much. Again, we cannot say much about the effects of racial desegregation, since our sample of Blacks is so unrepresentative.

Some high schools are more effective than others in boosting a student's occupational status and career plans, but a school which boosts a man's occupational prospects is not especially likely to help a woman. A school's impact on a student's eventual occupation does not depend on its effectiveness in raising test scores, but it does depend on its effectiveness in raising educational attainment. A school's social composition has a modest effect on a student's eventual occupational status, but that effect is not large in absolute terms. Teacher characteristics (masters' degrees and experience) and class size also have an independent relationship to occupational status, at least for males. The effects of small classes are perverse, however, in that small classes appear to lower a student's eventual status. This raises serious questions about the plausibility of the entire analysis, which is based on far fewer individuals than the analyses of test scores and educational attainment, and which contains no direct measures of at least one potentially important variable, local job opportunities.

High schools vary in their effectiveness at raising their graduates' test scores, educational attainment, and occupational status. But even when schools are unusually effective or ineffective, the reasons for these effects remain obscure. These findings suggest that neither educators nor social scientists know how to change high schools so as to raise students' test scores, educational attainment or occupational status.

Accountability

Our results imply that if legislatures or school boards want to hold high schools accountable for their students' achievement, they should be extremely careful to specify the outcomes that really interest them. High schools that do well at raising students' scores on one test will not necessarily do well at improving scores on other tests. High schools that do well at raising test scores will not necessarily improve their graduates' subsequent life chances. This means that unless there is a clear consensus on specific objectives, which there rarely is, no two evaluations of a given high school can be expected to yield the same judgment.

Equality of Opportunity

Most people define equality of opportunity as equalizing the mean level of success for certain visible social groups, such as males and females, Blacks and Whites, or children from high- and low-SES homes. We can assess the effect of equalizing high-school quality on the gap between such groups by looking at the gap within a single school. If the effects (i.e., coefficients) of Sex, Race, or SES are smaller within schools than in the sample as a whole, we can say that equalizing high-school quality might equalize the gap between these groups.

Since males and females typically attend the same schools, disparities in high-school quality as we have defined it cannot possibly account for differences in their test scores, educational attainment, or occupational status. But black and white students usually attended different high schools at the time of the Talent survey, so disparities in high-school quality could have contributed to racial inequality. For reasons already given, we did not analyze the effects of Race on test scores. Tables 5 and 6 show that after controlling SES and test scores, Blacks got *more* education and entered *higher*-status occupations than Whites. When we control high-school quality by adding the school dummies to the relevant equations in tables 5 and 6, Blacks lose their advantage. This implies that Blacks gain their advantage by attending better high schools. These results contradict almost everyone's a priori assumptions. But the black sample is so small and unrepresentative that we have little faith in these results.

Since high- and low-SES students often attend different schools, disparities in school quality could also contribute to the correlation between parental SES and a child's eventual test scores, educational attainment, or occupational status. So far as we can discover, SES has no significant effect on cognitive growth between ninth and twelfth grades, at least for the six Talent tests we investigated. This means that equalizing high-school quality cannot reduce the correlation between SES and twelfth-grade scores. SES does have a substantial effect on eventual educational attainment, even after all other measured ninth-grade traits have been controlled. Comparing equations 2 and 5 or 7 and 8 in table 5 shows, however, that this effect is not reduced when we control high-school quality. The gap is as large when high- and low-SES students attend the same high school as when they attend different schools. This means that equalizing high-school quality would not reduce inequality of educational opportunity for low-SES students.

SES has a substantial effect on both occupational status and career plans at age 23, even with ninth-grade test scores controlled. Table 6 shows that controlling high-school quality lowers the direct effect of parental SES by 19 to 26 percent for males but does not lower it at all for females. This means that high- and low-SES males end up more alike if they attend the same school. Unfortunately, it does not necessarily mean they end up more alike if they attend different schools of similar quality. High- and low-SES students attend different high schools largely because they live in different places. Local job opportunities are presumably better in affluent communities than in poor communities, at least for men, and local youngsters presumably have an advantage in getting local jobs. Equalizing the schools would do nothing to offset this situation. One would actually have to move high- and low-SES students into the same communities to eliminate this source of inequality. We cannot say how much impact high-school quality per se has on inequality in males' occupational opportunities.

Equality of Condition
While most people are concerned primarily with equalizing opportunity for visible social groups, some also want to reduce inequality within these groups. Inequality is generally measured by indices which relate the dispersion of outcomes to the average outcome. There are two ways to reduce such an index. One possibility is to raise the mean for everyone, while holding the dispersion constant. The other possibility is to reduce the dispersion while holding the mean constant. Various combinations of these two policies are obviously possible as well. We have already discussed the difficulties in identifying high-school policies that will raise mean test scores, educational attainment, or occupational status. It is equally difficult to reduce the dispersion of these outcomes. As we have seen, high-school quality accounts for only 1.0 to 3.4 percent of the variance in twelfth-grade test scores, 0.2 to 2.4 percent of the variance in educational attainment, and 2.5 to 4.8 percent of the variance in occupational status and career plans. This means that even if we knew how to eliminate all disparities in high-school quality, which we clearly do not, we could reduce the standard deviations of these outcomes by only one or two percent. Assuming the mean remained constant, this would imply a one to two percent reduction in the ratio of the standard deviation to the mean, and hence in inequality.

The modest contribution of high-school quality to adult inequality does not mean we should stop trying to equalize the schools. High schools are public institutions, and their contribution to inequality is symbolic as well as substantive. If a society accepts unnecessary and unreasonable disparities in high-school quality, it legitimates not only those inequalities but many others as well. Conversely, if a society commits itself to eliminating disparities in high-school quality, however small, it may encourage other institutions and individuals to reassess their behavior. The difficulty is that nobody knows how to eliminate disparities in high-school quality, at least when these are defined in terms of educational outcomes. The best we can do is eliminate disparities in inputs. As we have seen, this is unlikely to have much effect on test scores, educational attainment, or occupational status. We suspect that it may alter other outcomes to some extent, and that it may also alter how both students and communities feel about their schools. But this is mere speculation.

For those who want to alter not only symbols and feelings but individual outcomes, the data suggest a shift in emphasis from differences among high schools to differences within high schools. Most of the variation in adult characteristics arises among individuals who attend the same high school. Our data do not tell us whether schools can reduce such variation, much less how they can do so, but the data do show that progress on this front is potentially far more important than progress in reducing differences between schools.[31]

---

[31] For an analysis of the determinants of within-school variance of test performance see Byron W. Brown and Daniel H. Saks, "The Production and Distribution of Cognitive Skills Within Schools," *Journal of Political Economy*, 83 (1975), 571–593. Brown and Saks argue that schools actually try to increase the variance in scores, and that this helps explain the negligible relationship between school resources and changes in mean test score in studies such as ours. This possibility deserves more attention than we have given it.

Community Colleges and Social Stratification *

JEROME KARABEL

Harvard University

The expansion of the community colleges in recent years repeats an American pattern that couples class-based tracking with "educational inflation." Shaped by a changing economy and by the American ideology of equal opportunity, community colleges are moving toward vocational rather than transfer curricula and are channeling first generation college students into these programs. The author examines the social forces behind the community college movement and the social processes within the community colleges that have produced a submerged class conflict in higher education.

In recent years a remarkable transformation has occurred in American higher education, a change as far-ranging in its consequences as the earlier transformation of the American high school from an elite to a mass institution. At the forefront of this development has been the burgeoning two-year community college movement. Enrolling 153,970 students in 1948, two-year public colleges increased their enrollment by one million over the next twenty years to 1,169,635 in 1968 (Department of Health, Education, and Welfare, 1970, p. 75). This growth in enrollment has been accompanied by an increase in the number of institutions; during the 1960's, the number of community colleges increased from 656 to 1,100. Nationally, one-third of all students who enter higher education today start in a community col-

---

* I would like to thank Christopher Jencks, David Riesman, Russell Thackrey, and Michael Useem for their comments on an earlier draft of this paper. The author takes full responsibility for the views expressed in this article.

lege. In California, the state with the most intricate network of community colleges, students who begin in a community college represent 80 per cent of all entering students (Medsker & Tillery, 1971, 16-17). In the future, the role of community colleges in the system of higher education promises to become even larger.

A complex set of forces underlies this extraordinary change in the structure of American higher education. One critical factor in the expansion and differentiation of the system of colleges and universities has been a change in the structure of the economy. Between 1950 and 1970, the proportion of technical and professional workers in the labor force rose from 7.1 per cent to 14.5 per cent (Bureau of the Census, 1971a, p. 225). Some of this increase took place among traditional professions, such as law and medicine, but much of it occurred among growth fields such as data processing and the health semi-professions which frequently require more than a high school education but less than a bachelor's degree. Community colleges have been important in providing the manpower for this growing middle-level stratum and, if current projections of occupational trends are correct, they are likely to become indispensable in filling labor force needs during the next few years. Openings for library technicians and dental hygienists, for example, jobs for which community colleges provide much of the training, will number 9,000 and 2,400 respectively per year for the next decade. Overall, the largest growth area until 1980 will be the technical and professional category with a projected increase of 50 per cent (Bushnell and Zagaris, 1972, p. 135). Without these major changes in the American economy, it is extremely unlikely that the community college movement would have attained its present dimensions.

Although a change in the nature of the labor force laid the groundwork for a system of two-year public colleges, the magnitude and shape of the community college movement owe much to American ideology about equal opportunity through education. Observers, both foreign and domestic, have long noted that Americans take pride in their country's openness—in its apparent capacity to let each person advance as far as his abilities can take him, regardless of social origins. This perceived freedom from caste and class is often contrasted to the aristocratic character of many European societies.[1] America, according to the ideology, is the land of opportunity, and the capstone of its open opportunity structure is its system of public education.

---

[1] Contrary to popular perceptions, American and European rates of social mobility, at least as measured by mobility from manual to non-manual occupations, are very similar. For data on this point see Lipset and Bendix (1959).

Community Colleges
JEROME KARABEL

TABLE 1
Percentage of U. S. Younger Employed Males in Professional and Managerial Occupations, by Level of Educational Attainment, Latter 1960's

Level of Educational Attainment	Percentage, Professional and Managerial
High school graduation only	7
One or two terms of college	13
Three or four terms of college	28
Five to seven terms of college	32
Eight or more terms of college	82

Source: Unpublished tabulations of the October 1967, 1968, and 1969 Current Population Surveys of the Bureau of the Census, in which the occupations of younger persons, and the imputed earnings for the various occupations were related to levels of educational attainment. (Jaffe and Adams, 1972, p. 249)

Americans have not only believed in the possibility of upward mobility through education, but have also become convinced that, in a society which places considerable emphasis on credentials, the lack of the proper degrees may well be fatal to the realization of their aspirations. In recent years higher education has obtained a virtual monopoly on entrance to middle and upper level positions in the class structure. Table 1 shows that the probability of holding a high status job, in this case defined as a professional or managerial position, increases sharply with the possession of a bachelor's degree. This stress on diplomas has led to a clamor for access to higher education, regardless of social background or past achievements. The American educational system keeps the mobility "contest"[2] open for as long as possible and has been willing and able to accommodate the demands of the populace for universal access to college.

Response to the pressure for entrance led to greater hierarchical differentiation within higher education.[3] Existing four-year colleges did not, for the most part, open up to the masses of students demanding higher education (indeed, selectivity at many of these institutions has increased in recent years); instead, separate two-year institutions stressing their open and democratic character were created for these new students. Herein lies the genius of the community college movement: it seemingly fulfills the traditional American quest for *equality of opportunity* without sacrificing the principle of *achievement*. On the one hand, the openness of

---

[2] See Ralph Turner's "Modes of Social Ascent through Education" (1966) for a discussion of how differing norms in the United States and England lead to patterns of "contest" and "sponsored" mobility.

the community college[4] gives testimony to the American commitment to equality of opportunity through education; an empirical study by Medsker and Trent (1965) shows that, among students of high ability and low social status, the rate of college attendance varies from 22 per cent in a community with no colleges to 53 per cent in a community with a junior college. On the other hand, the community colleges leave the principle of achievement intact by enabling the state colleges and universities to deny access to those citizens who do not meet their qualifications. The latent ideology of the community college movement thus suggests that everyone should have an opportunity to attain elite status, but that once they have had a chance to prove themselves, an unequal distribution of rewards is acceptable. By their ideology, by their position in the implicit tracking system of higher education —indeed, by their very relationship to the larger class structure—the community colleges lend affirmation to the merit principle which, while facilitating individual upward mobility, diverts attention from underlying questions of distributive justice.

The community college movement is part of a larger historical process of educational expansion. In the early twentieth century, the key point of expansion was at the secondary level as the high school underwent a transition from an elite to a mass institution. Then, as now, access to education was markedly influenced by socioeconomic status.[5]

As the high school became a mass institution, it underwent an internal transformation (Trow, 1966). Formerly providing uniform training to a small group of relatively homogeneous students in order to enable them to fill new white-collar

[3] For an empirical study of hierarchical differentiation within higher education, see "Social Class, Academic Ability and College Quality" by Jerome Karabel and Alexander W. Astin (American Council on Education, Washington, D. C., forthcoming).

[4] The term "community college" is used in this study to refer to all *public two-year colleges*. Excluded from this definition are private two-year colleges and all four-year colleges and universities. In the text, the terms "junior college" and "two-year college" are used interchangeably with community college though they are not, strictly speaking, synonyms. The name community college has become the more frequently used because of the increasing emphasis of two-year public institutions on fulfilling local needs. Further, as the community college struggled to obtain a distinct identity and as greater stress was placed on two-year programs, the junior college label, which seemingly describes a lesser version of the four-year college geared almost exclusively to transfer, became increasingly inappropriate.

[5] Two of the most comprehensive recent studies of the influence of social class and ability on access to higher education are Sewell and Shah (1967) and Folger et al. (1970). George Counts (1922:149), in a classical empirical study of the American high school of a half century ago, concluded that "in very large measure participation in the privilege of a secondary education is contingent on social and economic status." Similarly, Michael Katz (1968), in a study of public education reform in nineteenth century Massachusetts, found that the early high school was overwhelmingly a middle class institution.

Community Colleges
JEROME KARABEL

jobs, the high school responded to the massive influx of students by developing a differentiated curriculum. The main thrust of this new curriculum was to provide terminal rather than college preparatory education.

Martin Trow places this "first transformation of American secondary education" between 1910 and 1940. During this period, the proportion of the 14 to 17 age group attending rose from about 15 per cent to over 70 per cent. Since World War II, a similar transformation has been taking place in American higher education: in 1945, 16.3 per cent of the 18 to 21 age group was enrolled in college; by 1968, the proportion had grown to 40.8 per cent (Department of Health, Education and Welfare, 1970, p. 67). This growth has been accompanied by increasing differentiation in higher education, with the community colleges playing a pivotal role in this new division of labor. In short, educational expansion seems to lead to some form of tracking which, in turn, distributes people in a manner which is roughly commensurate with both their class origins and their occupational destination.

The process by which the educational system expands without narrowing relative differences between groups or changing the underlying opportunity structure may be referred to as "educational inflation" (cf. Milner, 1972). Like economic inflation, educational inflation means that what used to be quite valuable (e.g., a high school diploma) is worth less than it once was. As lower socioeconomic groups attain access to a specific level of education, educational escalation is pushed one step higher. When the high school was democratized, sorting continued to take place through the mechanism of tracking, with higher status children taking college preparatory programs and lower status children enrolling in terminal vocational courses; similarly as access to college was universalized, the allocative function continued to occur through the provision of separate schools, two-year community colleges, which would provide an education for most students that would not only be different from a bachelor's degree program, but also shorter. The net effect of educational inflation is thus to vitiate the social impact of extending educational opportunity to a higher level.

If the theory of educational inflation is correct, we would expect that the tremendous expansion of the educational system in the twentieth century has been accompanied by minimal changes in the system of social stratification. Indeed, various studies indicate that the rate of social mobility has remained fairly constant in the last half-century (Lipset and Bendix, 1959; Blau and Duncan, 1967) as has the distribution of wealth and income (Kolko, 1962; Miller, 1971; Jencks, 1972). Apparently, the extension of educational opportunity, however much it may have contributed to other spheres such as economic productivity and the general cultural level of the society, has resulted in little or no change in the overall extent of social mobility and economic inequality.

To observe that educational expansion has not resulted in fundamental changes in the American class structure is in no way to deny that it *has* been critical in providing upward mobility for many individuals. Nor is the assertion that patterns of mobility and inequality have been fairly stable over time meant to reflect upon the intentions of those who were instrumental in changing the shape of the educational system; at work have been underlying social processes, particularly economic and ideological ones, which have helped give shape to the community college.

The thesis of this paper is that the community college, generally viewed as the leading edge of an open and egalitarian system of higher education, is in reality a prime contemporary expression of the dual historical patterns of class-based tracking and of educational inflation. The paper will examine data on the social composition of the community college student body, the flow of community college students through the system of higher education, and the distributive effects of public higher education. Throughout, the emphasis will be on social class and tracking. An analysis of existing evidence will show that the community college is itself the bottom track of the system of higher education both in class origins and occupational destinations of its students. Further, tracking takes place *within* the community college in the form of vocational education. The existence of submerged class conflicts, inherent in a class-based tracking system, will receive considerable attention, with special emphasis on the processes which contribute to these conflicts remaining latent. The paper will conclude with a discussion of the implications of its findings on class and the community college.

The Composition of the Community College Student Body

If community colleges occupy the bottom of a tracking system within higher education that is closely linked to the external class structure, the social composition of the two-year public college should be proportionately lower in status than that of more prestigious four-year institutions. Christopher Jencks and David Riesman, in *The Academic Revolution* (1968, p. 485), however, citing 1966 American Council on Education data, suggest that the "parents of students who enroll at community colleges are slightly *richer* than the parents of students at four-year institutions." This conclusion is derived from the small income superiority students at

Community Colleges
JEROME KARABEL

two-year public colleges had over students at four-year public colleges in 1966; it ignores public universities and all private institutions. Several other studies, most of them more recent, show that community college students *do* come from lower class backgrounds, as measured by income, occupation, and education, than do their counterparts at four-year colleges and universities (Medsker and Trent, 1965; Schoenfeldt, 1968; American Council on Education, 1971; Medsker and Tillery, 1971; Bureau of the Census, 1972).

Table 2 presents data showing the distribution of fathers' occupations at various types of colleges. Community colleges are lowest in terms of social class; they have the fewest children of professionals and managers (16 per cent) and the most of blue-collar workers (55 per cent). Private universities, the most prestigious of the categories and the one linked most closely to graduate and professional schools, have the highest social composition: 49 per cent professional and managerial and only 20 per cent blue-collar. Interestingly, the proportion of middle-level occupations shows little variation among the various types of colleges.

Having demonstrated the lower-middle and working-class character of community colleges, it would seem to follow that college type is also related to family income. Table 3, based on nationally representative American Council on Education data for 1971, reveals systematic income differences among the student bodies at various types of colleges. Over one-quarter of all community college students are from relatively low income families (under $8000) compared with about 11 per cent at private universities. Affluent students (over $20,000) comprise 12 per cent of the student body at community colleges but over 40 per cent at private institutions. The four-year public colleges show income distributions between community colleges and private universities.

TABLE 2
Father's Occupational Classification by Type of College Entered (percentages)

Type of College	Skilled, Semi-skilled Unskilled	Semi-professional, Small Business, Sales and Clerical	Professional and Managerial	Total
Public two-year	55	29	16	100
Public four-year	49	32	19	100
Private four-year	38	30	32	100
Public university	32	33	35	100
Private university	20	31	49	100

Source: Medsker and Trent (1965)

TABLE 3
Family Income by Type of College Entered (percentages)

Type of College	Under $8,000	$8,000–12,499	$12,500–20,000	Over $20,000	Total
Public two-year	27.2	34.8	26.4	11.5	100
Public four-year	25.4	31.7	28.3	14.7	100
Public university	15.1	29.7	32.8	22.3	100
Private university	10.6	20.4	27.3	41.8	100

Source: American Council on Education (1971, p. 39)

Prestige differences among colleges also correspond to differences in fathers' educational attainment. In Table 4, American Council on Education data for 1966 show that the proportion of students whose fathers graduated from college ranges from 15 per cent at community colleges to 72.6 per cent at elite institutions (colleges with average Scholastic Aptitude Tests over 650). Over one third of public two-year college students have fathers who did not graduate from high school compared with less than 5 per cent at elite colleges.

The data on occupation, income, and education all run in the same direction and testify to an increase in social class position as one ascends the prestige hierarchy of colleges and universities. Community colleges, at the bottom of the tracking system in higher education, are also lowest in student body class composition. That college prestige is a rough indicator of factors leading to adult occupational attainment and of adult socioeconomic status itself is borne out by a number of

TABLE 4
Father's Education by Type of College Entered (percentages)

Type of College	Grammar School or Less	Some High School	High School Graduate	Some College	College Graduate	Post-graduate Degree	Total
Public two-year	12.7	21.3	31.7	19.1	11.5	3.8	100
Public four-year	12.1	19.4	34.7	17.9	11.1	4.8	100
Public university	8.0	13.9	29.0	20.3	19.0	9.8	100
Private university	4.6	9.6	21.9	18.9	24.4	20.5	100
Elite[a]	1.2	3.5	10.6	13.1	31.3	40.5	100

Source: American Council on Education (1967, p. 22)
[a] Elite colleges are defined as institutions having average freshman SAT's over 650. For more data on elite colleges see Karabel and Astin (forthcoming).

Community Colleges
JEROME KARABEL

studies (Havemann and West, 1952; Reed and Miller, 1970; Wolfle, 1971; Pierson, 1969; Collins, 1971; Spaeth, 1968; Sharp, 1970; Folger *et al.*, 1970). Thus, the current tracking system in higher education may help transmit inequality intergenerationally. Lower class students disproportionately attend community colleges which, in turn, channel them into relatively low status jobs.

However related attendance at a community college may be to social origins, students are not explicitly sorted into the hierarchically differentiated system of higher education on the basis of social class. More important than class background in predicting where one goes to college is measured academic ability (Folger *et al.*, 1970, pp. 166-167; Karabel and Astin, forthcoming). Schoenfeldt (1968), using Project TALENT data, reports that junior college students are more like noncollege students in terms of academic ability and more like four-year college students in terms of socioeconomic status. A review of research on the ability of junior college students by Cross (1968) concludes that they show substantially less measured academic ability than their four-year counterparts although there is a great diversity in academic ability *among* junior college students. In a sample of 1966 high school graduates in four states who entered community colleges, 19 per cent were in the highest quartile of academic ability (Medsker & Tillery, 1971, p. 38). As is common with aggregate data, generalizations obscure important variations among individuals. In California, where admission to the state colleges and university are limited to the top 33 1/3 and 12 1/2 per cent in ability respectively, approximately 26 and 6 per cent of students who choose a junior college would have been eligible for a state college or university (Coordinating Council, 1969, p. 79).

There is evidence that many high ability students who attend community colleges are of modest social origins. In California, for example, the proportion of eligible students who choose to attend the state colleges or university varies from 22.5 per cent among students from families with incomes of under $4,000 to over 50 per cent in the $20,000-25,000 category (Hansen and Weisbrod, 1969, p. 74). It is assumed that many of these low-income students attend a nearby two-year college. Table 5 estimates the probability of a male student entering a junior college (public and private). The likeliest entrant at a two-year college is the person of high academic ability and low social status followed by the high status student of less than average ability. These data, however, cannot be construed as providing the relative proportion of intelligent, poor students as opposed to mediocre, rich students in the community college; instead, they merely show the probability of attending a two-year college *if* someone falls into a particular category. Table 5 also illustrates that there is a diversity of both social class and academic ability in the

TABLE 5
Probability of a Male Entering a Two-Year College

Socioeconomic Quarter	Ability Quarter			
	Low 1	2	3	High 4
Low 1	.04	.07	.06	.16
2	.03	.07	.10	.08
3	.07	.11	.10	.08
High 4	.11	.12	.11	.05

Source: Schoenfeldt (1968, p. 357)

community college. Internal diversity notwithstanding, the community college does indeed stand at the bottom of the tracking system in higher education not only from the perspective of social class, but also from that of academic ability.

The Flow of Community College Students Through the Educational System

A substantial body of research links the presence of a community college to increased utilization of higher education (Medsker & Trent, 1965; Cross, 1968; Willingham, 1970). The Medsker-Trent study, for example, shows that the existence of a community college increases the percentage of people who enter the system of higher education, especially among low status youth of high ability. This extension of the opportunity to attend college to persons of modest social origins or past achievements is unique to this nation and ranks as one of the community college movement's greatest accomplishments. Widely hailed as the "democratization of higher education" (Cross, 1968, p. 21; Fields, 1962, p. 55), the expansion of educational opportunity provided by two-year public colleges seemingly marks a giant stride toward the realization of the American ideal of upward mobility through education.

Increased access, however, does not automatically lead to a genuine expansion of educational opportunity. The critical question is not who gains access to higher education, but rather what happens to people once they get there. The distinction parallels the distinction between equal access (which is what many people mean by equal opportunity) and equal outcomes or results. For community college students, this interest in both access and outcomes leads naturally into an examination of patterns of aspirations, attrition, and transfer to four-year colleges.

Community Colleges
JEROME KARABEL

Patterns of Attendance

Despite the fact that community colleges offer no degrees or certificates higher than an associate of arts degree (A.A.), over 70 per cent of their students aspire to a bachelor's degree with more than 20 per cent aspiring to a degree beyond the B.A. Occupational aspirations are also high among these students with 64 per cent hoping to enter managerial and professional occupations (Cross, 1968, pp. 41-46). Students at two-year colleges, though generally of low to moderate economic and educational backgrounds, desire upward mobility in both education and career.[6] Indeed, high aspirations among community college students, at least upon entrance, is one of the most consistent findings in research on the topic.

In view of the community college's position within the tracking system of higher education, one would expect that unrealized aspirations through attrition would be quite high. Bruce Eckland (1964), in a seminal study of the college dropout, proposed a "diversity hypothesis" which suggested a link between social class and college graduation. The hypothesis is that "the rate of dropout at a college or university varies inversely with the class composition of its student population." Community colleges, with the lowest class composition among American institutions of higher education, are expected to show the highest dropout rate. Indeed, attrition among community college students is commonplace. In California, where the junior college movement is most advanced, the ratio of sophomores to freshmen among full-time students at community colleges is .36 (Jaffe & Adams, 1972, p. 229). While some of these students may transfer to a four-year college and others may later return to higher education, it remains true that there are almost three freshmen for every sophomore in California community colleges. Nationally, 38.4 per cent of two-year college students had received an A.A. degree in four years with only an additional 2 per cent still enrolled.[7] Among four-year college students, 46.7 per cent received a B.A. degree after four years with 11.8 per cent still

[6] We need to be cautious in interpreting this data; the aspirations of community college students may not be as deeply embedded as their counterparts at four-year colleges. There is a tendency in social research to reify data derived from questionnaires, even though the same response to an item may obscure differences in the intensity of the reply (e.g., two students may both check yes when asked if they aspire to a B.A., but one may merely like the idea while the other is committed to it). Further, there is a distinction between *aspirations*, which are frequently high, and *expectations*, which are often more realistic.

[7] Since these data include private two-year college students, they probably *underestimate* attrition at community colleges. Students at private junior colleges are somewhat higher than public two-year college students in both class background and academic ability (American Council on Education, 1971). A few of the studies reported in this paper aggregate public and private junior college data, but this poses little problem in that the inclusion of private institutions tends to provide a conservative estimate of differences between community colleges and four-year institutions. Fur-

enrolled. Noting that nearly 90 per cent of all junior college students expected to obtain at least an A.A. upon entrance to college, Astin (1972, p. 13) concludes that "it may certainly be said that unfilled expectations are the rule rather than the exception among two-year college students." For many community college students the "open door" turns out to be nothing more than a "revolving door."

With less than half of community college students receiving any kind of a degree at all, it is not surprising that few of them transfer to a four-year college and that even fewer obtain a bachelor's degree. The proportion of community college students who actually transfer to a four-year institution is difficult to determine, but estimates seem to range from 25 to 35 per cent. Clark (1960, p. 65) in a study of San José City College, found that one student in four transferred. Trent and Medsker (1968, p. 79), in a four-year follow-up of students who entered community colleges, found that 11 per cent had obtained a B.A., 22 per cent were still enrolled, and 67 per cent were no longer in college. Whatever the precise figures, we can surely say that no more than half of the over 70 per cent of community college students who aspire to a bachelor's degree upon entrance transfer to a four-year institution.

The number of community college entrants who obtain a B.A. is, of course, smaller than the number of transfers. Folger *et al.* (1970, p. 174) report that 22 per cent of junior college entrants obtain a B.A. within five years. Trent and Medsker (1968) find that slightly more than one junior college entrant in ten has a bachelor's degree four years after high school graduation. In comparison, 49 per cent of students who entered private colleges and universities have a B.A., with an additional 21 per cent still enrolled. Knoell and Medsker (1964), in the best study of students who do transfer from community colleges to four-year institutions, show that 62 per cent of these transfer students get a B.A. after three years and 9 per cent remain enrolled. For those community college entrants who succeed in transferring to a four-year college there is apparently a good chance that, despite a somewhat lower grade point average than native students, they will obtain a diploma.

Some indirect evidence suggests that the community college students who go on to a bachelor's degree are from higher socioeconomic backgrounds than students who never graduate. One indication of this is the finding that students enrolled in the transfer curriculum are from more affluent backgrounds than those in non-transfer programs (Cross, 1970, p. 191; Cohen, 1971, p. 72; Bushnell & Zagaris,

---

ther, since public colleges comprise well over 85 percent of total two-year college enrollment (HEW, 1970, p. 33), it is highly unlikely that the inclusion of private junior colleges seriously affects the results of these studies.

1972, p. 28). Unpublished ACE data from a 1969 follow-up of the entering class of 1966 show that the estimated probability of transferring from a junior college (public or private) to a four-year institution increases in linear fashion as father's educational attainment rises from less than high school (45 per cent transfer to a four-year college) to college graduate or higher (58 per cent). While the data relating social class at the community college to the attainment of a bachelor's degree are inadequate, they do suggest that the community college serves the middle class at least as well as it serves the working class. Christopher Jencks, in a personal communication, however, has suggested an alternative interpretation: "one of the primary functions of the two-year colleges is not to "cool out" (see pp. 536-540) the upwardly mobile working class, but to cool out the downwardly mobile middle class who are not so smart." This is a central question for students of higher education and stratification. It is one that is susceptible to empirical investigation, but existing research simply cannot settle the matter.

One of the most interesting findings to emerge from the research on community college attrition is that the sheer fact of attending a community college, *controlling for other variables,* seems to increase the likelihood of dropping out. Astin's recent longitudinal study, which controlled a myriad of variables (including aspirations, SES, and ability) applied the regression formula developed to predict returning for a second year at four-year college to two-year colleges and found that the expected rate of persistence exceeded the actual rate at 14 of 23 institutions. When he applied the formula for two-year colleges at four-year institutions, the actual persistence rates exceeded the expected ones in 151 out of 189 cases. Persistence, as measured by returning for a second year, seems negatively affected by attending a community college.[8]

The finding that community colleges have a negative impact on persistence, taking differential student characteristics at entrance into account, fits in with the repeated finding of a general positive relationship between institutional selectivity and the probability of staying in school. In a four-year national longitudinal study, Astin and Panos (1969) found that college selectivity is positively related to student persistence even when student inputs, including ability and

[8] The fact that community colleges are almost all commuter rather than residential institutions may contribute to their apparently negative impact on student persistence. Astin, in a personal communication, reports that much of the difference between two- and four-year colleges in attrition disappears when commuting is controlled. There may be a strain for the commuter student between the more academic world of college and the less intellectual world of family, neighborhood, and peers. One way to resolve this conflict is to move into a residential setting, but a more common resolution of the problem seems to be to drop out of college altogether.

SES, are controlled. Wegner and Sewell (1970), using Wisconsin data, have shown that type of college attended accounts for 3.1 per cent of the variance in graduation *beyond* the effects of academic ability, occupational aspiration, and SES. It is thus not surprising that community colleges, which are among the least selective institutions of higher education, have a negative impact on student persistence.

Since college selectivity negatively affects grades (Astin, 1971), the finding that attendance at a selective institution, even when controlling for student characteristics at entrance, increases the likelihood of remaining in college is somewhat surprising. Perhaps the greater the selectivity of the college the more likely the institution is to expect its students to graduate. Conversely, less selective colleges may exaggerate the differences between those who are "college material" and those who are not—flunking out students who might otherwise have skimmed by. The community colleges were designed, in part, to provide a limited number of transfer students to four-year colleges. Aware that its reputation as a transfer institution depends on the success of its students who attend four-year colleges and universities, the community college may "cool out" (see the next section) students who might have survived elsewhere. In short, low selectivity coupled with a built-in awareness of a sorting function may contribute to high rates of attrition.

The data presented in Table 6 show dramatically the negative impact of attending a community college, controlling separately for academic ability and socioeconomic status, on the probability of obtaining a bachelor's degree in five years. These data, though lacking a simultaneous control for SES and ability, provide evidence for massive differentials between junior and senior college entrants in rates of college completion within the same categories of class and intelligence. Among high aptitude men, for example, more than two-thirds of senior college entrants obtain a B.A. in five years compared with less than one- third among two-year college entrants. One could argue that these differentials will decrease over time as community college students have a chance to complete their degrees, but Eckland's (1964) study suggests that this may be dubious. Offering a "persistence hypothesis" which proposes that class differentials in rates of college completion increase over time, Eckland verifies this theory with empirical evidence. Since community colleges have a disproportionately large share of lower-class students, the persistence hypothesis suggests that the gap between two- and four-year college entrants in obtaining a four-year diploma may well increase over the years.

Another notable finding which emerges from studies of the progress of community college students through the educational system is the failure of massive systems of public two-year colleges to increase the number of people obtaining

TABLE 6
Proportion of Students Receiving Bachelor's Degrees Among Senior and Junior College Entrants with Similar Academic Aptitude, by Sex

Academic Aptitude and SES by Type of College	Percent Graduating from College Men	Percent Graduating from College Women
Academic aptitude		
High		
Senior College	70	74
Junior College	31	40
High-Medium		
Senior College	55	60
Junior College	19	20
Socioeconomic Status		
High		
Senior College	67	70
Junior College	21	26
High-Medium		
Senior College	57	63
Junior College	23	21

Source: Folger, et. al. (1970, p. 176)

bachelor's degrees. This finding is contrary to what we might expect; community colleges were supposed to increase the number of four-year degrees by increasing the number of low SES and high ability students who received bachelor's degrees. Jaffe and Adams (1972, pp. 230-231), using Census Bureau data from the late 1960's, find that the Pacific division (California accounts for 75 per cent of the young population) shows the second lowest proportion of the *age cohort* completing four years of college among the nine census divisions. California, with the largest system of community colleges in the nation, apparently provides four or more years of college to an unusually small proportion of its population (Knoell and Medsker, 1964, p. 3; Coordinating Council, 1969, p. 28; Jencks and Riesman, 1968, p. 489). The Rocky Mountain region, which also has a highly developed system of two-year colleges (but without the cultural milieu of the Pacific Coast states which, one could argue, might lead to high attrition) is the *lowest* of the nine regions in the proportion of the age group receiving bachelor's degrees.

The implications of the failure of the community college movement to expand opportunity for the attainment of the B.A., the credential which is critical for admission into the professional and managerial upper-middle class, are far-ranging.

The Folger Commission, reflecting on their findings regarding socioeconomic status and educational progress, expresses concern:

> Paradoxically, the community colleges appear to have increased college opportunity for low-status youth, and at the same time to have increased socio-economic differentials in college completion. They have been successful in getting low-income youth into college, but have not increased their chances of getting a degree nearly as much. (Folger et al., 1970, p. 319)

The complexity of the relationships among social class, attrition, and the community college should not be allowed to obscure their importance for an understanding of the stratification function of two-year public colleges. Eckland's "diversity hypothesis," stated at the beginning of this section, led us to expect high attrition among community colleges from the relatively low status composition of their student body. Notwithstanding high aspirations, attrition was shown to be prevalent among community college students. The fact of attending a two-year college, even controlling for ability, social class, and other variables, has a negative impact on persistence. Hence, the high attrition rate at the community college is not merely an outgrowth of the low status social composition of its student body. Tracking in higher education leads to disproportionately high attendance of low status students at community colleges which, in turn, decreases the likelihood that they will stay in school. Further, once a student is in a community college, both Eckland's persistence hypothesis and fragmentary evidence from transfer programs suggest that the high status student is more likely to remain in school, to transfer, and to obtain a bachelor's degree. This process does not contribute to equal educational opportunity, though it may contribute something to explaining the failure of community colleges to increase the proportion of college graduates. Writing in 1964, Eckland warned that "social-class differences will increasingly determine who graduates among the college entrants of the next few decades, since it is apparently among the less qualified students that class origins have the greatest impact" (p. 50). If current trends continue, his analysis will have been prophetic.

Cooling Out: Process and Functions

The preceding section on patterns of attendance among community college students showed large discrepancies between aspirations and their realization. Unrealized educational aspirations, almost always linked to a desire for upward mobility, reach genuinely massive proportions among community college students. Clearly, the social process which enables those who entered the junior college with high hopes never to be realized to adjust to their situation bears close investigation.

The key to this process is what Burton Clark (1960), in a classic case study of San José City College (a two-year institution), referred to as "cooling out." The community college, according to Clark, has three types of students; pure terminal (usually occupational), pure transfer, and latent terminal. The latent terminal student, the one who would like to transfer but who is not likely to meet the qualifications, poses a serious problem for the junior college. The crux of the dilemma is how to gently convince the latent terminal student that a transfer program is inappropriate for him without seeming to deny him the equal educational opportunity that Americans value so highly. Clark does not specify the class origins of these students, but since the modal community college student is of relatively low social status (Cross, 1971) and since SES is itself related to both academic ability and to the probability of dropping out of college, it seems fair to assume that many of them are working class or lower middle class. A great deal is thus at stake here: failure to give these students a "fair shake" would undermine American confidence in the democratic character of the educational system and, very possibly, of the larger society.

"Cooling out," the process described by Clark (pp. 71-76) of handling latent terminal students, begins even before the student arrives as a freshman. A battery of pre-entrance tests are given, and low scores lead to remedial classes which not only cast doubt on the student's promise, but which also slow his movement toward courses for credit. The second step is a meeting with a counselor to arrange the student's class schedule. In view of test scores, high school record, and the student's objectives, the counselor tries to assist the student in choosing a realistic program.[9]

The next step of the process Clark describes in his case study of San José is a specially devised course called "Psychology 5, Orientation to College." A one-unit mandatory course, it is designed to assist the student in selecting a program and places special emphasis on the problem of "unrealistic aspirations." Counselors

[9] In discussing the role of guidance in the junior college, it is interesting to observe the connection between the growth of the school counseling profession and educational tracking. As long as the curriculum at a particular level of schooling remains unified, there is relatively little need for guidance. However, when a number of curricula leading to occupations of varying prestige come into being, counseling becomes a virtual necessity. It is worth noting in this connection the long-standing enthusiasm of the business community for guidance programs. George S. Counts, in a study entitled *School and Society in Chicago* (1928), noted the fervor with which the Chicago Association of Commerce, the city's dominant business association, supported the establishment of a program of vocational guidance in the public schools in the early twentieth century.

report that the course provides an ideal opportunity "to talk tough" in an impersonal way to latent terminal students.

The cooling out process has, until this point, been gentle, and the latent-terminal student can refuse to heed the subtle and not-so-subtle hints he has been given. The fourth step of the process, however—dissemination of "need for improvement notices," given to students in courses where they are getting low grades—is impossible to ignore. If the student does not seek guidance, the counselor, with the authority of the disciplinary apparatus behind him, requests to see the student. All of this goes into the student's permanent record.

The fifth and possibly most decisive step of the process is the placing of a student on probation. This is to pressure him into a realistic program. "The real meaning of probation," says Clark, "lies in its killing off the hope of some of the latent terminal students" (p. 75).

The purpose of the drawn-out counseling procedure is not to bludgeon the student into dropping out, but rather to have the student himself decide to switch out of the transfer program. If the student can be persuaded to take himself out of the competition without being forced out of it (through being flunked out), he is much more likely to retain a benign view of the sorting process.

The opaqueness of the cooling out function is indispensable to its successful performance. In a revealing passage, Clark describes the nature of the problem:

A dilemma of this role, however, is that it needs to remain reasonably latent, not clearly perceived and understood by prospective clientele. Should the function become obvious, the ability of the junior college to perform it would be impaired. The realization that the junior college is a place where students reach undesired destinations would turn the pressure for college admission back on the "protected" colleges. The widespread identification of the junior college as principally a transfer station, aided by the ambiguity of the "community college" label, helps keep this role reasonably opaque to public scrutiny. (p. 165)

The implication of this passage, of course, is that the community college would be unable to perform its task of allowing high aspirations to gently subside if its social function were understood by those most directly affected by it. Clark considers "the student who filters out of education while in the junior college ... to be very much what such a college is about" (p. 84), and refers to the "transforming of transfer students into terminal students" as the community college's "operational specialty" (p. 146).

One problem with Clark's analysis of the community college is that he perceives the "situation of structured failure" to emerge out of a conflict between the rigour-

Community Colleges
JEROME KARABEL

ous academic standards of higher education and the non-selective open door. What Clark has failed to do here is to take his analysis a step further to analyze the social function of standards. Rothbart (1970) notes that "objective" academic standards also serve to exclude the poor and minorities from the university. The even-handed application of these standards to all groups gives each individual the feeling that he "had his chance." Academic standards, far from being the quintessential expression of an objective ivory tower concept, justify the university as a means of distributing privilege and of legitimating inequality. This is not to deny that academic standards have important intellectual substance, but it is to say that standards do have a class function. Indeed, what appears to Clark to be a conflict between professors committed to standards and students who do not "measure up" is, in a wider sense, a conflict between low-status students demanding upward mobility and a system unable to fully respond to their aspirations because it is too narrow at the top. Academic standards are located in the midst of this conflict and serve as a "covert mechanism" which, according to Rothbart, enables the university to "do the dirty work for the rest of society" (p. 174). The cooling out process, the opaqueness of which Clark himself stresses, is thus the expression not only of an academic conflict, but also of a submerged class conflict.

Community colleges, which are located at the very point in the structure of educational and social stratification where cultural aspirations clash head on with the realities of the class system, developed cooling out as a means not only of allocating people to slots in the occupational structure, but also of legitimating the process by which people are sorted. One of its main features is that it causes people to blame themselves rather than the system for their "failure." This process was an organic rather than a conscious one; cooling out was not designed by anyone but rather grew out of the conflict between cultural aspirations and economic reality. Commitment to standards, sincerely held by many academics, may have played a small part in this process, but professorial devotion to academic rigor could disappear and the underlying cultural and structural conflict would remain. Cooling out, or something very much like it, was and is inevitable given this conflict.

The cooling out process not only allows the junior college to perform its sorting and legitimation functions; given the class composition of the community college and the data on attrition, it also enables the two-year college to contribute to the intergenerational transmission of privilege (Bowles, 1971a and 1971b). At the bottom of an increasingly formalized tracking system in higher education, community colleges channel working-class students away from four-year colleges and into middle-level technical occupations. Having gained access to higher education, the low status student is often cooled out and made to internalize his structurally induced failure. The tremendous disjunction between aspirations and their realization, a potentially troublesome political problem, is thus mitigated and the ideology of equal opportunity is sustained. That community colleges have a *negative* impact on persistence, that they do *not* increase the number of bachelor's degrees, that they seem to provide the greatest opportunity for transfer (and hence mobility) to *middle* class students—these are all facts which are unknown to their clientele. The community college movement, seemingly a promising extension of equal educational opportunity, in reality marks the extension of a class-based tracking system into higher education and the continuation of a long historical process of educational escalation without real change.

Tracking Within the Community College—Vocational Education

The subordinate position of the community college within the tracking system of higher education has often been noted. What has been less frequently noted is that tracking also takes place *within* the community college. Two-year public colleges are almost always open door institutions, but admission to programs within them is often on a selective basis. What this generally means in practice is that students who are not "transfer material" are either tracked into vocational programs or cooled out altogether.

Class-based tracking, whether between schools, within schools, or both, is not new in American education. This pattern extends back into the early twentieth century, the period during which the American high school became a mass institution.[10] If the theory of class-based hierarchical differentiation in education is applied to the question of tracking within the community college, it would lead us to expect a relatively low class composition among students in vocational programs.

Data presented in Table 7 show a pronounced class bias in the composition of community college students enrolled in vocational programs. Compared with

[10] When George L. Counts examined class differences in secondary schools in the early twenties, he wrote:

> These differences in the extent of educational opportunity are further accentuated through the choice of curricula. As a rule, those groups which are poorly represented in the high school patronize the more narrow and practical curricula, the curricula which stand as terminal points in the educational system and which prepare for wage-earning. And the poorer their representation in high school, the greater is the probability that they will enter these curricula. The one- and two-year vocational courses, wherever offered, draw their registration particularly, from the ranks of labor (Counts, 1922, p. 143). See also Trow, 1966; Cohen and Lazerson, 1972; Greer, 1972.

TABLE 7
Selected Characteristics of Students Enrolled in Three Curriculums in 63 Comprehensive Community Colleges (percentages)

Characteristics	College Parallel	Technical	Vocational
Father's occupation			
Unskilled or semiskilled	18	26	35
White collar	46	35	25
Parental income			
Less than $6,000	14	14	24
More than $10,000	36	28	21
Father's formal education			
Less than high school graduation	27	34	50
Some college or more	31	20	14
Race			
Caucasian	91	79	70
Negro	5	7	14
Oriental	1	7	7
Other	1	4	6

Source: Comparative Guidance and Placement Program, 1969. (Cross, 1970, p. 191)

students in transfer programs, vocational students are markedly lower in family income, father's education, and father's occupation. While almost half of community college students in the transfer curriculum are from white-collar families, only one-fourth of the students in vocational programs are from such backgrounds. Students enrolled in technical programs fall in between vocational and transfer students along various measures of socioeconomic status. Black students show themselves to be considerably more likely than white students to enroll in community college vocational programs.[11]

The relatively low social origins of vocational and technical students are likely to be reflected in their adult occupations. Community college occupational programs are broadly designed to prepare people for entrance into the growing technical and semi-professional stratum. Estimates as to the size of this expanding class suggest that it may comprise one-third of the labor force by 1975 (Harris, 1971, p. 254). This stratum occupies the lower-middle levels of the system of social strat-

[11] Minority students are also disproportionately enrolled in two of the lower rungs of the higher education tracking system—community colleges and unselective black colleges. Patterns of enrollment, of course, vary from region to region with community colleges dominant in the West and black institutions more prominent in the South. For data showing that the proportion of minority students decreases as one progresses up the three-track California system see Coordinating Council (1969: 23) and Jaffe and Adams (1972: 232).

TABLE 8
Yearly Income of U. S. Younger Employed Males, by Level of Educational Attainment, Late 1960s (Base: High school graudation income = 100)

Level of Educational Attainment	Income	Percentage of All College Dropouts
High school graduation	100	—
One or two terms of college	110	40
Three or four terms of college	119	37
Five to seven terms of college	121	23
Eight or more terms of college	150	—

Source: Unpublished tabulations of the October 1967, 1968, and 1969 Current Population Surveys of the Bureau of the Census, in which the occupations of younger persons, and the imputed earnings for the various occupations were related to levels of educational attainment. (Jaffe and Adams, 1972, p. 249)

ification, but it creates a sensation of upward mobility among its members because it is representative of the change from a blue-collar (or secondary) to a white-collar (or tertiary) economy. Since many members of this "new working class" originate from blue-collar backgrounds, their movement into this stratum does in fact represent mobility. Yet it may be conjectured that this perception of mobility is only temporary; as more and more people move into these jobs, the prestige of a white-collar position may undergo a corresponding decline in status.[12]

Evidence on the economic returns of these vocational programs is, at best, indirect, and empirical studies on this topic would be extremely useful. Yet it is apparent that, in general, having two years of college is not half as good as having four years (Bowles, 1971b, Jaffe & Adams, 1972). Table 8, based on recent Census Bureau data, indicates that the recipient of five to seven terms of college is closer in income to a high school graduate than to a college graduate. Possibly, there is some sort of "sheepskin effect" associated with the attainment of a bachelor's degree. But whatever the reasons, having part of a college education seems to be

[12] At the same time, however, it is easy to forget that *absolute* changes in occupation, income, and educational attainment can have important consequences in everyday life and may raise general levels of satisfaction. Having more people attend college, while not narrowing the educational gap in relative terms, may lead to a more enlightened populace. Keniston and Gerzon (1972) attack the narrowly economic view of higher education and argue that important non-pecuniary benefits accrue from college attendance. Similarly, a change from a blue-collar to a white-collar economy may eliminate many menial tasks and hence lead to greater job satisfaction. Finally, an absolute increase in the standard of living, while not necessarily abolishing poverty (which, as Jencks argues, is primarily a relative phenomenon), may result in a higher quality of life than was possible under conditions of greater scarcity.

of limited economic value. Whether this is also true for community college students in programs specially designed to prepare them for an occupation remains to be seen.[13]

The Sponsors of the Vocational Movement

Unlike the movement for open admissions to college, which received much of its impetus from mass pressure, there has been little popular clamor for community college vocational programs. Indeed, most junior college entrants see the two-year college as a way-station to a four-year college and shun occupational programs (see the next section). Despite this, there has been an enormous push to increase enrollment in community college occupational programs. This push from the top for more career education marks one of the major developments in the evolution of the community college movement.

The interest of the business community in encouraging occupational training at public expense is manifest. With a changing labor force which requires ever-increasing amounts of skill to perform its tasks and with manpower shortages in certain critical areas, private industry is anxious to use the community college as a training ground for its employees. An associate of the Space Division of the North American Rockwell Corporation makes the corporate viewpoint clear: "industry . . . must recognize that junior colleges are indispensible to the fulfillment of its needs for technical manpower" (Ryan, 1971, p. 71). In the Los Angeles area, Space Division personnel and junior college faculty work together to set up curricular requirements, frame course content, determine student competence, and formulate "on-the-job performance objectives."

The influence of the business community on the junior college is exerted in part through membership of local industrial notables on community college boards

---

[13] Grubb and Lazerson (1972) report that economic returns to vocational education are almost uniformly low, but their review does not include studies of programs at community colleges. Some skepticism as to the allegedly high incomes of graduates of occupational programs for blue-collar jobs may, however, be expressed. Contrary to popular mythology about the affluent worker, the proportion of male blue-collar workers earning more than $15,000 in 1970 was a miniscule 4 percent (Bureau of the Census, 1971: 30). Only 3 out of 10 blue-collar workers earned more than $10,000 in 1970.

We do not know what economic rewards accrue to graduates of community college vocational programs, nor do we know much about the occupational and economic status of the community college drop-out. This is fertile ground for empirical inquiry. A longitudinal study of three groups of high school graduates—students who do not enter college, community college drop-outs, and community college entrants who obtain a degree (A.A. or B.A.)—matching students with similar personal characteristics, would do much to illuminate the effects of attending a community college.

of trustees. Hartnett (1969, p. 28) reports that 33 per cent of public junior college trustees are business executives and that over half of all community college trustees agree that "running a college is basically like running a business." Overt business interference in the affairs of the community college is, however, probably rare; the ideological influence of the business community, with its emphasis on pragmatism and economic efficiency, is so pervasive in the two-year college that conflicts between the industrial and educational communities would not normally arise. One imagines that Arthur M. Cohen (1971b, p. 6), Director of the ERIC Clearinghouse for Junior Colleges, is hardly exaggerating when he says that when "corporate managers . . . announce a need for skilled workers, . . . college administrators trip over each other in their haste to organize a new technical curriculum."

Foundations have also shown an intense interest in junior college vocational programs, an interest which is somewhat more difficult to explain than that of business and industry. The Kellogg Foundation, which over a period of years, has made grants to the community college movement totaling several million dollars (Gleazer, 1968, p. 38), has a long-standing interest in career training. In 1959, the general director of the Kellogg Foundation noted approvingly that the "community college movement can do much to supply the sub-professionals, the technicians so necessary to the professions and industry in the years ahead" (Powell, 1965, p. 17). Kellogg followed up on this interest in career education with grants to Chicago City Junior College in 1963 and 1964 for associate degree programs in nursing and business which came to $312,440 and $112,493 respectively (Sunko, 1965, p. 42). In addition, in the late 1950's, Kellogg made a several hundred thousand dollar commitment to support the American Association of Junior Colleges, the national organization of the two-year college movement which has itself been a long-time advocate of vocational programs (Brick, 1964).

The Carnegie Commission on Higher Education, financially sponsored by, but independent of, the Carnegie Corporation of New York, has also been active in sponsoring career education. In its widely read pamphlet, *The Open-Door colleges,* the Carnegie Commission (1970), made explicit policy proposals for community colleges. Members of the Commission came out strongly for occupational programs, and stated that they "should be given the fullest support and status within community colleges" and should be "flexibly geared to the changing requirements of society" (1970, p. 1). Later in the report (pp. 15-16) the Commission recommended that community colleges remain two-year institutions lest they "place less emphasis on occupational programs." Community colleges, the Com-

Community Colleges
JEROME KARABEL

mission said, "should follow an open-enrollment policy, whereas access to four-year institutions should generally be more selective." The net impact of these recommendations is to leave the tracking system of higher education intact. Considering the class composition of the community college, to maintain the status quo in higher education tracking is, in essence, to perpetuate privilege (see Wolfe, 1971).

The influence of foundations in fostering vocational education in community colleges is difficult to measure precisely, but it is clear that they have been among its leading sponsors.[14] State master plans (see Hurlburt, 1969; Cross, 1970) have also done much to formalize the subordinate status of the community college within higher education and to encourage the growth of their vocational curricula. The federal government, too, has promoted vocational training in the two-year institutions. Federal involvement dates back at least to 1963. At that time, Congress authorized the spending of several hundred million dollars to encourage post-secondary technical education. More recently, the Higher Education Act of 1972 (pp. 77-78) authorized $850,000,000 over the next three years for post-secondary occupational education. In comparison, the entire sum authorized for the establishment of new community colleges and the expansion of old ones is less than one-third as much—$275,000,000.

The language of the Higher Education Act of 1972 makes clear just what is meant by vocational education:

The term 'postsecondary occupational education' means education, training, or retraining . . . conducted by an institution . . . which is designed to prepare individuals for gainful employment as semi-skilled or skilled workers or technicians or sub-professionals in recognized occupations (including new and emerging occupations) . . . but excluding any program to prepare individuals for employment in occupations . . . to be generally considered professional or which require a baccalaureate or advanced degree. (p. 87)

The import of this definition of occupational education is to exclude four-year programs leading to a B.A. from funding. The intent of this legislation, which provides enormous sums of money for community college career education, is obvious: it is designed to fill current manpower shortage in the middle and lower-middle levels of the occupational structure.

The idea of career education which the U.S. Office of Education is "working to

---

[14] Karier (1972) has written a provocative essay on the role of foundations in sponsoring educational testing. The role of far-sighted foundations in fostering educational reform, possibly as a means of rationalizing the social order, is a topic worthy of careful investigation.

spread throughout elementary, secondary and at least community college circles" (Marland, 1972, p. 217) is that the student, regardless of when he leaves the educational system, should have sufficient skills to enable him to be gainfully employed. The idea is a worthy one, but it implicitly accepts the existing system of social stratification. The philosophy of career education is that the proper function of the educational system is to respond to current manpower needs and to allocate people to positions characterized by large disparities in rewards. Commissioner of Education, Sidney Marland, observes that no more than 20 per cent of all jobs in the 1970's will require a bachelor's degree; apparently, this is supposed to provide a rough index as to how many people should attend college for four years. Further, it is worth noting that career education does not seem to extend above the community college level. An idea whose "time has come," it somehow does not seem applicable to the sons and daughters of the middle and upper classes who attend four-year colleges and universities.

Federal sponsorship of vocational programs in the community college may have contributed to the development of a rigid track system (Cohen, 1971a, p. 152). By prohibiting the allocation of funds to non-vocational programs, federal laws have deepened the division between transfer and occupational programs. This division fosters separate facilities, separate brochures, and separate administrations. The result is a magnification of the differences between transfer and vocational programs leading to a decline in the desirability of occupational training.

Also at the forefront of the movement to expand vocational programs in community colleges have been various national higher education organizations. The American Association of Junior Colleges (AAJC), almost since its founding in 1920, has exerted its influence to encourage the growth of vocational education. Faced with the initial problem of establishing an identity for two-year colleges, the AAJC set out to describe the unique functions of the junior college. Prominent among these was the provision of two-year occupational training at the postsecondary level. In 1940 and 1941 the AAJC sponsored a Commission on Junior College Terminal Education. According to Ralph Fields (1962), a long-time observer of the junior college, this commission was instrumental in lending legitimacy to vocational training in the community college.

In recent years, the AAJC has continued its active encouragement of occupational programs in the community college. Numerous pamphlets, training programs, and conferences on vocational training in the two-year college have been sponsored by AAJC. In that the AAJC, the leading national association of junior colleges, has probably done more than any other single organization to give definition to the community college movement, its enthusiasm for vocational training takes on particular importance.

The American Council on Education, the umbrella organization for the various associations of higher education, is considered by many to be the leading spokesman for American higher education. It, too, has given major support to postsecondary technical education. In 1963, the Council sponsored a study of the place of technical and vocational training in higher education. One of the conclusions of the report was that "two-year colleges, if they are to assume their proper and effective role in the educational system of the nation, should make vocational and technical education programs a major part of their mission and a fundamental institutional objective" (Venn, 1964, p. 165). Edmund Gleazer, Jr. (1968, p. 139), Executive Director of AAJC, points to this report as critical in gaining acceptance for vocational training within the higher education community.

Finally, many American universities have looked with favor on the development of the community college into a "comprehensive" institution with occupational programs in addition to its more traditional transfer programs. From the origins of the junior college in the late nineteenth and early twentieth centuries as an institution designed to extend secondary education for two years in order to keep the university pure, there has been a recognition among many university academics that it is in their interest to have a diversity of institutions in higher education (Thornton, 1960, pp. 46-50). A number of observers have noted that the community colleges serve as a safety valve, diverting students clamoring for access to college away from more selective institutions (Clark, 1960; Jencks and Riesman, 1968; Cohen, 1971b). Elite colleges neither want nor need these students; if separate institutions, or, for that matter, vocational programs within these institutions help keep the masses out of their colleges, then they are to be given full support.[15] Paradoxically, the elite sector of the academic community, much of it liberal to radical, finds itself in a peculiar alliance with industry, foundations, government, and established higher education associations to vocationalize the community college.[16]

---

[15] Amitai Etzioni (1970), chairman of the Department of Sociology at Columbia University, expresses this point of view well: "If we can no longer keep the floodgates closed at the admissions office, it at least seems wise to channel the general flow away from four-year colleges and toward two-year extensions of high school in the junior and community colleges." Vice President Agnew (1970), in a speech attacking open admissions, approvingly cited this quotation.

[16] See Riessman's "The Vocationalization of Higher Education: Duping the Poor" for an analysis of the movement to turn the community college into a technical institution. For a brilliant article on the elitism of leftist academics toward working-class students see McDermott (1969).

The Response to Vocational Education: Submerged Class Conflict
Despite the massive effort by leading national educational policy-makers to encourage the development of occupational education in the community college, student response to vocational programs has been limited. Estimates vary as to how many community college students are enrolled in career education programs, but the figures seem to range from 25 to 33 per cent (Cross, 1970; Ogilvie, 1971; Medsker and Tillery, 1971). Over two-thirds of two-year college entrants aspire to a bachelor's degree, and a similar proportion enroll, at least initially, in college-parallel or transfer programs. Many of these students, of course, are subsequently cooled out, but few of them seem to prefer a vocational program to leaving the community college altogether.

Leaders of the occupational education movement have constantly bemoaned the lack of student enthusiasm for vocational education (Venn, 1964; Gleazer, 1968; Carnegie, 1970; Medsker and Tillery, 1971; Cross, 1971). The problem, they believe, is the low status of career training in a society that worships the bachelor's degree. Medsker and Tillery (p. 140), for example, argue that "negative attitudes toward vocational education . . . are by-products of the academic syndrome in American higher education." Marland (1972, p. 218) refers to the difficulty as "degree fixation." The problem, then, since it is one of an irrational preoccupation with obtaining a traditional four-year education, leads to an obvious solution: raising the status of vocational education. This proposed solution has been suggested by the Carnegie Commission on Higher Education, the Office of Education, the American Association of Junior Colleges, the American Council on Education, leaders of industry, and scholars in the field of community colleges.

Despite the apparent logic and simplicity of raising the status of vocational education, the task presents enormous difficulties. Minority students, though more likely to be enrolled in occupational programs than white students, seem especially sensitive to being channeled into vocational tracks. Overall, students are voting with their feet against community college vocational programs.

This is not an irrational obsession with four-year diplomas on the part of the students. It is not just snobbish prejudice; there are sound structural reasons for the low status of career education in the community college. At the base of an educational institution's prestige is its relationship to the occupational and class structure of the society in which it operates (Clark, 1962, pp. 80-83). The community college lies at the base of the stratification structure of higher education both in the class origins of its students and in their occupational destinations. Within the

Community Colleges
JEROME KARABEL

community college, the vocational curriculum is at the bottom of the prestige hierarchy—again, both in terms of social composition and likely adult status.

It is unrealistic, then, to expect that community college vocational programs, the bottom track of higher education's bottom track, will have much status. It is worth noting that the British, generally more hardheaded about matters of social class than Americans, faced the matter of educational status directly some years ago. In the 1950's in Great Britain, there was a great deal of talk about "parity of esteem" in English secondary education. The problem was to give equal status to grammar schools (college preparatory), technical schools (middle level managerial and technical), and secondary modern schools (terminal). After considerable debate, the British realized that "parity of esteem" was an impossible ideal given the encompassing class structure (Banks, 1955; Marshall, 1965).

The educational establishment's concern with the low status of occupational programs in the community colleges reveals much more about its own ideology than it does about the allegedly irrational behavior of students resistant to vocational education. A great deal of emphasis is placed on improving the public image of vocational education, but little attention is paid to the substantive matter of class differences in income, occupational prestige, power, and opportunities for autonomy and expression at the workplace. The Carnegie Commission, whose ideology is probably representative of the higher education establishment, blurs the distinction between *equality* and *equality of opportunity* (Karabel, 1972a, p. 42). Discussing its vision of the day when minority persons will be proportionately represented in higher occupational levels, the Commission hails this as an "important signal that society was meeting its commitment to equality." The conception of equality conveyed in this passage is really one of equality of opportunity; the Commission seems less interested in reducing gross differences in rewards than in giving everyone a chance to get ahead of everyone else. The Carnegie Commission, reflecting the values not only of the national educational leadership but also of the wider society, shows concern about opportunities for mobility, but little concern about a reduction in inequality.

The submerged class conflict that exists between the sponsors of vocational education in the junior college, who represent the interests and outlook of the more privileged sectors of society, and community college students, many of them working class, occasionally becomes overt. At Seattle Community College in 1968-1969, the Black Student Union vigorously opposed a recommendation to concentrate trade and technical programs in the central (Black) campus while the "higher" semiprofessional programs were allocated to the northern and southern (white) campuses (Cohen, 1971a: 142). Rutgers (Newark) was the scene in 1969 of extensive demonstrations to gain open admissions to a branch of the state university. The import of the case of Rutgers (Newark) was that the protests took place in a city where students already had access to an open-door community college (Essex) and a mildly selective state college (Newark State). What the students were resisting here was not being tracked within the community college, but rather being channeled into the community college itself.[17] The well-known struggle for open admissions at CUNY in the spring of 1969 was not primarily for access per se, but for access to the more prestigious four-year institutions: City, Brooklyn, Queens, and Hunter.

The pattern in these isolated cases of manifest resistance to tracking within or between colleges is one of minority student leadership. In the United States, where race is a much more visible social cleavage than class, it is not surprising that Black students have shown the most sensitivity to tracking in higher education. Channeling of Black students to community colleges and to vocational programs within them is, after all, fairly visible; in contrast, the *class* character of the tracking system is much less perceptible. Were it not for the militancy of some minority students, it is likely that the conflict over vocational education would have long continued to manifest itself in enrollment patterns without becoming overt.

The class nature of the conflict over tracking has, however, not always been invisible. In Illinois in 1913, there was a battle over a bill in the state legislature to establish a separate system of vocational schools above the sixth grade. Business strongly backed the bill, sponsored by Chicago School Superintendent Edwin G. Cooley. The Chicago Federation of Labor, lobbying against the bill, expressed fear that it reflected

an effort on the part of large employers to turn the public schools into an agency for supplying them with an adequate supply of docile, well-trained, and capable workers [which] ... aimed to bring Illinois a caste system of education which would shunt the children of the laboring classes at an early age first into vocational courses and then into the factories (Counts, 1928, p. 167).

After a bitter fight, the bill was defeated in the legislature.

The tracking which takes place in the community college is, however, much more invisible than that proposed in the Cooley Bill. For one thing, the commu-

---

[17] I am indebted to Russell Thackrey for pointing out the implications of the interesting case of Rutgers (Newark).

Community Colleges
JEROME KARABEL

nity college, by the very use of the word "college" in its title, locates itself squarely within the system of higher education and gives it at least the minimal status which comes from being a college rather than a technical school. For another, the apparent emphasis of the junior college on the transfer function leads to a perception of it as a way station on the road to a four-year college. This view of the community college as a place of transfer rather than a track is strengthened by the subtlety and smoothness of the cooling out process. The community college is a "comprehensive" institution; like the high school before it, it provides preparatory and terminal education in the same building and offers sufficient opportunities for movement between programs to obscure the larger pattern of tracking. Finally, the very age at which students enter the community college makes tracking a less serious issue; there *is* a difference between channeling an eleven-year-old child and channeling a young adult of eighteen.

Whatever the differences between high school and college tracking, there is a marked similarity in the rationales given in each case for curricular differentiation. The argument is that a common curriculum denies equality of opportunity by restricting educational achievement to a single mode which will inevitably lead to some form of hierarchy. In 1908, the Boston school superintendent argued:

Until very recently [the schools] have offered equal opportunity to receive *one kind* of education, but what will make them democratic is to provide opportunity for all to receive such an education as will fit them *equally well* for their particular life work. (Cohen and Lazerson, 1972: 69)

Similarly, K. Patricia Cross (1971: 162), a leading researcher on the junior college, argues more than 60 years later:

Surely quality education consists not in offering the same thing to all people in a token gesture toward equality but in maximizing the match between the talents of the individual and the teaching resources of the institution. Educational quality is not uni-dimensional. Colleges can be *different* and excellent too.

In principle, colleges can be different and excellent, too. But in a stratified society, what this diversity of educational experiences is likely to mean is that people will, at best, have an equal opportunity to obtain an education that will fit them into their appropriate position in the class structure. More often than not, those of lower class origins will, under the new definition of equality of educational opportunity, find themselves in schools or curricula which train them for positions roughly commensurate with their social origins.

The current movement to vocationalize the community college is a logical outgrowth of the dual historical patterns of class-based hierarchical differentiation in education and of educational inflation. The system of higher education, forced to respond to pressure for access arising from mobility aspirations endemic in an affluent society which stresses individual success and the democratic character of its opportunity structure, has let people in and has then proceeded to track them into community colleges and, more particularly, into occupational programs within these two-year colleges. This push toward vocational training in the community college has been sponsored by a national educational planning elite whose social composition, outlook, and policy proposals are reflective of the interests of the more privileged strata of our society. Notably absent among those pressuring for more occupational training in the junior college have been the students themselves.

The Distributive Effects of Public Higher Education

One of the benefits supposed to result from the democratization of access to higher education accompanying the growth of community colleges is a more just distribution of resources in the public sector of higher education. Before the advent of open-door junior colleges, the argument goes, access to a college education was closely related to family income. However, now that everyone has a chance to go to college, class differences in attendance patterns should diminish, and we might expect differences in subsidies received from the public system of higher education to be minimized.

Hansen and Weisbrod (1969), in a study of the California system of public higher education, find that the three-track system of state university, state college, and community college results in poor people's paying for the education of the affluent. Position within the California tracking system is related to the amount of money spent on one's education; the cost of the first two years of education in the tripartite system is $2970, $2700, and $1440 at the university, state college, and community college levels respectively. Thus the higher ranking the institution, the more public money spent on the student.

Eligibility to attend the high-cost state university or the middle-cost state college system shows a generally linear relationship with family income. Table 9 shows that students from families with incomes of over $25,000 are about four times as likely to be eligible for the university and twice as likely to be eligible for the state colleges as are students from families with incomes under $4000. Further, the prob-

Community Colleges
JEROME KARABEL

TABLE 9
Distribution of High School Graduates by Eligibility for Public Higher Education in California, by Type of Education and Family Income, 1966

	Percentage Distribution of High School Graduates by Eligibility for	
Family Income	University of California	University of California and State Colleges
$ 0–3,999	10.7	28.0
4,000–5,999	11.5	26.3
6,000–7,999	11.9	30.5
8,000–9,999	16.2	33.2
10,000–12,499	19.4	37.1
12,500–14,999	22.5	39.8
15,000–17,499	27.9	45.4
17,500–19,999	29.5	45.1
20,000–24,999	33.3	46.1
25,000 and Over	40.1	54.3
Not Reported	13.3	28.0
All	19.6	36.3

Source: Hansen and Weisbrod (1969, p. 72)

ability that a student will take advantage of his eligibility to enter the upper two tracks is also substantially related to his family income (Hansen & Weisbrod, 1969: 74). Family income is thus related to which track a student attends and, indeed, to whether a student attends college at all. Among California high school graduates, 41 per cent of all high school graduates do not enter the system of public higher education.

Students in the higher tracks are more likely to persist in college and hence to get larger subsidies. Figures for the total higher education subsidy given to students in the three tracks are $4870, $3810, and $1050 from top to bottom. Since taxes in California are approximately proportional to income and since the probability of attending an expensive school is positively related to income, the net effect of the California system is to redistribute income from poor to rich.[18] Table 10 shows the net distributive effects of possibly the most celebrated state system of American

---

[18] A minor reversal of this pattern takes place in occupational programs within the community college. Morsch (1971: 33) presents data showing that occupational programs in two-year colleges cost $756 annually compared with $557 for transfer programs. Since low status students are disproportionately enrolled in vocational programs, there may be some minor redistribution of resources from rich to poor occurring.

TABLE 10

Average Family Incomes, Average Higher Education Subsidies Received, and Average State and Local Taxes Paid by Families, by Type of Institution Children Attend, California, 1964

	All Families	Families Without Children in California Public Higher Education	Families With Children in California Public Higher Education			
			Total	Junior College	State College	University of California
1. Average Family Income	$8,000	$7,900	$9,560	$8,800	$10,000	$12,000
2. Average Higher Education Subsidy Per Year	—	0	880	720	1,400	1,700
3. Average Total State and Local Taxes Paid	620	650	740	680	770	910
4. Net Transfer (Line 2–Line 3)	—	−650	+140	+40	+630	+790

Source: Hansen and Weisbrod (1969, p. 76)

public higher education. The real losers in this system are the families (average income $7900) without children in the Californian system of public higher education who receive a negative subsidy of $650. Junior college families, with average incomes of $8800 do slightly better than break even while families with children at the university, with incomes of $12,000, get an annual subsidy of $790.[19]

Again, the pattern revealed by examining the distributive effects of public higher education is part of a recurring historical process.[20] Katz (1968: 53), analyzing the

---

[19] For a critique of Hansen and Weisbrod which uses family income rather than college type as the independent variable see Pechman (1970). Using Hansen and Weisbrod's own figures, Pechman argues that the California system of public higher education does *not* result in a redistribution of resources from poor to rich. Windham (1970), however, applies Pechman's method of using family income rather than college type as the unit of analysis in a study of the Florida system and finds the state of Florida does indeed redistribute resources in a regressive fashion. Whatever the net gains and losses by income class which occur when state tax systems are taken into account, it seems clear that the affluent *do* receive more benefits from state-supported systems of higher education than do the poor. Insofar as California and Florida have unusually large systems of free-access community colleges, the effects may be even more pronounced in states with more limited access to higher education.

[20] The case of public higher education, in which the middle class gains the greatest benefits, may be typical of the distributive effects of many social services in the modern Welfare State. See Titmuss (1964), Marshall (1965), and Blackburn (1969) for evidence showing that the prime beneficiaries of the British Welfare State are members of the middle class.

founding of the American high school in mid-nineteenth century Massachusetts, observes how the middle class was "spreading throughout the whole community the burden of educating a small minority of its children." The study by George S. Counts in the early twenties (1922: 152) strikingly illustrates the historical parallel:

> At the present time the public high school is attended quite largely by the children of the more well-to-do classes. This affords us the spectacle of a privilege being extended at public expense to those very classes that already occupy the privileged positions in modern society. The poor are contributing to provide secondary education for the children of the rich, but are either too poor or too ignorant to avail themselves of the opportunities which they help to provide.

Thus the stratified system of public higher education, like the class based system of secondary education before it, results in a redistribution of resources from poor to rich.

Discussion

The recent Newman Report on Higher Education (1971; 57) noted that "the public, and especially the four-year colleges and universities, are shifting more and more responsibility onto the community colleges for undertaking the toughest tasks of higher education." One of the most difficult of these tasks has been to educate hundreds of thousands of students, many of them of modest social origins, in whom more selective colleges and universities showed no interest. Community colleges have given these students access to higher education and have provided some of them a chance to advance their class position.

Despite the idealism and vigor of the community college movement, there has been a sharp contradiction between official rhetoric and social reality. Hailed as the "democratizers of higher education," community colleges are, in reality, a vital component of the class-based tracking system. The modal junior college student, though aspiring to a four-year diploma upon entrance, receives neither an associate nor a bachelor's degree. The likelihood of his persisting in higher education is *negatively* influenced by attending a community college. Since a disproportionate number of two-year college students are of working-class origins, low status students are most likely to attend those institutions which increase the likelihood that they will drop out of college. Having increased access to higher education, community colleges are notably unsuccessful in retaining their students and in reducing class differentials in educational opportunity.

If current trends continue, the tracking system of higher education may well become more rigid. The community college, as the bottom track, is likely to absorb the vast majority of students who are the first generation in their families to enter higher education. Since most of these students are from relatively low status backgrounds, an increase in the already significant correlation between social class and position in the tracking system of higher education is likely to occur. As more and more people enter postsecondary education, the community college will probably become more distinct from the rest of higher education both in class composition and in curriculum. With the push of the policy-planning elite for more career education, vocational training may well become more pervasive, and the community college will become even more a terminal rather than a transfer institution. These trends, often referred to as expressions of higher education's "diversity" and of the community college's "special and unique role" are the very processes which place the community college at the bottom of the class-based tracking system. The system of higher education's much-touted "diversity" is, for the most part, hierarchy rather than genuine variety (see Karabel, 1972a and 1972b), a form of hierarchy which has more to do with social class than educational philosophy.

The high rate of attrition at community colleges may well be functional for the existing social system. The cooling out function of the junior college, as Clark puts it, is what "such a college is about." Community colleges exist in part to reconcile students' culturally induced hopes for mobility with their eventual destinations, transforming structurally induced failure into individual failure. This serves to legitimize the myth of an equal opportunity structure; it shifts attention to questions of individual mobility rather than distributive justice. Cooling out, then, can be seen as conflict between working class students and standards that legitimize the position of the privileged—a veiled class conflict. Similarly, there is class conflict implicit in the differences over vocational education between the aspirations of students and the objectives of policy-makers. This has occasionally become overt, but the community colleges seem to serve their legitimizing function best when the conflict remains submerged.

Can the inability of the community college movement to modify the American class structure be overcome? An assessment of some specific reforms that have been proposed may yield some insight. One obvious reform would be to reverse the pattern that Hansen and Weisbrod (1969) document—simply to invest more money in the community colleges than in the four-year public institutions. The idea of this reform would be both to provide the highest quality education to those who have socioeconomic and cognitive disadvantages to overcome and to put an end to the pattern of poor people subsidizing relatively affluent people through public systems of higher education. This proposal, which may be justified on grounds of equity, is unlikely to make much difference either in terms of education or social class. A repeated finding in social science research, confirmed by both the Coleman Report (1966) and the recent Jencks (1972) study, is that educational expenditures seem to be virtually unrelated to cognitive development at the elementary and secondary levels, and there is no reason to believe that money is any more effective in colleges. However desirable a shift in resources from four-year colleges to community colleges might be on other grounds, it is unlikely to seriously affect the larger pattern of class-based tracking in higher education.

Another possibility would be to transform the community college into a four-year institution—the very proposal that the Carnegie Commission on Higher Education strongly opposes. The purpose of this reform would be to upgrade the status of the community college and to diminish the rigidity of the tracking system. Yet it is highly questionable whether making the junior college into a senior college would have any such effect; there are marked status distinctions among four-year colleges and, in all likelihood, the new four-year institutions would be at the bottom of the prestige hierarchy. Further, the creation of more four-year colleges would probably accelerate the process of educational inflation.

The proposal to vocationalize the community college exemplifies the dilemma faced by those who would reform the public two-year college. Noting that many community college students neither transfer nor get an associate degree, proponents of vocational education argue that the students should stop engaging in a uni-dimensional academic competition which they cannot win and should instead obtain a marketable skill before leaving the educational system. If one accepts the existing system of social stratification, there is an almost irresistible logic to the vocational training argument; there are, after all, manpower shortages to be filled and it *is* true that not everyone can be a member of the elite.

In a sense, the community colleges are "damned if they do and damned if they don't." The vocational educational reform provides a striking example of their dilemma, for the question of whether community colleges should become predominantly vocational institutions may well be the most critical policy issue facing the two-year institutions in the years ahead. If they move toward more career education, they will tend to accentuate class-based tracking. If they continue as "comprehensive institutions" they will continue to be plagued by the enormous attrition in their transfer curricula. Either way, the primary role of the colleges derives from their relation to the class structure and feasible reforms will, at best, result in minor changes in their channeling function.

That the community colleges cannot do what many of their proponents claim they are supposed to do does not mean that they can do nothing at all. They do make a difference for many students—providing them opportunities for better lives than their parents had. They are able to introduce some students, particularly those who are residential rather than commuter students, to ideas, influences, and ways of life that broaden their view of the world. And surely it is not beyond reason to think that better staff, counseling, and facilities could somewhat reduce the rate of attrition in the transfer curricula. It is not beyond hope to think that reform of the vocational tracks could encourage students not to fit like cogs into rigid occupational roles but to have some faith in themselves, their right to decent working conditions, and to some control over their own work so that they could shape the roles they are supposed to fit into. It may be that students and teachers intent on changing society could raise the consciousness of community college students about where they fit in the social system and why they fit where they do. All this is possible, important, and underway in many community colleges.

But as for educational reform making this a more egalitarian society, we cannot be sanguine. Jencks (1972) has shown that the effects of schooling on ultimate income and occupation are relatively small. Even if the community colleges were to undergo a major transformation, little change in the system of social stratification would be likely to take place. If we are genuinely concerned about creating a more egalitarian society, it will be necessary to change our economic institutions. The problems of inequality and inequality of opportunity are, in short, best dealt with not through educational reform but rather by the wider changes in economic and political life that would help build a socialist society.

Writing in favor of secondary education for everybody many years ago, R. H. Tawney, the British social historian, remarked that the "intrusion into educational organization of the vulgarities of the class system is an irrelevance as mischievous in effect as it is odious in conception." That matters of social class have intruded into the community college is beyond dispute; whether the influence of class can be diminished not only in the community college but also in the larger society remains to be seen.

References

Agnew, S. Toward a middle way in college admissions. *Educational Record* 51 (Spring, 1970), pp. 106-111.

American Council on Education, Office of Research. National norms for entering college freshmen—Fall 1966. ACE Research Reports, Vol. 2, No. 1. Washington, D.C.: 1966.

American Council on Education, Office of Research. The American freshman: National norms for Fall 1971. ACE Research Reports, Vol. 6, No. 6. Washington, D.C.: 1971.

Astin, A. W. *Predicting academic performance in college.* New York: Free Press, 1971.

Astin, A. W. College dropouts: A national profile. ACE Research Reports, Vol. 7, No. 1. Washington, D. C.: American Council on Education, 1972.

Astin, A. W. & Panos, R. J. *The educational and vocational development of college students.* Washington, D.C.: American Council on Education, 1969.

Banks, O. *Parity and prestige in English secondary education.* London: Routledge and Kegan Paul, Ltd., 1955.

Blackburn, R. The unequal society. In H. P. Dreitzel (Ed.), *Recent sociology No. 1.* London: Macmillan Company, 1969.

Blau, P. M. & Duncan, O. D. *The American occupational structure.* New York: Wiley, 1967.

Bowles, S. Contradictions in U. S. higher education. James Weaver (Ed.) *Political economy: radical vs. orthodox approaches.* Boston: Allyn & Bacon, 1972.

Bowles, S. Unequal education and the reproduction of the social division of labor. *Review of radical political economics,* 3 (Fall), 1971.

Brick, M. *Forum and focus for the junior college movement.* New York: Bureau of Publications, Teachers College, Columbia University, 1964.

Bureau of the Census. *The American almanac.* New York: Grosset & Dunlap, 1971a.

Bureau of the Census. Educational attainment: March 1971. Series P20, No. 229. Washington, D.C.: U. S. Government Printing Office, 1971b.

Bureau of the Census. Undergraduate enrollment in two-year and four-year colleges: October 1971. Series P20, No. 236. Washington, D.C.: U. S. Government Printing Office, 1972.

Bushnell, D. S. & Zagaris, I. *Report from Project FOCUS: Strategies for change.* Washington, D. C.: American Association of Junior Colleges, 1972.

Carnegie Commission on Higher Education. *The open-door colleges.* New York: McGraw-Hill, 1970.

Clark, B. R. *The open door college.* New York: McGraw-Hill, 1960.

Clark, B. R. *Educating the expert society.* San Francisco: Chandler, 1962.

Cohen, A. M. et al. *A constant variable.* San Francisco: Jossey-Bass, 1971a.

Cohen, A. M. Stretching pre-college education. *Social Policy* (May/June, 1971b), pp. 5-9.

Cohen, D. K. & Lazerson, M. Education and the corporate order. *Socialist Revolution,* 2 (March/April, 1972), pp. 47-72.

Coleman, J. S., et al. *Equality of educational opportunity.* Washington, D. C.: U. S. Government Printing Office, 1966.

Collins, R. Functional and conflict theories of stratification. *American Sociological Review* 36 (December, 1971), pp. 1002-19.
Coordinating Council for Higher Education. *The undergraduate student and his higher education: Policies of California colleges and universities in the next decade.* Sacramento, Cal. 1969.
Counts, G. S. *School and society in Chicago.* New York: Harcourt, Brace, 1928.
Counts, G. S. *The selective character of American secondary education.* Chicago: University of Chicago Press, 1922.
Cross, K. P. The junior college student: A research description. Princeton, N. J.: Educational Testing Service, 1968.
Cross, K. P. The role of the junior college in providing postsecondary education for all. In *Trends in postsecondary education.* Washington, D. C.: U. S. Government Printing Office, 1970.
Cross, K. P. *Beyond the open door.* San Francisco: Jossey-Bass, 1971.
Department of Health, Education, and Welfare. *Digest of educational statistics.* Washington, D. C.: U. S. Government Printing Office, 1970.
Eckland, B. K. Social class and college graduation: Some misconceptions corrected. *American Journal of Sociology,* 70 (July, 1964), pp. 36-50.
Etzioni, A. The high schoolization of college. *Wall Street Journal,* March 17, 1970.
Fields, R. R. *The community college movement.* New York: McGraw-Hill, 1962.
Folger, J. K., Astin, H. S., & Bayer, A. E. *Human resources and higher education.* New York: Russell Sage, 1970.
Gleazer, E. J., Jr. *This is the community college.* Boston: Houghton Mifflin, 1968.
Greer, C. *The great school legend.* New York: Basic Books, 1972.
Grubb, W. N. & Lazerson, M. *Education and industrialism: Documents in vocational education.* New York: Teachers College, Columbia University, in press.
Hansen, W. L. & Weisbrod, B. A. *Benefits, costs, and finance of public higher education.* Chicago: Markham, 1969.
Harris, N. C. The middle manpower job spectrum. In W. K. Ogilvie, and M. R. Raines (Eds.), *Perspectives on the Community-Junior College.* New York: Appleton-Century-Crofts, 1971.
Hartnett, R. T. College and university trustees: Their backgrounds, roles, and educational attitudes. Princeton, N. J.: Educational Testing Service, 1969.
Havemann, E. & West, P. *They went to college.* New York: Harcourt, Brace, 1952.
Higher Education Act of 1972. Public Law 92-318. 92nd Congress, 659, June 23, 1972.
Hurlburt, A. L. *State master plans for community colleges.* Washington, D. C.: American Association of Junior Colleges, 1969.
Jaffe, A. J. & Adams, W. Two models of open enrollment. In L. Wilson and O. Mills (Eds.), *Universal higher education.* Washington: American Council on Education, 1972.
Jencks, C. & Riesman, D. *The academic revolution.* Garden City, N. Y.: Doubleday, 1968.
Jencks, C. et al. *Inequality: a reassessment of the effect of family and schooling in America.* New York: Basic Books, 1972.

Karabel, J. Perspectives on open admissions. *Educational Record,* 53 (Winter, 1972a), pp. 30-44.
Karabel, J. Open admissions: Toward meritocracy or equality? *Change,* 4 (May, 1972b), pp. 38-43.
Karabel, J. & Astin, A. W. Social class, academic ability, and college quality. Washington: American Council on Education, Office of Research, in press.
Karier, C. J. Testing for order and control in the corporate liberal state. *Educational Theory,* 22 (Spring, 1972), pp. 154-180.
Katz, M. B. *The irony of early school reform.* Boston: Beacon Press, 1968.
Keniston, K. & Gerzon, M. Human and social benefits. In L. Wilson and O. Mills, *Universal Higher Education.* Washington, D. C.: American Council on Education, 1972.
Knoell, D. M. & Medsker, L. L. *Articulation between two-year and four-year colleges.* Berkeley: Center for the Study of Higher Education, 1964.
Kolko, G. *Wealth and power in America.* New York: Praeger, 1962.
Lipset, S. M. & Bendix, R. *Social mobility in industrial society.* Berkeley: University of California Press, 1959.
Marland, S. P., Jr. A strengthening alliance. In L. Wilson and O. Mills (Eds.), *Universal higher education.* Washington, D. C.: American Council on Education, 1972.
Marshall, T. H. *Class, citizenship, and social development.* Garden City, N.Y.: Anchor, 1965.
McDermott, J. The laying on of culture. *The Nation,* March 10, 1969.
Medsker, L. L. & Trent, J. W. *The influence of different types of public higher institutions on college attendance from varying socioeconomic and ability levels.* Berkeley: Center for Research and Development in Higher Education, 1965.
Medsker, L. L. & Tillery, D. *Breaking the access barriers.* New York: McGraw-Hill, 1971.
Miller, H. *Rich, man, poor man.* New York: Thomas Y. Crowell, 1971.
Milner, M., Jr. *The illusion of equality.* San Francisco: Jossey-Bass, 1972.
Morsch, W. O. *Costs analysis of occupational training programs in community colleges and vocational training centers.* Washington, D. C.: Bureau of Social Science Research, 1971.
Newman, F., et al. *Report on higher education.* Reports to the U. S. Department of Health, Education, and Welfare. Washington, D. C.: U. S. Government Printing Office, 1971.
Ogilvie, W. K. Occupational education and the community college. In W. K. Ogilvie & M. R. Raines (Eds.), *Perspectives on the Community-Junior College.* New York: Appleton-Century-Crofts, 1971.
Pechman, J. A. The distributional effects of public higher education in California. *Journal of Human Resources,* 5 (Summer, 1970), pp. 361-37.
Pierson, G. W. *The education of American leaders.* New York: Praeger, 1969.
Powell, H. B. The foundation and the future of the junior college. In *The foundation and the junior colleges.* Washington, D. C.: American Association of Junior Colleges, 1965.
Reed, R. & Miller, H. Some determinants of the variation in earnings for college men. *Journal of Human Resources,* 5, Spring, 1970, pp. 177-190.

Riessman, F. The 'vocationalization' of higher education: Duping the poor. *Social Policy*, 2, (May/June, 1971), pp. 3-4.

Rothbart, G. S. The legitimation of inequality: objective scholarship vs. black militance. *Sociology of Education*, 43 (Spring, 1970), pp. 159-174.

Ryan, P. B. Why industry needs the junior college. In W. K. Ogilvie & M. R. Raines (Eds.), *Perspectives on the Community-Junior College*. New York: Appleton-Century-Crofts, 1971.

Schoenfeldt, L. F. Education after high school. *Sociology of Education*, 41 (Fall 1968), pp. 350-369.

Sewell, W. H. and Shah, V. P. Socioeconomic status, intelligence, and the attainment of higher education. *Sociology of Education*, 40 (Winter, 1967), pp. 1-23.

Sharp, L. M. *Education and employment*. Baltimore, Johns Hopkins, 1970.

Spaeth, J. L. The allocation of college graduates to graduate and professional schools. *Sociology of Education*, 41 (Fall, 1968), pp. 342-349.

Sunko, Theodore S. Making the case for junior college foundation support. In *The Foundation and the junior college*. Washington, D. C.: American Association of Junior Colleges, 1965.

Thornton, J. W., Jr. *The community junior college*. New York: John Wiley, 1960.

Titmuss, R. M. The limits of the welfare state. *New Left Review*, 23 (September/October, 1964), pp. 28-37.

Trent, J. W., & Medsker, L. L. *Beyond high school*. San Francisco: Jossey-Bass, 1968.

Trow, M. The second transformation of American secondary education. In R. Bendix and S. Lipset (Eds.), *Class, status and power*. New York: Free Press, 1966.

Turner, R. Modes of social ascent through education. In R. Bendix and S. Lipset (Eds.), *Class, status and power*. New York: Free Press, 1966.

Venn, G. *Man, education and work*. Washington, D. C.: American Council on Education, 1964.

Watson, N. Corporations and the community colleges: a growing liaison? *Technical Education News*, Vol. 29, No. 2 (April/May 1970), pp. 3-6.

Wegner, E. L. & Sewell, W. H. Selection and context as factors affecting the probability of graduation from college. *American Journal of Sociology*, 75 (January, 1970), pp. 665-679.

Willingham, W. *Free-access higher education*. New York: College Entrance Examination Board, 1970.

Windham, D. M. *Education, equality and income redistribution*. Lexington, Mass.: D. C. Heath, 1970.

Wolfe, A. Reform without reform: the Carnegie Commission on Higher Education. *Social Policy*, 2 (May/June, 1971), pp. 18-27.

Wolfle, D. *The uses of talent*. Princeton, N. J.: Princeton University Press, 1971.

Gatekeeping and the Melting Pot: Interaction in Counseling Encounters

FREDERICK ERICKSON
Harvard University

To what extent do junior college counselors advise students on the basis of nominally objective criteria such as grades, aptitude scores and available job or college slots? To what extent do they judge students' potential on other grounds generated interactionally, such as race, ethnicity, appearance or communication style? This article explores the relationship of social identity, cultural communication style and the gatekeeping process. By analyzing films, videotapes and the participants' reactions, the author tested the hypotheses that the more alike counselors and students were in terms of social identity and communication style, the more smoothly the counseling interaction would proceed and the more special help counselors were likely to give students. While the hypotheses were confirmed in general, the author found that race, ethnicity and cultural style could be overridden by other factors. After a discussion of the theories behind interactional dynamics, the author presents the data collected in this study of junior college counseling and discusses the implications of his findings for reorganizing gatekeeping encounters.

* The study was made possible by grants from the Center for Studies of Metropolitan Problems, NIMH (MH18230 and MH21460) and the Ford Foundation. Their support is gratefully acknowledged. My principal colleagues were Carolyn Leonard-Dolan and Jeffrey Shultz, who worked in the first and second halves of the research, respectively. Leonard-Dolan developed the techniques for microanalysis of body motion rhythm whose results are reported here. Shultz developed the "Overall Behavior Symmetry" coding procedures and conducted the statistical analysis reported. I also wish to thank Victoria Steinitz, Courtney Cazden, Beatrice Whiting, John Gumperz and Edward T. Hall for helpful criticism and advice. Responsibility for defects in analysis and reporting is entirely mine.

At various points in people's lives, decisions affecting social mobility are made. The decisions usually are made jointly: individuals may exercise some degree of choice over their own future, but given a scarcity of positions in some areas of society, their qualifications are usually evaluated by others who decide whether or not they can do what they wish. This decision-making process is known as gatekeeping. The people who tend the gates are often professionals with experience and credentials in the fields they monitor. They are found in schools, colleges, employment agencies and personnel offices of business and government. Such decisions can carry enormous weight for individuals. When individual cases form patterns, such decisions may have consequences for society as a whole, especially if these patterns are determined by race and ethnicity.

I gradually noticed patterns in gatekeeping encounters when, from 1963 through 1966, I worked first as a volunteer, and then as a staff member at a Y.M.C.A. in a predominantly black neighborhood in a large American city. I learned quickly that daily living for people in the neighborhood involved an inside-outside polarity: children learned at a young age that they had "to meet the Man"—the white outsider—each day. As they grew up they recognized that white people had power and influence and that black people did not. Survival often depended on the disposition of the Man: at critical times, he could help or greatly hinder a black person in dealing with the larger, white society.

In the early and mid-1960's most gatekeepers were white. They still are. Many black professionals and community organizers with whom I worked believed that black people were routinely victimized by white gatekeepers. Whether the gatekeepers were malevolent or well-intentioned, their attempts to understand and communicate with black people were seen as inept and leading to faulty judgments. This charge caused me to wonder what the Man actually did as gatekeeper. Did he deal with people from his own ethnic group differently from black or Latino interviewees and, if so, how did these differences affect the interaction? I also wondered whether black gatekeepers, as many Blacks argued, would end the victimization of black interviewees by providing them with special understanding and help.

During the late 1960's ethnic and racial awareness developed among many groups in response to the original movement begun by Blacks. As a teacher in an urban university and someone who lived and worked with white ethnic students and adults, I found that many of them also perceived an inside-outside polarity and believed that they too were being victimized in encounters with outsiders who did not understand them. White ethnics felt that they could trust and understand gatekeepers who were fellow ethnics more than gatekeepers who were ethnically different (see also Suttles, 1968).

Gatekeeping
FREDERICK ERICKSON

With several colleagues I decided to examine school gatekeeping encounters for people in junior colleges where counselors are supposed to guide students in making important future school and career choices. At this time in students' lives, gatekeepers can greatly influence what students believe about themselves and their options.

Gatekeeping and School Counseling

The task of school counselors is to let some students through gates within the organization to courses and course sequences of higher rank and prevent others from passing through these gates. School gatekeeping decisions also have consequences beyond the school organization; they can facilitate or block access to the wider society. Since our society places high value on credentials, school gatekeeping decisions can be crucial.

School gatekeeping is complex because counselors function not only as gatekeepers but as advisors. This can be thought of as teaching about the social structure; as advisor, the counselor is a "social structure coach." He or she describes mobility channels and explains how current decisions about courses will have future consequences for advancement in the larger society.

A fundamental conflict between these two roles potentially places school counselors in a double bind—as advisors they are supposed to act on behalf of the students as advocates, while as gatekeepers they are supposed to act on behalf of the organization as judges. This is the classic role dilemma of the educational practitioner, described in reference to teachers by Waller (1933). Counselors face this dilemma because they have considerable latitude in the way they perform their functions. Both gatekeeping and advising behavior can be used by counselors to advocate students' interests or to promote the interests of school and society at the students' expense. While counselors rarely tell students explicitly that their goals are unattainable, counselors can influence students in other ways, e.g., the manner in which they describe the social structure. To some students, school and society can be described as an open structure in which they will be able to decide what they want and act effectively to reach their goal. To others, the social structure can be presented as a closed one in which individuals do not choose for themselves, in which many hurdles and problems lie ahead. Depending on what counselors select to emphasize about society, students may experience counselors' advice as encouragement or as restraint.

Counselors also may actively assist students, by writing letters, making telephone calls, or breaking or bending organizational rules. Dispensing favors, however, is a significant deviation from the routine of a busy counselor. Many of the favors available to counselors are owed them by teachers and other administrators and staff. Counselors must reciprocate to maintain a capital reserve of favors. Help costs time and effort; it cannot be given to all students. Thus, a counselor can perform a different mix of functions with different students; he might be advocate to some and impartial judge or even prosecutor to others. Each counselor must decide, consciously or not, *who he is to be* with each student. I believe that this decision is worked out interactionally and depends in part on the counselor's judgment of *who the student is.*

Social Identity in Counseling Encounters

A person has many attributes or features of social identity. A student, for example, may be simultaneously well-dressed, Italian-American, working class, a 3.8 grade-average, male and athletic. In an encounter, however, only some of a person's total range of attributes will be relevant to the other participant. In a school setting, the attributes that define who a person is ought to be universalistic and salient to school performance and future job success. Such characteristics should be achievable by all, given the required talent and motivation. Ideally, then, academic skill, experience, effort and punctuality should be relevant features in gatekeeping encounters. Particularistic attributes, those which apply only to some and are determined by birth or are not considered relevant to school performance, should not be noticed or measured.

In reality, however, counseling interviews are more complicated than this. Formally irrelevant attributes are not always ignored. Cicourel and Kitsuse (1963), for example, in their study of gatekeeping, interviewed high school counselors to determine how they decided to tell black and white students of various socio-economic backgrounds whether or not they should apply to college (and consequently anticipate a professional or nonprofessional occupation). They found that black students who had average-to-high academic performance were consistently dissuaded from attending college, while white students of high socio-economic rank who had mediocre and even low academic performance were consistently encouraged to attend college. The authors argued convincingly that attributes of social identity such as race and social class—formally defined as irrelevant—became informally relevant to counselors' decisions about students.

Two examples from my own work also show that factors other than universalistic attributes influence the counselor's decision of who the student is and conse-

Gatekeeping
FREDERICK ERICKSON

quently how much help he should receive. The first interchange took place when an Italian-American counselor talked with an Italian-American student about the previous semester's grades:

Counselor: Data Processing 101. Whadja get for a grade?
Student: A "B."
Counselor: Data Processing 111?
Student: An "F."
Counselor: (Stops smiling momentarily, looks straight across at the student and then resumes smile) That's your major, data processing, right?
Student: (Smiling) Yeah, well I was . . . I just talked with him and he said it was 'cause of excessive absences.
Counselor: (Smiling, speaking with a slightly sarcastic tone) Good for you, good for you . . . Math 101?
Student: A "B."

Now according to formal standards, this student should have been in serious trouble—he failed a course in his major area of study. Yet the counselor did not reprimand him for the failure. He merely asked why it occurred and then indicated by going on to other courses that he would overlook the "F." Moreover, the interview continued in a friendly vein and ended with the counselor giving the student a low-numbered access ticket for registration to replace the high-numbered ticket he had drawn originally. This favor enabled the student to register early and therefore sign up for a course he needed before its enrollment was filled. Such deviation from a regular business-like demeanor was unusual, even for students of good academic standing. Clearly, the counselor had decided that this student was someone worthy of special attention, and the factors which determined that decision were not universalistic standards of achievement.

The same counselor interacted quite differently with a Polish-American student who spoke with a slight nonstandard accent. Again, the topic was grades from the previous semester:

Counselor: (Unsmiling and formal) What did you get in your Biology 101 last semester?
Student: Whad' I get?
Counselor: What did you get for a grade?
Student: "B."
Counselor: "B"?
Student: Yeah.
Counselor: How about Speech 101?
Student: Speech, ah . . . ah, I th . . . , I think, I didn't get that one.

99

Counselor: (Looks straight at the student without smiling) What do you mean you "didn't get it?"
Student: I got some incomplete.
Counselor: Ah, . . . how come?
Student: Th . . . then I, ah, ma . . . I did complete them. You know, then I make up the test . . . and then they give me tha . . .
Counselor: Did you make up the tests?
Student: The grades . . . yes, I did.
Counselor: (Looks down at the student's transcript) You don't know all the grades you got, though.
Student: I didn't (unintelligible) and "C."
Counselor: (Looks up at student without smiling) You didn't fail anything did you?
Student: No. No fail.

When the Polish-American student indicated confusion at the beginning of the exchange by responding to a question with a question, the counselor seemed to take that to mean that the student was not intelligent or attentive. From then on he challenged the student's answers even when they were not ambiguous. The resulting tone was unfriendly and at times intimidating. Also, because the student had trouble communicating, the counselor inferred incorrectly that he was having trouble academically. While this student's interview was very different from the first student's, in both cases the decisions about who the students were, and therefore about whether they were worthy of help and attention, were made on bases other than universalistic standards of achievement.

Despite societal norms and organizational rules, particularistic attributes do influence the participants' decisions of who the other person is in an encounter. This is supported by general theories of interaction, especially the work of Bateson (1956), Goffman (1961, 1974), Goodenough (1965), Garfinkel (1967), Cicourel (1972) and Mehan and Wood (in press), and the theories of inter-ethnic relations of Barth (1969, 1972) and Vincent (1974). According to these theories, encounters are dynamic systems in which participants create their own interactional rules and meanings. Rules of relevance (that is, decisions about which attributes of a person will be important to the interaction), or conversely as Goffman (1961) calls them, rules of irrelevance (those features which should be ignored), become part of the participants' definition of the situation. Also, as Cicourel (1972) suggests, the definition of a situation is not a stable feature set at the beginning of an encounter, but a dynamic feature negotiated in the process of interaction. In a counseling encounter a student may be for the counselor at

Gatekeeping
FREDERICK ERICKSON

one moment an "Italian-American medical technology major" and at the next moment an "Italian-American medical technology major who just told me he got an F." If the new feature of the student's social identity becomes situationally relevant, the counselor's role may change.

The notion of encounters as partially bounded social settings as described by Goffman (1961; 1974, pp. 38-39) and Handelman (1972) is useful in thinking about what the relevance rules will be. Encounters are partially bounded in the sense that some of the rules are shared with the larger society while others are generated ad hoc by the participants in the situation. In the case of counseling interviews, the rules shared with the society are the universalistic standards of academic achievement, and the ad hoc rules are the particularistic attributes which formally should be ignored. Since different rules hold in different situations, in some encounters counselors notice a student's grades and ignores his or her ethnicity, while in others they may be more influenced by ethnicity or some other feature of social identity than by grades.

Previous research on gatekeeping, examples from my own work and interactional theory provide a framework for understanding how race and ethnicity might influence a counseling interaction despite formal rules to the contrary. We turn now to a more detailed consideration of how these factors affect an interaction.

The Influence of Particularistic Social Identity

It is clear that ethnicity and race cannot be viewed simply as background variables which constantly affect interaction in the same ways across all encounters. Assuming there is a semipermeable boundary between the encounter and the larger world, it follows that particularistic factors may, or may *not,* leak into the encounter, and that background factors that are relevant outside the encounter may, or may *not,* be relevant in it. In other words, while ethnicity and race may be salient features of a counseling encounter, they are not automatically salient. One needs more differentiated ways of considering the functions of ethnicity and other particularistic attributes of social identity in social relations face-to-face. (For simplicity of presentation I will use the term ethnicity to include racial differences as well as differences of national origin, even though there are important distinctions between these two forms of social labeling.)

Ethnicity seems to influence counseling encounters in two ways: through a feeling of commonality and solidarity between the participants and through a shared style of communication and self-presentation. The feeling of commonality is based on assumptions the participants make about who the other person is: if a counselor and a student are both black or both Italian, they may assume that they are more alike or have more interests in common than if they are from different backgrounds. They may feel more comfortable and expect the interaction to proceed more easily than otherwise. Also, they may have greater loyalty and obligation to a person of their own background.

I would expect that such a sense of commonality would exist to some extent within pan-ethnic as well as ethnic groups. Pan-ethnicity is a category that emerged from my research. It became apparent as the data were analyzed that some ethnic groups interacted more smoothly with each other than others. Two individuals who differed considerably in terms of ethnicity and cultural style, such as a Polish-American and an Irish-American, might nonetheless establish solidarity in an encounter in terms of general features of similarity as white ethnics. The same might hold true for a black counselor meeting a Chicano student. On one level, they are racially and culturally different, but on another they share the characteristic of being members of Third World minority groups. The two pan-ethnic groups I studied were called White Ethnic and Third World. (These terms were the best available without reverting to social science jargon.)

As my research progressed, it also became apparent that participants employed some means of establishing commonality within an encounter which cut across ethnic and pan-ethnic lines. I call this more inclusive category of shared social identity *particularistic co-membership*. Co-membership can be based on a wide variety of similarities, including comprehensive categories such as Catholic or male, or more narrow categories that come up during the conversation, such as "people whose shirts were wrinkled in the wash" or "people who took driver's tests yesterday." In either case they are attributes of social identity that are formally defined as irrelevant to gatekeeping, but become informally relevant on an ad hoc basis. While the counselor and student reveal the most ad hoc co-memberships when they are of the same ethnic or racial group (ethnicity and race tend to predict additional kinds of particularistic sharing), ad hoc co-memberships sometimes make up for the lack of ethnic and pan-ethnic similarities. (See Shultz, 1975 for an extended discussion of co-membership.)

The shared attributes of co-membership are often topics of small talk. For example, later in the interview of the student who failed data processing, a relevant discussion about the student's registration in a physical education class touched off a seeming digression about the student having been a wrestler:

Counselor: You wrestlin'?
  Student: Naw, I have a bad knee, I just had it operated on.
  Counselor: (Smiling) You sure it was the knee? (Implying, "And not your head?")

Student: (Smiling) Sure it was, I got a big cut and big scar to prove it. (Counselor laughs)
Counselor: (Smiling) Okay, now this semester.

While such small talk seems trivial, in fact it is very important. In this case, the counselor had formerly been a wrestling coach at a Roman Catholic high school where the student had been enrolled and where the student's brother had been a member of the counselor's wrestling team. The brief reference to wrestling was a shorthand way of alluding to many co-memberships shared by the counselor and student. Encounters in which counselor and student identify themselves by some form of sharing, whether ethnicity, pan-ethnicity or other co-memberships, usually seem quite different from those encounters in which they do not.

Just as establishment of co-membership affects counseling encounters, so do the communication and self-presentation styles of the participants. Communication styles tend to differ among ethnic groups. Styles vary in terms of gesticulation, eye contact, speech rhythm, kinesic (body motion) rhythm and listening behavior (how listeners show that they are paying attention and are understanding what is being said). Ethnic and pan-ethnic styles are not limited to first-generation immigrants but may persist for many generations. Early work by Efron (1941) and Birdwhistell (1952), later work by Hall (1959, 1966) and my own current work suggest that even after many members of a group speak standard English (or "Boston Irish" or "New Yorkese") cultural differences in nonverbal behavior may continue to be passed on to the next generation, usually without conscious awareness by group members.

In short, the American melting pot may not have melted as thoroughly as many people think. Persons of differing ethnicity may bring subtle cultural differences to encounters without realizing it. Shared or divergent communication styles influence a gatekeeping encounter by affecting its behavioral organization, that is, whether a conversation proceeds smoothly or by fits and starts, whether a counselor and student continually interrupt each other or are both able to talk simultaneously without interrupting, and whether their styles of listening behavior match.

A number of researchers have noted a relationship between the kinesic rhythm of speakers and listeners. Birdwhistell first reported this (1952); more recently Condon and Ogsten (1967) and Kendon (1970) have demonstrated that listeners move in synchrony with the voice accents and body motion of speakers, and Byers and Byers (1972) have studied behavior symmetry and the organization of speaking turns in the classroom. Byers (1972) has also shown that this behavior symmetry is rhythmically organized and that when a conversation is proceeding smoothly, speech and body motion patterns fall into a regular rhythm that is almost metronomic.

Behavior is asymmetric when an interaction proceeds by fits and starts; the kinesic rhythm becomes less regular. Verbally, asymmetry is characterized by hesitating, stuttering or repeating a phrase. Speakers interrupt each other frequently because the rhythm of taking turns at speaking becomes unstable. Nonverbal asymmetry includes distortions in the kinesic rhythm, sudden changes of posture or distance between speakers and behaviors we ordinarily describe as squirming and fidgeting.

Behavior asymmetry often occurs during what Goffman (1961, p. 45) terms an incident—one member of an encounter reveals something new and disturbing about herself or himself. Such moments of asymmetry or, more subjectively, *uncomfortable moments,* are important interactionally, because the issues being talked about then are often crucial to the counselor's gatekeeping function. An example of this occurs when the student majoring in data processing revealed that he got an "F" in a data processing course.

When participants share a communication style, I expect that there will be fewer uncomfortable moments and those that do occur will not be so asymmetric as they would if participants had different styles. Shared communication styles seem to influence not only the ease with which an interaction proceeds but the ability of the participants to read each other accurately. Accuracy is particularly important in the counseling situation where it is often inappropriate for a counselor or a student to deal with problems explicitly, and especially inappropriate to do so if the counselor and student are pan-ethnically or racially different. In our sample if a white ethnic counselor thought a black or Chicano student's major courses would not transfer to a four-year college, it was very unlikely that he would say so directly. Because he feared being perceived as sending global messages that Third World students were not capable of finishing a four-year college, the counselor tended not to deal with specific problems. Similarly, the student could not say "I think your advice is nonsense and I refuse to follow it." Both counselor and student rely heavily on implicit cues, and the more ethnically different they are the more implicit the cues become. Even the manner in which advice is given—grudgingly, with many reservations, routinely or with encouragement—can function as an implicit message about the nature of society, the student's place in it and the counselor's attitude toward the student.

Student and counselor must continually read one another's words, gestures and

Gatekeeping
FREDERICK ERICKSON

tone of voice to infer intent. Rist's work (1970) in the classroom suggests that such reading does take place. He reports that teachers judged students according to their nonverbal as well as verbal behavior. They communicated their opinions implicitly by nonverbal means and by using language to mean more than what literally was said to students. The student and counselor also keep track of the figurative meaning behind what is said—and behind what is left unsaid. When something goes wrong in the encounter there is always the possibility that the counselor or student is saying no.

When cultural styles do not match, the dangers of participants misreading each other multiply. This occurred in the present study in an interview with a white counselor and black student:

Counselor: ... as far as next semester ... Why don't we give some thought to what you'd like to take there. ... (Leans forward) Do you plan on continuing along this P.E. major?

Student: Yeah, I guess so. I might as well keep it up ... my P.E., and (Shifts in chair) I wanna go into counseling too, see ... you know, to have two way ... like equal balance.

Counselor: I see, Ah ... What do you know about counseling?

Student: Nothing. (Smiles and averts eyes, then looks up)

Counselor: Okay ...

Student: (Shifts in chair, smiles and averts eyes) I know you have to take psychology courses of some sort ... and counseling.

Counselor: (Leans back) Well, ... (Student stops smiling, looks directly at counselor and sits almost immobile while counselor talks and shifts in chair repeatedly) it's this is a ... It'll vary from different places to different places ... But essentially what you need ... First of all you're gonna need state certification ... state teacher certification ... in other words you're gonna have to be certified to teach in some area ... English or history, or whatever happens to be your bag ... P.E. Secondly, you're gonna have to have a Master's Degree ... in counseling ... which as you know is an advanced degree. (Short laugh) That's what you have to do to get a counseling ... to be a counselor.

Although this seems like a fairly straightforward interchange, the counselor and the student had very different reactions when they separately viewed a tape of the interview. The counselor's account of what occurred was relatively positive:

Right now we both seem to be concentrating on giving information. ... He on the other hand is concentrating ... on accepting the information and putting it together ... he's got aspirations for the future, P.E. and uh ... uh counseling ... he's a little bit ahead of himself as far as the counseling ... as the year progressed, I guess I got the question so often

105

that it became one of my favorite topics an' I was ready to uh numerate . . . essentially what he did was he started me off on my information.

The student did not share the counselor's view of the interchange. He interpreted it negatively. When asked whether the information given him was satisfactory he responded, "Not especially," and when asked why he felt that way he stated,

Well . . . well I couldn't really say, but I wasn't satisfied with what he wanted to push. . . . I guess he didn't think I was qualified, you know. That's the way he sounded to me. . . . This guy here seems like he was trying to knock me down, in a way, you know. Trying to say no . . . I don't think you can handle anything besides P.E. You know he just said it in general terms, he just didn't go up and POW like they would in the old days, you know. This way they just try to use a little more psychology . . . they sugar coat it this way.

The counselor did not literally tell the student not to go into counseling. But the counselor's hesitant and circuitous talk about certification and other academic requirements to be acquired before the goal was reached discouraged the student from sharing more of his interests or pursuing the goal. Apparently the student correctly assessed the counselor's intent, but the counselor seemed unaware that his remarks were being interpreted that way by the student. Hence implicit messages—intended or not, read accurately or not—are important in the counseling situation. Differences in communication style accompanying differences in ethnic background probably will increase the chances that these implicit messages will be overlooked or misread.

In thinking about the effect of communication style, however, it is necessary to keep intra-ethnic cultural diversity in mind. There may be considerable variation within ethnic groups because members are not acculturated to the same degree. All Italian-Americans do not habitually "talk with their hands" any more than all American Blacks speak nonstandard English. Even if such features of cultural style were shared widely among members of an ethnic category (and they often are), they would not be performed by all members at all times and in all places. A theory of intra-group and inter-group communication styles must allow for situational exceptions to its general rules. Failure to acknowledge these complexities results only in stereotyping. Even though it is reasonable to expect that people of similar ethnicity are more likely to bring similar cultural communication styles to an encounter, and that therefore it is less likely that things will go wrong interactionally just because of cultural differences, it does not work out this way invariably in actual encounters.

The same holds true for persons who are ethnically different, but are members of the same pan-ethnic category. There may be pan-ethnic situational styles, like

Gatekeeping
FREDERICK ERICKSON

the male-white-ethnic-Catholic-school-or-work style and the male-teenage-black-Chicano-Puerto-Rican-street style found in the large American city I studied. Or members of one ethnic group may acculturate to styles of another group within the same pan-ethnic category; for example, second-generation Italian-Americans in Boston speak "Boston Irish." Finally, because of patterns of residence, school attendance and employment, city people who are ethnically different but pan-ethnically similar are likely to be familiar with each other's ethnic styles and be able to "style-switch" to adapt to one another. At the same time, smooth interaction does not occur automatically in intra-pan-ethnic encounters.

Also, encounters between people of different ethnic backgrounds are not necessarily disastrous. A number of possibilities exist. In some inter-ethnic encounters, cultural differences may go unnoticed because acculturation or adaptive style switching averts interactional trouble. Sometimes cultural differences go unnoticed yet cause underlying discomfort or distrust. At other times the differences may cause trouble, and even be noticed, yet may be overridden by other features of the situation such as co-membership.

In summary, I propose that ethnicity can influence gatekeeping through a display of commonality and the obligations of solidarity evoked by that display and through a shared communication style. If a counselor and student are from the same ethnic or pan-ethnic group, they may feel more friendly toward each other than they would if they were from different backgrounds, and the counselor may be more inclined to give the student special help. A feeling of solidarity, or co-membership, can also be established within an encounter by revealing some shared attribute or interest, even if counselor and student are not of the same group. Also, if the communication styles of a counselor and student match, the interaction should proceed more smoothly than it would otherwise. The match in communication styles is also important in increasing the counselor's and student's ability to read correctly the implicit messages the other sends.

In filling the double role of advisor and gatekeeper, counselors have a choice about how to treat the students with whom they work: depending on their decision of who the student is, they may act as advocate for the student or as defender of the system. Their decision is determined within the interaction and may be influenced by features of the student's social identity such as ethnicity and race as well as by the formal standards of academic achievement.

In the study reported here, I examined the relationships between social identity, emotional tone, behavioral smoothness, the match of communication styles and special help given to the student.

Procedures and Data

The work discussed here is part of a larger study in which my co-workers and I studied eighty-two encounters in junior colleges, high schools and industry. The larger study and the technical procedures described here are discussed in greater detail in Erickson et al. (1973).

In the junior colleges, we videotaped and filmed counselors and students in the normal course of the advising routine. No scripts or special questions were written; no special student assignments were made. Some of the students meeting with a counselor belonged to the same ethnic or racial group as their counselors, others did not. Data from twenty-five encounters, involving four male counselors and twenty-five male students from two junior colleges, are reported here. Two of the counselors were white; two were black. Although a few counselors and students had met previously, their acquaintance seemed to have had no systematic effect on the interaction.

A videotape and a film camera were placed on a tripod in a corner of the interviewer's office and operated by remote control from another room. Since the counseling encounters naturally involved two people seated across a desk from each other in a room or partitioned space, they were easy to record unobtrusively. The participants knew they were being filmed and gave their permission in advance. Only two students and one counselor reported that the cameras made them nervous. In each case, this occurred only at the beginning of an interview. Since the interviews were real, all counselors and students soon became absorbed in the genuine business at hand. After the actual interview, often within a week, the counselor and student viewed the videotape of their encounter in separate viewing sessions. They could stop the videotape whenever they wanted and comment on what was happening at that point. Their comments were audiotaped. Transcripts were made of each interview and viewing session, and the points in the viewing session at which counselors or students made comments were noted.

Overview of Variables

The raw data proved difficult to analyze. To tap subtle features of interactional quality or character we needed sensitive indices, and therefore developed our own procedures. Raters read transcripts and listened to audiotapes; they watched films with sound and without, at regular speed and slow motion. We studied three categories of variables: social identity, outcomes, and interactional character.

Social Identity Variables. The social identity variables were ethnicity or race, pan-ethnicity and co-membership. Ethnicity—Italian-American, Polish-American,

Irish-American, Chicano, Puerto Rican, and Black—was determined by last name and skin color of the participants. We then labeled each encounter: intra-ethnic encounters were those in which the counselor and the student were of the same ethnic group and inter-ethnic encounters were those in which counselor and student were of different ethnic groups. In addition, each encounter was labeled either intra-pan-ethnic, if the counselor and student were of the same pan-ethnic group (White Ethnic or Third World) or inter-pan-ethnic if the counselor and student were of different pan-ethnic groups. Each encounter also was categorized according to high, medium or low co-membership. The co-membership score was an index of situationally defined similarities including but not limited to ethnicity and pan-ethnicity.

In our analyses and in the tables that follow, each encounter was counted and sorted according to each of these three categories of shared social identity so that we could see the relationship between *different levels of inclusiveness in shared social identity* and *measures of interactional character and outcome*.

Outcome Variable. One convenient way to evaluate the outcome of an interaction is to measure the special help each student receives from a counselor. We defined *special help* as assistance which went beyond the counselor's regular routine or involved bending organizational rules.

Interactional Character Variables. We coded three aspects of interactional character for each encounter: the overall behavioral smoothness, the smoothness of behavior during the most uncomfortable moment in an encounter and the overall emotional tone of each encounter.

The overall smoothness was assessed by a summary score, the Overall Behavior Symmetry Coefficient (OBSC), which counted the total number of uncomfortable moments, asymmetric verbal interruptions and symmetric verbal overlaps within each encounter. The frequency of uncomfortable moments in an interview turned out to be an appropriate and useful index of overall interactional symmetry. Raters trained to watch films of the interviews were able to identify uncomfortable moments with high agreement.

The second interactional character variable was the Rhythmic Symmetry Code (RSC). It was derived from a detailed analysis of the most uncomfortable of all the uncomfortable moments in the encounters. In all cases for which we had viewing session data (23 out of the 25 cases reported here), the uncomfortable moment our raters designated most uncomfortable was the one which the counselor, or the student, or both, had also identified as an uncomfortable moment. These moments, usually between 45 seconds and a minute and a half in length, were then analyzed frame by frame in slow motion. Charts showing the timing of speech and body motion were prepared, and these charts were categorized according to high, medium or low symmetry in interactional rhythm.

The third interactional character variable, overall emotional tone, was an indication of the degree of friendliness of an encounter, rated on a scale from hostile to very friendly. Rating turned out to be a complex decision process because the deviations from a business-like manner on the part of the interviewer were slight. Moreover, since each counselor had his own personal style, it was sometimes difficult for the raters to make comparable judgments. Generally, however, there was fairly good agreement among raters.

Results

To test our working hypotheses that the social identities and communication styles of the counselor and student affect the character and outcome of the interaction, we looked first at the relationship between social identity and special help. The data in Table 1, despite individual differences among counselors, generally supported our hypothesis. As can be seen from the overall means in the first two rows of the table, students of the same ethnic background as the coun-

TABLE 1
Mean Special Help by Different Social Identity Classifications

Social Identity	Number of Encounters	Counselors A	B	C	D	Overall Means
Intra-ethnic	9	13.0	12.7	—	12.0	12.7
Inter-ethnic	16	12.7	6.8	5.8	8.0	8.0
Intra-pan-ethnic	15	13.0	10.5	5.3	11.2	10.4
Inter-pan-ethnic	10	11.7	—	6.2	7.4	8.6
High Co-membership	7	10.8	18.0	7.9	11.8	12.6
Med Co-membership	9	16.2	9.8	7.3	11.5	10.5
Low Co-membership	9	11.5	6.2	3.8	5.2	6.6

selor tended to receive more special help than students of different ethnic backgrounds (12.7 as opposed to 8.0). Similarly, intra-pan-ethnic encounters resulted in somewhat more special help for the student than inter-pan-ethnic encounters (10.4 to 8.6). Analyses of variance for each social identity category showed that the differences in the amount of special help received were statistically significant when the encounters were classified according to co-membership (12.6 to 10.5 to 6.6, $p < .025$, see Table 6). This suggests that some shared attribute other than ethnicity can evoke advocacy from a counselor.

Since the character of the interaction conveys messages of encouragement or discouragement, even when no special help has been given, we were also interested in the relationship between social identity and interactional character. Looking first at the OBSC, the measure of the overall smoothness of the encounter, Table 2 shows that again the results generally supported our hypothesis. Sharing particularistic attributes of social identity was associated with higher OBSC scores. This suggests that the social identity of the counselor and student is related to the relative ease and smoothness with which the encounter takes place. Interestingly, the differences between high and low co-membership (16.9 to 11.7) were greater than between intra- and inter-ethnicity (14.4 to 13.6). We originally had expected that the OBSC would be an index of shared cultural communication style: encounters between people of the same ethnic group would have high OBSC scores while encounters with high co-membership, including people who are ethnically and culturally different, would have lower OBSC scores. This was not the case. Table 2 suggests that factors of social identity independent from cultural style-sharing influenced the overall ease of the encounter.

TABLE 2
Mean OBSC by Different Social Identity Classifications

Social Identity	Number of Encounters	Counselors A	B	C	D	Overall Means
Intra-ethnic	9	16.2	14.7	—	8.0	14.4
Inter-ethnic	16	11.8	11.5	14.4	15.2	13.6
Intra-pan-ethnic	15	16.2	13.5	17.6	12.3	14.4
Inter-pan-ethnic	10	11.8	—	12.3	14.8	13.2
-High Co-membership	7	18.2	16.0	16.8	16.3	16.9
Med Co-membership	9	11.5	14.7	18.4	10.7	13.9
Low Co-membership	9	12.2	10.7	9.2	15.0	11.7

The RSC, the detailed measure of the most uncomfortable moment in an encounter, confirmed our original expectation: differences for ethnicity were greater than for co-membership. Table 3 contrasts these two measures. Because the RSC is categorical, contingency tables are presented instead of means; the OBSC is presented in a comparable form. The effect of shared social identity as measured by the RSC is significant only for ethnicity ($\chi^2=6.86$; $p<.05$), while

TABLE 3

Incidence of RSC and OBSC Levels by Different Social Identity Classifications

	Overall Behavior Symmetry Scores				Rhythmic Symmetry Codes			
Social Identity	High	Med	Low		High	Med	Low	
Intra-ethnic	4	2	3	9	8	1	0	9
Inter-ethnic	5	5	6	16	6	3	7	16
	9	7	9	25	14	4	7	25
	(χ^2 = 0.47; NS)				(χ^2 = 6.86; p < .05)			
Intra-pan-ethnic	7	3	5	15	10	3	2	15
Inter-pan-ethnic	2	4	4	10	4	1	5	10
	9	7	9	25	14	4	7	25
	(χ^2 = 0.47; NS)				(χ^2 = 4.02; NS)			
High Co-membership	5	2	0	7	5	1	1	7
Med Co-membership	3	3	3	9	6	1	2	9
Low Co-membership	1	2	6	9	3	2	4	9
	9	7	9	25	14	4	7	25
	(χ^2 = 9.10; p < .10)				(χ^2 = 3.12; NS)			

Cell entries are the number of encounters in each category.

the effect as measured by the OBSC approaches significance only for co-membership (χ^2 = 9.10; p<.10). These tables suggest that the RSC is more sensitive to cultural influences in communication style than the OBSC.

The third indicator of interactional character is emotional tone. In Table 4, the overall means show a pattern similar to that found with the OBSC. There were some differences between intra- and inter-ethnic (7.9 to 6.2) and intra- and inter-pan-ethnic encounters (7.5 to 5.8), but the differences were greatest for co-membership (9.0 to 7.0 to 4.8): on the average, the warmest encounters were those where high co-membership was established. These findings support the other analyses in showing both that social identity does influence gatekeeping encounters and that commonality in social identity can be established on grounds other than ethnicity.

Because the RSC tapped the match of cultural communication styles between counselor and student, it seemed to measure social identity as well as general interactional character in a way that the OBSC and emotional tone measures did

TABLE 4
Mean Emotional Tone by Different Social Identity Classifications

Social Identity	Number of Encounters	Counselors A	B	C	D	Overall Means
Intra-ethnic	9	8.6	7.8	—	—	7.9
Inter-ethnic	16	6.8	7.0	5.6	7.1	6.2
Intra-pan-ethnic	15	8.6	7.6	6.8	5.7	7.5
Inter-pan-ethnic	10	6.3	—	2.7	7.3	5.8
High Co-membership	7	9.0	9.4	9.1	8.6	9.0
Med Co-membership	9	7.8	7.7	6.2	6.1	7.0
Low Co-membership	9	6.4	6.4	0.2	5.5	4.8

not. We therefore decided to see whether the RSC was related to the outcome of the encounter in the same way that our other measures of social identity were. The relation between RSC and special help is shown in Table 5. Although the re-

TABLE 5
Incidence of RSC Levels by Special Help Levels

		Rhythmic Symmetry High	Med	Low	
Special Help	High	6	2	1	9
	Med	5	1	3	9
	Low	3	1	3	7
		14	4	7	25

(x^2 = 2.32; NS)

Cell entries are the number of encounters in each category.

lationships were not statistically significant, they did show a trend of high symmetry being associated with high or medium special help. This implies that in some cases a match in communication styles may result in a counselor deciding that a student was someone to be advocated.

Table 6 is a summary of the overall means in each social identity grouping for special help, OBSC and emotional tone. (Again, the RSC is not included in this table because its analysis does not yield means.) The differences in the scores were most significant for co-membership. Also, encounters characterized by high co-membership have the highest overall means on all three measures. They

TABLE 6
Mean Special Help, OBSC and Emotional Tone by Different Social Identity Classifications

Social Identity	Number of Encounters	Special Help	OBSC	Emotional Tone
Intra-ethnic	9	12.7 (5.0)	14.4 (3.7)	7.9 (1.7) ⎫ *
Inter-ethnic	16	8.0 (4.2)	13.6 (3.4)	6.2 (2.7) ⎭
Intra pan-ethnic	15	10.4 (5.0)	14.4 (3.5)	7.5 (1.6)
Inter pan-ethnic	10	8.6 (5.0)	13.2 (3.5)	5.8 (3.2)
High Co-membership	7	12.6 (4.2) ⎫	16.9 (1.8) ⎫	9.0 (0.7) ⎫
Med Co-membership	9	10.5 (5.0) ⎬ **	13.9 (3.4) ⎬ *	7.0 (1.3) ⎬ ***
Low Co-membership	9	6.6 (4.2) ⎭	11.7 (2.9) ⎭	4.8 (2.7) ⎭

*$p < .05$ **$p < .025$ ***$p < .005$
Standard deviations are shown in parentheses.

were the smoothest and most friendly, and students received the most special help. These findings suggest that neither ethnicity nor cultural communication style alone is a necessary condition for positive interactional character and outcomes. While ethnicity usually made a big difference in how the counselor and student treated each other, sometimes it did not. This is consistent with the earlier theoretical discussion.

For each counselor we studied, there were encounters in which a student who differed in ethnicity and cultural communication style from the counselor received as much friendliness and special help as did a student who was similar to the counselor. But these were exceptions, and in almost every one of them situationally relevant, particularistic co-membership was established between counselor and student. This suggests a fundamental principle underlying the data reported in Table 6: If a student is ethnically different from the counselor and wants special help and friendliness, he or she must make up for ethnic differences by establishing some other form of co-membership. For example, if a student is Polish-American and the counselor is Italian-American, it helps if they both happen to be wrestlers and reveal themselves as such.

It also follows that lacking co-memberships, a student might make up for background differences in other situational ways, such as acting especially deferential or attentive toward the counselor. There were students in our sample who had extremely low co-membership with their counselor but who displayed high deference and attention and received a moderate amount of special help. Conversely, there were cases in which students sharing ethnicity or pan-ethnicity and additional co-memberships with the counselor (such as the Italian-American wrestler) received high special help with low deference. The number of instances showing in these patterns is small but they suggest that in some cases the more different the counselor and student are in social background, the more special help "costs" in deference. This can be expressed less formally as "When you talk to the Man you sometimes have to 'Uncle Tom,' but when you talk to 'a brother,' you don't." Since for everyone, white ethnic, Latino, and Black alike, there is always somebody who is the Man, the possibility of demonstrating differential deference costs according to social identity is intriguing. An *increments of deference* hypothesis should be framed and tested more systematically.

Expectations Confirmed and Disconfirmed
When my co-workers and I began our study of gatekeeping encounters, our anthropological training led us to expect that cultural style in communication behavior would be the most powerful single factor affecting the outcomes of gatekeeping encounters. By the end of the study, this formulation of the research problem seemed too simple. Ethnicity and communication style influenced gatekeeping outcomes in many encounters, but had little influence in others. These findings help explain how laymen and social scientists can get into such bitter arguments about how important ethnicity and cultural style are compared to intelligence, temperament or social class. Those who believe in either side always can find instances to support their position.

Similarity between counselor and student in cultural communication style and social identity had a strong effect on the character and outcomes of the gatekeeping encounters in our sample. This was always true, even though in some situations ethnicity or communication style were salient in an encounter, while in others they were overridden by co-membership.

One could argue that the reported differences in interactional character and outcome are attributable to factors other than social identity, such as other characteristics of the student, or to inadequacies of the research design. One such factor is social class. Admittedly there is some overlap between the pan-ethnic categories, white ethnic and Third World, and social class categories. But there were intra-ethnic differences within and inter-ethnic similarities across social class ranks; and when the cases were sorted by social class rather than by ethnicity, pan-ethnicity and co-membership, the relationship between social background and interactional character and outcome was not clearly patterned. Furthermore, the high degree of association between co-membership and interactional character and outcome suggests that, in face-to-face interaction, people use *various combinations of ways of being alike,* including social class, but also including nationality group, race, cultural sharing, pan-ethnicity and a host of other commonalities. No one index of social identity explains the data as well as combinations of indices do, and so an emphasis on social class by itself (or ethnicity or race by themselves) as the main factor would be misleading.

Another confounding variable might be student grades. The range of grade-point averages was small—most of the students in our sample were average in performance. Conceivably, some small differences in grades could have been important for particular counselors. We failed to interview them about this. But we doubt that it was true since in some cases students with the highest and lowest grades had RSC and emotional tone scores that were inconsistent with their grade rank but consistent with their ethnic similarity to the counselor. Still, it is possible that at the extremes of the grading scale, grades might be more important than social identity. For students in the middle of the grade range, however, ethnicity, pan-ethnicity and co-membership were better predictors of interactional character and outcome than were student grades.

A third possible confounding factor is practice effects, here defined as the position of an encounter in the series that was filmed for each counselor and the number of times the counselor and student had met before they were filmed together. However, there were no systematic differences between encounters attributable to their position in the series. Although encounters in which the counselor and student were meeting for the first time did tend to receive lower scores on the OBSC and emotional tone measures than did encounters in which both parties had met before, there were still large differences according to ethnicity and pan-ethnicity, and having met before seemed not to have any effect on the RSC.

One possible methodological weakness is the sample size. Because there were twenty-five students but only four counselors, it could be argued that, even if our findings are correct, we should not generalize from them. A response to this charge is that the findings reported here are supported in our other work. We also studied a number of encounters involving participants other than male junior college counselors: two high school counselors, one female junior college counselor, four job interviewers and twenty-five pairs of students (Erickson et al., 1973). Across all encounters, there were sharp differences in behavior symmetry and emotional tone attributable to social identity and communication style. This is not to say that a larger sample size is not desirable. I have discussed procedures for doing a less intensive but more extensive study elsewhere (Erickson, 1974). Although the findings reported here must be considered tentative, they are not entirely so: despite small sample size and somewhat nonstandard methods, a kind of collective reliability was apparent in the data. The diverse pieces of evidence fit together in patterns showing regularities not likely to be caused by chance or by repeated measuring of the same things in different ways. Our loosely defined working hypothesis was supported: *ethnicity and other forms of co-membership and cultural communication style in some combination predict the emotional tone of encounters and the amount of special help junior college students can expect to receive.*

Conclusions

The gatekeeping function of counselors in junior colleges has been described by others. Clark (1960) maintained that the main functions of counseling in the junior college are to discourage students and to lower their expectations. He based his argument on Goffman's concept (1952) of "cooling out the mark"—con men convincing the sucker that it was his own fault for allowing himself to be deceived. Cooling out, according to Clark, is not only the junior college counselor's function but that of the junior college as a whole. Those students organizationally designated as unworthy must come to believe that the failure is their fault, not the school's. The junior college processes students whom society defines as marginal (lower class, white ethnics and Third World students being heavily overrepresented in this category). A few are allowed access to the upper middle class, but at least two thirds are redirected toward alternative goals, usually of lower social rank (see Karabel, 1972).

What criteria did counselors use—consciously or unconsciously—to perform their gatekeeping functions? In our data we saw a few instances of cooling out in intra-ethnic encounters, more instances in inter-ethnic encounters and even more in encounters with low co-membership. Cooling out rarely occured in encounters with high co-membership. Even though school policy says that counselors should use only universalistic criteria, some particularistic criteria were used in each encounter. It may be that without the "leakage" of ethnicity and other particularistic factors, face-to-face interaction simply could not proceed. If particularistic factors cannot be removed from a gatekeeping encounter, a policy dilemma arises: counselors are required to be *fair* to students (as fairness is defined by the 1964 Civil Rights Act prohibiting discriminatory treatment because of race, color, religion or national origin) in ways that are interactionally impossible.

One way to resolve this dilemma would be for schools to relax the pressure put on gatekeepers so they could give more special help to all students. This might increase the likelihood that a higher percentage of Third World and white ethnic students would be let through the school gates into the middle and upper occupational strata of the society. But unless more occupational slots are created than presently exist, then one would only shift the white ethnic-Third World conflict over scarce resources from the school to the employment office.

In the absence of widespread social change, gatekeeping will not be eliminated. Perhaps, then, gatekeepers should be trained to exclude ethnicity and race from the particularistic factors that enter their decisions to dispense special help. I think that such training would be impossible. Even if it were possible, it would be extremely difficult because in order to conduct everyday life, people must "size each other up" according to all kinds of cues, a skill which is learned in early childhood and performed unconsciously. There is no way that skin color, accent or demeanor can be ignored in face-to-face encounters. The process by which particularistic attributes of social identity enter into interactions seems too complex to be performed reflectively, or stopped at will. Thus, training would probably need to be intensive and continuous (analogous to psychotherapy) and would be prohibitively expensive for a school. Training which fell short of this, in my opinion, would be just "window dressing"—conducting in-service training whose manifest aim is to change the status quo, but whose latent function is to legitimize the organization and its standard operating procedures.

General consciousness raising about the effects of particularism on face-to-face interaction might be useful. This would not be skill training but would make counselors, administrators and teachers more aware of how they act toward and make judgments about students.

Another option would be to have schools make public the ethnicity, race and other background attributes of counselors and to allow students to choose their own. This does not mean students invariably would find it in their interest to pick a counselor of their own ethnicity, since we found that under certain conditions,

Gatekeeping
FREDERICK ERICKSON

inter-ethnic and even inter-pan-ethnic encounters produced fair and helpful treatment. Rather, this option would allow students who are ill at ease with a non-co-member (however the students define that term) to remove themselves from those encounters by permitting these students to select a co-member as counselor. If students wanted practice in strategies for talking to the Man, they could select a non-co-member as counselor. Because there are still relatively few Third World counselors in schools, this option would entail hiring enough Third World counselors in schools with large numbers of Third World students to guarantee that the choice of an ethnic co-member is possible.

In our research, we found that counselors and students with marked differences in social identity often did not experience ease in their encounters. It appears that, usually without realizing it, counselors and students were playing out, in microcosm, social relations similar in form to those found within their own group and between their own group and others. The difficulties that ethnically and especially pan-ethnically different counselors and students experienced did not result from any special malevolence on the part of the counselors; they just *happened*. The counselors we studied were not trying to cheat their students or their school; nor were they incompetent. They were doing their job professionally despite a heavy work load.

Conversely, ethnically or pan-ethnically similar counselors and students, meeting as strangers in junior colleges, tended to treat each other cordially and with mutual helpfulness, almost as if they were kin or fictive kin—members of the same urban village. This did not occur because of planned humanization of the school; it just *happened*. If everyday life in the counselor's office proceeded according to the ideal norms of a universalistic, rationally ordered organization, we would not expect this.

While our research does not imply that ethnically segregated educational settings are superior to desegregated ones, it does show that ethnicity cannot be ignored. We have found that ethnicity, race and communication style can affect the quality of counseling students receive. Because these factors are an integral part of face-to-face interaction, they probably affect other interactions in the school and therefore are important educational variables. It seems that our schools would profit greatly if they discovered and used the distinctive educational possibilities of both inter-group and intra-group contact among adults and young people in schools.

Considered most broadly, race, ethnicity and communication style may affect other gatekeeping, caretaking and supervisory decisions. Charges of "institutional racism" and "cultural genocide" brought by Third World peoples against white Americans and of "effete snobbery" brought by white ethnics against predominantly English-American, upper-class whites should not be dismissed. Our research suggests, it seems to me, that such charges are more than empty rhetoric. They may reflect the unsupportiveness and arrogance experienced by many Americans in everyday life at school and at work.

References

Barth, F. *Ethnic groups and boundaries: the social organization of culture difference.* Boston: Little, Brown, 1969.
Barth, F. Analytical dimensions in the comparison of social organizations. *American Anthropologist,* 1972, **74,** 207-220.
Bateson, G., Jackson, D., Haley, J., & Weakland, J. Toward a theory of schizophrenia. *Behavioral Science,* 1956, **1,** 251-264. Also in G. Bateson, *Steps toward an ecology of mind.* New York: Ballantine Books, 1972.
Birdwhistell, R. *Introduction to kinesics.* Louisville, Ky.: University of Louisville Press, 1952. See also, Birdwhistell, R. *Kinesics and context.* Philadelphia: University of Pennsylvania Press, 1970.
Byers, P. *From biological rhythm to cultural pattern: A study of minimal units.* (Doctoral dissertation, Columbia University) Ann Arbor, Mich.: University Microfilms, 1972, No. 73-9004.
Byers, P., & Byers, H. Nonverbal communication and the education of children. In C. Cazden, V. John, and D. Hymes (Eds.) *Functions of language in the classroom.* New York: Teachers' College Press. 1972.
Cicourel, A. Basic and normative rules in the negotiation of status and role. In D. Sudnow (Ed.), *Studies in social interaction.* New York: Free Press, 1972.
Cicourel, A., Jennings, K., Jennings, S., Leiter, K., MacKay, R., Mehan, H., & Roth, D. *Language use and school performance.* New York: Academic Press, 1974.
Cicourel, A., & Kitsuse, J. *The educational decision-makers.* Indianapolis: Bobbs-Merrill, 1963.
Clark, B. *The open door college.* New York: McGraw-Hill, 1960.
Condon, W., & Ogsten, W. A segmentation of behavior. *Journal of Psychiatric Research,* 1967, **1,** 221-235.
Efron, D. *Gesture and environment.* New York: King's Crown, 1941. Reissued as Efron, D., *Gesture, race and culture.* New York: Humanities Press, 1973.
Erickson, F. Using simple quantitative measures in urban anthropology: A case study. In P. Sanday (Ed.), *Anthropology and public policy.* New York: Academic Press, forthcoming.
Erickson, F., with Shultz, J., Leonard-Dolan, C., Pariser, D., Erder, M., Marchese, J., and Jean, C. *Inter-ethnic relations in urban institutional settings.* Final Technical Report, December 30, 1973, Harvard Graduate School of Education, Projects MH 18230, MH 21460, National Institute of Mental Health.
Garfinkel, H. *Studies in ethnomethodology.* Englewood Cliffs, N.J.: Prentice-Hall, 1967.

Goffman, E. Cooling the mark out: Some aspects of adaptation to failure. *Psychiatry,* 1952, **15,** 451-63.
Goffman, E. *Encounters: Two studies in the sociology of interaction.* Indianapolis: Bobbs-Merrill, 1961.
Goffman, E. *Frame analysis: An essay on the organization of experience.* New York: Harper Colophon, 1974.
Goodenough, W. Rethinking status and role: Toward a general model of the cultural organization of social relationships. In M. Banton (Ed.), *The relevance of models in anthropology.* London: Tavistock, 1965.
Hall, E. *The silent language.* New York: Fawcett, 1959.
Hall, E. *The hidden dimension.* New York: Doubleday, 1966.
Handelman, D. Gossip in encounters: The transmission of information in a bounded social setting. *Man,* 1973, **8** (2), 210-227.
Karabel, J. Community colleges and social stratification. *Harvard Educational Review,* 1972, **4,** 521-562.
Kendon, A. Movement coordination in social interaction: Some examples described. *Acta Psychologica,* 1970, **32,** 100-125.
Mehan, H., & Wood, H. *The reality of ethnomethodology.* New York: Wiley-Interscience, in press.
Rist, R. Student social class and teacher expectations: The self-fulfilling prophecy in ghetto education. *Harvard Educational Review,* 1970, **40,** 411-450.
Shultz, J. *The search for potential co-membership: An analysis of conversations among strangers.* Unpublished doctoral dissertation, Harvard Graduate School of Education, 1975.
Suttles, G. *The social order of the slum: Ethnicity and territory in the inner city.* Chicago: University of Chicago Press, 1968.
Vincent, J. The structuring of ethnicity. *Human Organization,* 1974, **33,** 375-379.
Waller, W. *The sociology of teaching.* New York: John Wiley, 1932.

Some Comparative Principles of Educational Stratification

RANDALL COLLINS
University of California, San Diego

During the 1950s and early 1960s functionalism, which held that education socializes the young and provides socially necessary technical skills, provided the dominant explanation for the genesis and role of educational systems. In the late 1960s, various neo-Marxist positions appeared which pointed to education's role in maintaining class inequality. Drawing on the work of Max Weber, Randall Collins proposes to move beyond both types of explanation by demonstrating the role of three sources of demand for education—the demand of individuals for practical skills, the desire of groups for social solidarity and high status, and the concern of states for effective political control. These sources and their consequences can be conceptualized as operating within a market for cultural goods which behaves much like the market for economic goods.

What determines the structures and contents of educational systems? A great deal of research in the sociology of education has taken an existing structure and its content for granted and concentrated on describing the social processes that occur within it. We are left with the question of why a given educational system exists—what conditions or forces produce it, sustain it, change it, or even abolish it. This theoretical question has often been answered from a functionalist or social-order perspective, which explains education by citing its contributions to the integration or productivity of society. Alternatively, education may be explained as a weapon in the struggles for domination that make up the phenomenon of stratification, whether considered from the viewpoint of Marxist theory, Weberian theory, or some mixture of the two.

The social-order approach, long accepted rather uncritically by many American social theorists, has a number of crucial weaknesses. In its most general formulation—that education socializes young people into the existing social order[1]—the theory is causally underdetermined. Its apparent truth is tautological. The propo-

[1] Robert Dreeben's *On What Is Learned in School* (New York: Addison-Wesley, 1968) is a recent formulation of this position.

sition justifies *any* educational structure after the fact; it does not explain why one particular structure exists rather than some other, and therefore it is not subject to empirical validation. Some functionalist theorists have attempted to evade this difficulty by formulating more specific kinds of social demands that education fulfills: they assert either that education provides specific technical skills or that educational history follows an empirically demonstrable series of stages which evolve from primitive to advanced forms. The evidence usually cited for the first model is the rise over the last century in a given Western country's educational attendance; for the second model, the standard evidence is a set of educational-attendance figures for societies differing on a measure of economic productivity such as per-capita gross national product.[2] The two specifications of functionalist theory often overlap, since many evolutionary models posit that schooling expands to meet the increasing need for technically skilled workers in industrial and especially in advanced or "post-industrial" societies.

These efforts to salvage functionalist theory are not very successful, in my opinion. A close look at the evidence indicates that schooling does not supply specific technical skills, as functionalists contend.[3] Furthermore, as we shall see, historical patterns of educational development have been caused by factors other than increasing sophistication of industrial techniques.

These problems with the functionalist viewpoint lead me to believe that the most fruitful new developments in the attempt to explain the evolution and change of educational systems involve the stratification or domination approach. Like the functionalist approaches, the approaches to education which focus on domination have also varied. The Marxist approach has several versions. In the *Communist Manifesto,* Marx and Engels demanded free and universal access to education, a theme that has persisted in liberal as well as radical critiques of class differences in educational access and attainment. More sophisticated Marxist positions have emerged in recent years. Louis Althusser theorizes that education is a mechanism of domination that reproduces the unequal relationship of capitalist production.[4] Samuel Bowles and Herbert Gintis, arguing from a detailed empirical basis, stress education's role in producing a compliant labor force.[5] Standing at least one tenet of Marxism on its head, Alain Touraine interprets the class struggle of each historical period as a conflict between the ruling class, which controls productive skills, and the subordinate classes, which possess only labor power.[6] In this view,

---

[2] Use of the second type of evidence involves the fallacy of assuming that static cross sections present a historical sequence actually followed by all societies; the historical approach shows that this assumption is not justified. See Daniel Bell, *The Coming of Post-Industrial Society* (New York: Basic Books, 1973); and Frederick Harbison and Charles A. Myers, *Education, Manpower, and Economic Growth* (New York: McGraw-Hill, 1964).

[3] Randall Collins, "Functional and Conflict Theories of Educational Stratification," *American Sociological Review,* 36 (1971), 1002–19.

[4] Louis Althusser, "Ideology and Ideological State Apparatuses," *Lenin and Philosophy and Other Essays* (London: New Left Books, 1971), pp. 123–73.

[5] Samuel Bowles and Herbert Gintis, *Schooling in Capitalist America: Educational Reform and the Contradictions of Economic Life* (New York: Basic Books, 1976).

[6] Alain Touraine, *Production de la Société* Paris: Éditions du Seuil, 1973).

Educational Stratification
RANDALL COLLINS

education is the basis of modern class domination, and struggles over educational access become the new focus of class struggle.

These Marxist approaches thus include a simple view of education as an unequally distributed good, a sophisticated view of education as a mechanism of domination, and a technocratic, evolutionary view of educationally derived skills as the prime basis of modern stratification. In my view, exponents of the domination approach are on the right track. Althusser's theory, however, shares functionalism's weakness of treating education as part of a given structure without showing, by empirical detail or historical comparison, the conditions for one sort of education rather than another. Bowles and Gintis provide the most specified and empirically bolstered theory, but their single causal dynamic, I shall argue, needs to be incorporated into a larger set of stratifying processes.

Although the Weberian approach rejects the Marxian emphasis on the causal preponderance of the economic structure and its historical evolution, the Weberian approach is, to a degree, a sophisticated version of the Marxian tradition. That is, Weberians do see economic interests based on property divisions as key bases of group organization, of intergroup conflict, and of historical change.[7] But, in contrast to Marx, Weber also pointed out that organizational resources, especially those of state and private bureaucracies, and cultural resources, above all religious traditions (but also secular ones such as education), can create and channel additional interest groups and conflicts.[8] Three lines of societal division—economic, organizational-political, and cultural (or in Weber's terms, "class," "party," and "status")—mesh, so that economic classes or organizational politicians are stronger if they also possess the unity that comes from common cultural resources. But the three types of resources may be differentially distributed; strong ethnic, national, religious, or other cultural divisions can shape struggles for economic or political domination into patterns very different from those emerging along class lines. There are many kinds of stratification systems, and with the proper conceptual tools one may show the conditions for each.

My approach may be broadly characterized as Weberian. I see education as part of a multisided struggle among status communities for domination, for economic advantage, and for prestige. This approach allows the incorporation of a multiplicity of particular causes into an overall explanation, since it regards social structure as the result of the mobilization of a variety of resources and interest groups within a common arena. It even permits us to salvage the main intellectual contribution of the social-order tradition as it applies to education—Durkheim's theory of education as an agent of moral socialization and hence as the secular equivalent of religion in modern society.[9] Durkheim shows that participation in rituals—whether religious, political, or educational—promotes group identifica-

[7] See Max Weber, *Economy and Society* (New York: Bedminster Press, 1968), especially pp. 932–37 and 998–1002.

[8] Pierre Bourdieu develops this tradition in a highly original manner. He views the realm of symbolic status as a market for cultural capital in which social struggle is shaped not only by the various competing classes, but also by the autonomous structure of the cultural marketplace itself. *Esquisse d'une Théorie de la Pratique* (Geneva: Droz, 1972), pp. 227–43.

[9] Emile Durkheim, *Moral Education* (New York: Free Press, 1961).

tion, and that myths or symbols that are the focus of rituals become marks of membership in distinctive social groups and the referents of moral legitimacy. Put in this fashion, the Durkheimian theory points the way out of its own major weakness, its obliviousness to the stratifying effects of education and to the social struggles that surround it. For procedures inculcating social membership can be used by particular groups in a stratified society both to cement their own boundaries and to morally legitimate themselves in the eyes of others.[10] In its overgeneralized form, the Durkheimian theory simply asserts that education integrates entire, undifferentiated societies; in a more limited form, it is useful in showing education's contribution to integrating particular groups in situations of conflict and domination. This version of Durkheim fits naturally with the Weberian concept of stratification through status groups.

In what follows, I will attempt to show how the positive insights of the Durkheimian, Marxian, and even practical-skills approaches to education may contribute to a multidimensional Weberian model of stratification. I will also try to specify the types of educational systems to which each approach applies. My overall concern will be with the interaction of the economic, organizational, and cultural aspects of stratification; I shall attempt to show that in the long run the interaction of these spheres generates a market-like structure. Since this pattern is difficult to see except at a macroscopic level, a word about comparative historical evidence and method is in order.

The Uses of Comparative Evidence

The wealth of historical information about educational systems throughout the world in the last three thousand years or more is crucial for building a theory of the evolution and change of educational systems. Historical materials reveal a range of educational structures within which modern ones fall as special types, and this range of structures allows long-term processes to be put in a comparative context that permits causal generalizations about their dynamics.

We can take a comparative vantage point on education in half a dozen major civilizations (Chinese, Japanese, Indian, Islamic, Greco-Roman, and northern European), as well as in a number of tribal societies and early literate civilizations (such as the Egyptian and Mesopotamian). Our information is not equally good on each of these. There is good documentation on the structure, content, and clientele of education in the more centralized periods in China and Japan and in most of Mediterranean and European history since the rise of the Greek city-states. Much less research has been done on education in the Islamic world, and Indian educational history is a matter of somewhat distant inference. For the early literate civilizations, surviving documentation is limited to certain aspects of the education of scribes. Yet, overall, we are in a favorable position to establish general outlines of the main types of education and of the social processes that condition their

---

[10] This process is explained in Randall Collins, *Conflict Sociology* (New York: Academic Press, 1975), chs. 2-4.

Educational Stratification
RANDALL COLLINS

existence as institutions. Analyzing education from a general perspective helps us to move with greater confidence in historical areas where information is sketchy; patterns found in the whole body of evidence allow us to make sense of facts that otherwise might not rise to the level of hints.

The disadvantages of the comparative historical approach lie in researchers' distance from their subjects. In some areas even the main outlines are unclear, and almost everywhere detail is less available and sampling less controllable than in contemporary research. These problems are not insurmountable. An interest in structures directs us to the most often repeated aspects of human behavior; greater detail is not always necessary, and, in the absence of an overview, detail might well obscure the very structures that most call for explanation. Empirical evidence, whether contemporary or historical, detailed or summarized, is meaningful only in the context of theoretical propositions, and the value of these propositions can be established only by their capacity to order a whole range of materials. In this sense, the coherence among theoretical propositions and pieces of evidence is the test of any empirical method. By the same token, contemporary data do not lose their relevance; they are available to test further, or suggest extensions or alternatives to, the models arising from historical materials. Comparative historical analysis and contemporary research are not only complementary but are parts of the same enterprise.

I shall deal with the historical evidence under three main headings, each of which is associated with different demands for education—practical skills, status-group membership, and bureaucracy. In a conclusion I shall discuss how these types of educational demands combine and what their long-term dynamics are. The three categories may be thought of as corresponding in spirit with Weber's three bases of stratification—class, status, and party. Education has been part of struggles for practical economic skills, for cultural integration and prestige of particular associational groups, and for political control by and within formal organizations. I shall attempt to show that education for *practical skills* has largely involved informal procedures of work apprenticeship or family settings; such training has included formal credentials and ceremonial procedures only if a skilled group has had the political power to create a monopoly. Education for *status-group membership,* on the other hand, has been characterized by ceremonies dramatizing the unity of the educated group and its status vis-à-vis outsiders; the content of such education has been based upon cultural ideals, usually of an explicitly impractical sort, which reflect the ethos of the particular kind of status group involved. Education which has arisen as part of the process of *bureaucratization* has been shaped by efforts of elites to establish impersonal methods of control; the content of education here is irrelevant (and hence a variety of contents can be incorporated), but the structure of grades, ranks, degrees, and other formal credentials is of central importance as a means of discipline through hierarchy and specialization.

Finally, I shall examine the combinations of these demands that have emerged in particular historical periods. Because education can meet several demands simultaneously, we find some historical cases appearing under a number of headings. In the long run, these three kinds of demands for education may be seen as interacting with various sources of supply so as to constitute a market. Within this market we can note dynamic processes of inflation and deflation in the value of educational credentials. The long-range historical perspective on education leads us to a conceptualization of social stratification in which struggles for domination resemble an economic system not only in the material base but also in the cultural superstructure.

Practical Skills

The most common modern interpretation of the role of education is that it meets the demand for technical skills. Most contemporary evidence, however, contradicts this interpretation.[11] The content of most modern education is not very practical: educational attainment and grades are not much related to work performance, and most technical skills are learned on the job. Although work skills are more complex in *some* modern jobs than in most preindustrial jobs, in many modern jobs they are not. Similar patterns appear in an overview of societies throughout history.

In tribal societies, children are trained for adult work primarily through informal apprenticeship in which they watch and later help their parents or other relatives.[12] The more complex and advanced crafts, such as metal working or the art of the shaman or medicine man, may be learned by secret apprenticeship outside the family. The same pattern characterizes the training of craftsmen in literate civilizations. Greco-Roman artisans, for example, learned their skills solely through apprenticeship, usually within the family; this approach was used for medicine (at that time, as in all areas until the late nineteenth century, a craft with little real effectiveness), for such advanced crafts as architecture and construction engineering, and for the various arts.[13] After the conquest of Greece by the Romans (circa 190 B.C.), many skilled craftsmen were slaves, who were excluded from any formal schooling. This exclusion did not detract from the quality of their practical work, although it did keep the power and prestige of their occupations low.

The pattern of learning the most useful and complex practical skills by apprenticeship is common to the civilizations of China, Japan, India, Islam, and medieval and early modern Europe. Although probably illiterate and certainly not formally educated, the craftsmen of these civilizations were not sharply different in skill or innovativeness from those of the industrial world. After all, it was the craftsmen of medieval Europe and China who produced the beginnings of the machine revolution over a long period starting at least as far back as A.D. 900.[14] Even during

---

[11] Collins, "Functional and Conflict Theories."
[12] Robert J. Havighurst, "Education in Hopi Society," in *Comparative Perspectives on Education*, ed. Robert J. Havighurst (Boston: Little, Brown, 1968), pp. 3–10; and Mircea Eliade, *The Forge and the Crucible* (New York: Harper & Row, 1957), pp. 53–108.
[13] Henri Irenée Marrou, *A History of Education in Antiquity* (New York: New American Library, 1964), pp. 262–66.
[14] Lynn White, Jr., *Medieval Technology and Social Change* (New York: Oxford Univ. Press, 1962); and Joseph Needham, *Science and Civilization in China* (Cambridge, Eng.: Cambridge Univ. Press, 1954–1956), I–IV.

Educational Stratification
RANDALL COLLINS

England's full-scale takeoff into industrialism in the early nineteenth century, the level of education was generally low, and what education did exist was by and large nontechnical in content.[15]

The one practical skill often taught in specialized schools has been literacy. The origins of literate education are in the priestly administrations of ancient Mesopotamia and Egypt, where children were trained in schools for the career of scribe.[16] Some of these schools were attached to temples; others were probably run by private schoolmasters. The scribe might be a government administrator, especially in the rather totalitarian Egyptian dynasties, or an independent practitioner who engaged in letter writing for the populace. Some merchants also were literate. Apparently, however, literacy training usually approximated an apprenticeship, since the assistant (in Mesopotamia often an adopted son) of an independent scribe accompanied his trainer, practiced the fundamentals of the trade, and gradually came to copy and then share in his trainer's work.

Such practical education almost always has been highly unritualized. Even in the more formal schools, we know of no attendance requirements, examinations, grades, or degrees; proficiency was sufficiently tested in practice. In highly commercial periods, the middle classes have attempted to acquire skills in literacy and arithmetic. Thus we find education for these ends among the commercial classes of Japan's Tokugawa period and of the prosperous periods in European history since the High Middle Ages.[17] But practical education of this sort has generally been quite different from the ritualized and status-ostentatious education of elites of those societies. Arithmetic and the reading and writing of the vulgar languages have usually been taught in family or apprenticeship settings or in low-status private schools without the formalized public credentials of official, high-status institutions.

At times, though, practical education has involved a ritualized superstructure. This generally has occurred where an occupational group has been politically powerful and has possessed strong collective organization, as in the case of a guild or self-regulating profession. Under these conditions, the occupation group can monopolize skills and require a lengthy period of servitude for trainees through formal requirements for length of apprenticeship, examinations (such as producing a master-work), and ceremonial procedures of promotion. In Italy and Germany in the late Middle Ages, training was sometimes lengthened so artificially that

---

[15] In 1837, for example, only 20 to 25 percent of the children in the larger English industrial towns were attending schools for any length of time, and the proportions were doubtless lower in the countryside. English science in this period was overwhelmingly developed and carried out by amateurs, and there was little formal teaching of science in the schools and universities. Brian Simon, *Studies in the History of Education, 1780–1870* (London: Lawrence & Wishart, 1959), p. 170; and John Theodore Merz, *A History of European Thought in the Nineteenth Century* (New York: Dover, 1965), I, 250–67.

[16] Marrou, pp. xv–xix; Henri Frankfort, John A. Wilson, and Thorkild Jacobsen, *Before Philosophy* (Baltimore: Penguin Books, 1949), pp. 71–102; and Edward Chiera, *They Wrote on Clay* (Chicago: Univ. of Chicago Press, 1938).

[17] Ronald P. Dore, *Education in Tokugawa Japan* (Berkeley: Univ. of California Press, 1964), pp. 214–90; D. E. Smith, *History of Mathematics* (New York: Dover, 1958), I, 194–268; Bernard Bailyn, *Education in the Forming of American Society: Needs and Opportunities for Study* (Chapel Hill: Univ. of North Carolina Press, 1960).

journeymen revolted, producing some of the earliest instances of overt class warfare.[18] In contrast, the politically powerless Greco-Roman craftsmen were apprenticed informally and promoted to full active status solely on the basis of adequate performance.

Perhaps ritualized training first appeared in tribal societies where cohorts of young people underwent ritual segregation, ordeals, and formal initiation into the society of adults.[19] Specialists in magic and witch doctoring, whose skills were heavily dependent on the psychological effects of their ceremonies, often underwent very ritualized secret apprenticeships. The same was true of iron workers in many West African tribes and in medieval Japan, who derived a great deal of prestige from their ability to make weapons.[20]

In summary, most practical education has involved students working as assistants to experienced workers.[21] Schools have sometimes been established in cases where the fundamental components of a practical skill could be learned by repetitious drill, such as in the acquisition of literacy and arithmetic skills. Usually such schooling has been unritualized and aimed at developing proficiency in the most efficient manner. This has been particularly true where dominant social classes have had a ritualized form of education and practical work has been relegated to unprivileged middle or lower classes. At times, though, powerful groups have incorporated practical education into a ritualized educational system. In the United States, for example, a formal structure surrounds elementary education, which alone among all levels of modern education bears a clear relationship to economic productivity.[22] The more elaborate organizational form, though, must be explained by factors other than the demand for practical skills, and to these social factors we now turn.

Status-Group Membership

Weber defined a status group as a community based on a common culture that provides a consciousness of membership (and hence of the boundaries with nonmembers) and, usually, some claim to prestige and legitimacy in the social order.[23] The key resource for the creation and maintenance of such communities, then, is a common culture. It should be borne in mind that Weber acknowledged the importance of both status-group and class stratification. Cultural resources frequently are stratified by economic class and are one of the weapons that classes can use to become powerfully organized. Cultural resources may also produce status-group divisions within classes or even across them, most notably in the forms

---

[18] Max Weber, *General Economic History* (New York: Free Press, 1961), pp. 107–27.
[19] Shmuel N. Eisenstadt, *From Generation to Generation* (Glencoe, Ill.: Free Press, 1956).
[20] Eliade, *The Forge and the Crucible*.
[21] This has been the case not only for heavy manual pursuits, but also for the skilled crafts and administrative and ritual skills. The training of priests in both Eastern and Western religions has historically been primarily by apprenticeship, even in the case of the literate churches. See Marrou, pp. 419–51; and Melford E. Spiro, *Buddhism and Society* (New York: Harper & Row, 1970).
[22] Collins, "Functional and Conflict Theories," p. 1006.
[23] Weber, *Economy and Society*, pp. 926–39.

Educational Stratification
RANDALL COLLINS

of nationalism and ethnicity. In every case, we should remember that cultural resources are *means* and that groups organized on their basis may have a variety of *ends:* groups are not confined to struggling for prestige but may also try to use their culturally based organization to monopolize economic and power positions.

In historical perspective, education has been used more often for organizing status groups than for other purposes. Since the defining locus of status-group activity is leisure and consumption, status-group education has been sharply distinguished from practical education by the exclusion of materially productive skills. Because status groups have used a common culture as a mark of group membership, status-group education has taken the form of a club and has included much ceremony to demonstrate group solidarity and to publicly distinguish members from nonmembers. This club aspect characterized the activities of Chinese gentlemen who met for genteel conversation and poetry writing, as well as the periodic festivals put on for the Greek public by students, an elite sector of the population.[24]

Status-group education, then, has been ceremonial, aesthetic, and detached from practical activities. Its rituals rarely have dramatized rankings within the group; formal grades, competitive examinations, and degrees usually have been absent. Where competitions have occurred, as in the games and contests of the Greeks, they have shown the group as a whole and have emphasized the leisure of group members and spectators. The main distinctions have been between insiders and outsiders, not among members of the group. Frequently, there have been no formal attendance requirements, and the absence of formal degrees has reflected the fact that acquisition of the status group's culture is the object of education. In contrast with bureaucratic forms of education, the test has come in one's participation in the leisure activities of the status group, and the organization of the schools has been only incidental to that end.

Status-group education has predominated in societies controlled by aristocracies and other wealthy, leisured classes. In Greece and Rome, it arose out of the age-group initiations of the quasi-tribal period.[25] With the development of highly stratified city-states, warrior training evolved into a set of games (what we now call the basic track and field events), singing, and eventually reading and writing traditional poetry, especially the warrior epics of Homer. Participation in this culture, particularly in the games and festivals of the schools, became the mark of upper-class status, especially as a middle class of merchants and soldiers developed due to changes in the economy and in warfare. The exclusiveness of education was threatened during the fifth century B.C., when, in the midst of political revolutions and expanding commerce, wandering teachers known as sophists offered instruction in the art of argument, or rhetoric, to all who could pay the price. This threat to the cultural domination of the upper classes was headed off, however, as education in rhetoric and grammar was added to the standard sequence of school-

[24] Max Weber, *The Religion of China* (New York: Free Press, 1951), pp. 119–33; Marrou, *History of Education*, pp. 147–64.
[25] Marrou, *History of Education;* and Ramsey MacMullen, *Roman Social Relations* (New Haven, Conn.: Yale Univ. Press, 1974), pp. 81, 107–15.

ing involving sports and festivals. This form of education lasted for eight hundred years, through the Roman conquest of Greece, and was eventually adopted with only minor changes by the Romans. The Greek upper classes in cities throughout the eastern Mediterranean used possession of this culture to distinguish themselves from the surrounding "barbarians," even if the latter might be cultivated Syrians, Egyptians, or Romans.

In China, the first educated men were diviners or sages, who read oracles for the court and probably passed their skills along through appenticeship.[26] Since these skills eventually developed into a full-fledged writing system, this early education may be seen as a form of "practical" training. The period of Confucius, Lao Tzu, and other teachers (circa 500–200 B.C.) was also one of predominantly practical training in that education was usually directed to training advisors for the competing courts. With the unification of China under the Han dynasty (circa 200 B.C.–A.D. 200), the Confucian form of education developed into a bureaucratic selection device. Selection, though, was based largely on aesthetic skills, and, as social status outside as well as within government service came to depend on education, the aesthetic elements in education developed still further. In later dynasties formal examinations were judged exclusively on the bases of literary skill and beauty of calligraphy. The leisure pursuits of Chinese gentlemen of this era centered on poetry writing and painting; the prestigious form of sociability was the "literary gathering" where literature was read and discussed. This emphasis on aesthetics was even more pronounced during periods of weak dynasties or of political decentralization. An example was the period of A.D. 200–600, when Confucianism was displaced by a highly poetic and artistic form of Taoist mysticism, whose practitioners cultivated an individualism which entailed a total disregard for formal educational requirements or doctrines.

There are many other examples of aesthetic education for the gentry. In India, from the beginnings of literacy, education was closely associated with status-group prestige. Brahmin priests monopolized knowledge of the Vedic traditions and thereby helped not only to close off entry to their caste but also to legitimate the caste system.[27] For the original Brahmins, education was a "practical" training in religious and magic skills. As a complex commercial society developed, however, the Brahmin caste became less an occupational group of priests and more an educated caste of landholders and administrators for the various princes. Among the lower castes, religious movements developed which emulated the old Brahmin religious purity and mystical doctrine, because this was a route toward improving one's social prestige. Within the upper levels, both the Brahmin and the warrior and the merchant castes developed a more secular culture, including poetry, drama, dance, a science of love-making, and art, which displayed their membership in the privileged leisure classes. The height of this culture, in which private teachers apparently taught the rich, occurred during the wealthy Gupta period from A.D. 300 to 700.

[26] Fung Yu-lan, *A Short History of Chinese Philosophy* (New York: Free Press, 1966).
[27] Romila Thapar, *A History of India* (Baltimore: Penguin Books, 1966), pp. 136–66; Max Weber, *The Religion of India* (New York: Free Press, 1958), pp. 123–33; and Mysore N. Srinivas, "Sanskritization," in *Social Change in Modern India* (Berkeley: Univ. of California Press, 1955), pp. 1–45.

Educational Stratification
RANDALL COLLINS

Similarly, in the Heian court of early Japanese civilization (A.D. 1000), men and women courtiers developed an elaborate culture of poetry writing and art appreciation and even produced the first great Japanese works of prose fiction, largely through informal family education.[28] In the Islamic world, education developed from religious training in the holy scriptures and laws to a form of culture that, in the cosmopolitan cities of prosperous periods, provided entertainment and status for the wealthy.[29] Especially in the court circles of centers such as Baghdad and Cordova, this culture included not only a pious acquaintance with religious tradition, but also a knowledge of semi-religious and even secular traditions of poetry, philosophy, and science.

In Europe, informal education as the basis of status emulation was most prominent during the Renaissance, especially in the wealthy commercial cities of Italy, but also in Germany, the Netherlands, France, and England.[30] Poetry writing and allusions to the classics were marks of prestige in everyday social life. Status groups were further organized around the patronage of artists, scientists, and scholars, and around "academies" that held formal meetings for members to discuss and be entertained by their own culture. The schooling involved in acquiring this culture was largely individual and private and was carried out in rivalry with the formal organization of the universities. Eventually, however, the status culture based on aesthetic activities began to be inculcated more formally as schools were established, and for several centuries (from 1500 to 1800) the schools succeeded in attracting the children of the elite. These schools included the "colleges" organized by the Jesuits, which in France became the *lycées*; the English boarding schools that came to be known as public schools; and similar schools in Germany that originally were called academies and, later, gymnasia. They became secondary schools only when the combination of bureaucratization and incorporation of humanistic culture into the universities made university education a more important foundation of elite status. For the German universities, this occurred around 1800; for the French, English, and American universities, after 1870. In modern university systems, high social prestige has usually been attached to schools that have concentrated, in their curricula, on the classics or on a literary and relatively impractical form of modern culture—schools such as Oxford and Cambridge in England and the Ivy League schools in the United States.

Well-organized status groups have not been confined to the upper classes, however. Under conditions of an expanding commercial economy and a political system with some dispersion of authority, less dominant classes have been able to claim greater prestige and to organize their communities more strongly by developing their own cultures. Such middle-class education (as among the "merchant princes" of the Renaissance) sometimes has emulated the aesthetic culture of the upper class, but more usually it has taken a religious form. Examples of the latter

---

[28] Ivar Morris, *The World of the Shining Prince: Court Life in Ancient Japan* (Oxford: Oxford Univ. Press, 1964).

[29] William H. McNiell, *The Rise of the West* (Chicago: Univ. of Chicago Press, 1963), pp. 476–80.

[30] Joseph Ben-David, *The Scientist's Role in Society* (Englewood Cliffs, N.J.: Prentice-Hall, 1971), pp. 59–65, 80–82; and Collins, *Conflict Sociology*, pp. 485–87.

were the academies of dissenting Protestant sects in England and Germany during the early Industrial Revolution.[31] We can even see this religious form in the educational movements of the English working class during the nineteenth century—the Sunday schools and Workingmen's Improvement Associations.[32] The workingmen's movement was oriented towards enhancing its discipline and used rituals to increase its social respectability. Education in the movement was used not to enhance work skills, but to make a claim for higher social status and even to assist in political organizing. Similarly, in Islam, the upper-class education provided by the *ulema*—the teacher-judges who interpreted the holy law and were patronized by the wealthy—was challenged by the mystical Sufi cults among metal workers, rug makers, and other urban artisans.[33] These Sufi secret societies, which combined craft apprenticeship with religious learning, were often vehicles for political opposition to the dominant classes, and in Baghdad in the eleventh century they discredited and destroyed the secular, aesthetic culture of the courts.

There have been times when a rebellious class, sensing a shift in the resources that underlie the organization of power, has gone to the extreme of developing a culture which is the opposite of the existing dominant culture. Thus the *philosophes* of eighteenth-century France mocked the traditional religious culture and the classical culture and promoted in their stead the ideal of a modern culture based on science and technology.[34] This cultural ideal appealed to a new status group, which included the emerging administrators of the state, especially members of the new technical branches of the military. This group provided the organizational basis for the revolution of 1789–1800. In England, the utilitarians espoused a similar ideal, although less successfully; their technocratic ideology, although embodied in a number of schools, failed to overthrow the traditional culture of the elite. Still, technocratic ideology has remained a unifying theme in middle-class and, to some extent, labor politics since the early 1800s.[35] This ideology has influenced Communist doctrine, as shown in the Soviet educational system's emphasis on technical education as the sole legitimate qualification for dominant positions.[36]

The contents of status-group education, then, vary predictably with the class situations of the groups that espouse them. We find aesthetic education, often combined with games and a reverence for tradition, in the status cultures of privileged upper classes. Moral respectability, usually in the form of religious doctrine, has

---

[31] Nicholas Hans, *New Trends in Education in the 18th Century* (London: Routledge & Kegan Paul, 1951). The disciplined, upward-striving tone of the German dissenting academics is noted by Max Weber in *The Protestant Ethic and the Spirit of Capitalism* (New York: Scribners, 1930).

[32] Edward P. Thompson, *The Making of the English Working Class* (Harmondsworth, Eng.: Penguin Books, 1968).

[33] A. J. Arberry, *Sufism: An Account of the Mystics of Islam* (London: Allen & Unwyn, 1940); and Bernard Lewis, "The Islamic Guilds," *Economic History Review*, 8 (1937), 20–37.

[34] Ben-David, *The Scientist's Role in Society*, pp. 88–97; and James K. Finch, *The Story of Engineering* (New York: Doubleday, 1960), pp. 137–38, 159–60.

[35] Elie Halévie, *The Growth of Philosophical Radicalism* (Boston: Beacon Press, 1955); and William H. G. Armytage, *The Rise of the Technocrats* (London: Routledge & Kegan Paul, 1965).

[36] Nigel Grant, *Soviet Education* (Baltimore: Penguin Books, 1968); David Granick, *The Red Executive* (New York: Doubleday, 1960), pp. 46–73; and Zbigniew Brzezinski and Samuel P. Huntington, *Political Power: USA/USSR* (New York: Viking Press, 1965), pp. 129–90.

been the cultural ideal of moderately aspiring middle classes or upper working classes. Rising classes in revolutionary periods have often taken practical and scientific education as their cultural ideal. Perhaps, though, we are generalizing about rebellious groups from a set of cases that is too historically limited; the more universal principle might be that revolutionary groups draw on whatever cultural form can be claimed to be both progressive and sharply distinct from traditional status claims.

Bureaucracy

Bureaucracy is a style of organization based on rules and regulations, written reports, and files of records. The use of such written materials tends to make control appear abstract and generalized; bureaucracy makes possible the separation of the individual officeholder from the powers of the position. Bureaucracy helps to solve the crucial problem of rulers and other leaders of organizations: the tendency to lose control of subordinates because they appropriate their positions as their own and thus become independent of their chiefs. Other characteristics of bureaucracy also serve the purpose of control. The specialization of tasks limits the individual's powers and makes him or her more dependent on the cooperation of other specialists. The multiplication of ranks and the setting of regular career sequences with limited periods in each office keep officials concerned with their organizational futures and motivated toward higher offices. Formal examinations maximize the impersonality and competitiveness of the system when they are the basis for entrance into the bureaucracy or promotion within it. Not all bureaucratic organizations have used all these control devices, however. There have been many quasi-bureaucracies which have mixed bureaucratic controls with mechanisms of hereditary aristocracy, purchase of position, or various informal arrangements; research tends to confirm that no organization is without some informal structure.[37]

Early Bureaucracy
Bureaucracy depends on literacy and the availability of writing materials. The first versions of bureaucratic organization arose in the administration of temples in early Mesopotamia and Egypt (and in the horticultural Mayan civilization of Yucatan), where early forms of writing and numbers were applied to keeping inventories and astronomical records.[38] Later, as rule by priests amalgamated with rule by military aristocracies, writing was used for diplomatic and commercial correspondence and for the machinery of government, particularly the administration of taxes. Schools for scribes were supported at the temples and perhaps sometimes by secular rulers, although, as we have noted, there also was much private education. Scribes themselves often rose to high administrative positions in government, especially in many Egyptian dynasties, where the priesthood was particularly prominent.

---

[37] Weber, *Economy and Society*, pp. 956–1110; and Collins, *Conflict Sociology*, ch. 6.
[38] See fn. 16.

How bureaucratic were these early organizations? The aristocracy was hereditary and largely illiterate. The priesthood appears to have been usually hereditary, and, since much of the ritual and belief was oral, it is quite possible that many priests were also illiterate and hence outside the bureaucratic system. There does seem to have been some specialization of offices within the administrations of the temples and of the larger governments, possibly a certain amount of rotation in office, and even some regular career channels. These characteristics varied from time to time, with the centralizing rulers and the scribes favoring bureaucratization and the priests and hereditary aristocrats opposing it. The generally unsettled military situation, especially in Mesopotamia, worked against extensive bureaucratization. Probably the unwieldiness of the clay tablets used for writing and the expense of the papyrus used in Egypt also militated against the development of a full-fledged system of bureaucratic reports. Scribes at times rose to very high positions, but acquisition of literacy was not the only career route and perhaps not even the most important one. We know of no system of formal examinations for entrance into or promotion in office, although such a system may have existed in the form of secret rituals in the periods of Egyptian history more dominated by priests.

Chinese and Japanese Bureaucracy

A more elaborate bureaucracy appeared in China.[39] At its center was the examination system, which began in the Han dynasty when the emperor required feudal lords to present themselves for examination in order to serve as his officials. During subsequent periods of political division, the examination system broke down along with the rest of the bureaucracy. But in the second great unifying dynasty, the T'ang (A.D. 618–907), the examination system was reintroduced and strengthened as a means of controlling the aristocracy. From then on, it remained in place; shifts in power occurred within the context of the examination system. In principle, the system was more or less meritocratic; it was to the advantage of the ruler to offer opportunities of advancement to everyone rather than to allow a small class to monopolize these opportunities and thus grow strong enough to become his rivals. In fact, members of the landed gentry were able to gain control by adopting the Confucian culture and by extending the examination system.

The system gradually developed from a single examination to a series. Eventually, a candidate had to pass three exams at the district schools to become a *sheng-yuan*, a member of the gentry class; then the provincial exam to gain the rank of *chu-jen*; and, finally, the metropolitan exam, given at Peking, to become a *chin-shih*. The examinations were given every three years, and only a small quota, 1 or 2 percent of the candidates, was allowed to pass each one. The average age for taking the degree of *sheng-yuan* was twenty-four, for that of *chu-jen* thirty, and for

---

[39] Knight Biggerstaff, *The Earliest Modern Government Schools in China* (Ithaca, N. Y.: Cornell Univ. Press, 1961); Wolfgang Franke, *The Reform and Abolition of the Traditional Chinese Examination System* (Cambridge, Mass.: Harvard Univ. Press, 1960), pp. 1–14; Chung-li Chang, *The Chinese Gentry* (Seattle: Univ. of Washington Press, 1955); and Max Weber, *Religion of China*, pp. 107–41.

the *chin-shih* thirty-five.[40] Naturally only the wealthy could afford to devote themselves to this pursuit of gentry status. Rewards for success were commensurate with the effort, since China had no hereditary aristocracy. Only those who had passed the higher exams were allowed to wear distinguishing buttons on their hats, to be exempt from corporal punishment and forced labor, and to receive the homage of the kow-tow, or ritual prostration, instead of giving it to others. Government officials were drawn from the higher gentry, with their ranks depending on how many examinations they had passed. In later dynasties, officeholders also had to take periodic examinations to maintain their status.

The government almost never intervened in the schools themselves but only held examinations. School attendance was not a prerequisite for taking the examinations; many individuals studied by themselves or with parents or private tutors. Still, during periods when the examination system was in force, many schools did exist. They were supported sometimes by a clan and sometimes by the personal contributions of parents or students. These schools seem to have been very simple in form. Each had a single teacher, generally a scholar without government office; there were no special hours, attendance requirements, or examinations. In China, bureaucratic government fostered extensive education but did not bring bureaucracy into the schools.

In Japan, during the period when government was strongest, we find something of the opposite pattern, with the government using the schools, and not just education, as a means of control. The Tokugawa regime (circa 1600–1850), which unified the country after a highly fragmented feudal period, had organized a strong military coalition among the regional clans. Unable to replace the clans with a centralized officialdom or to end the hereditary appropriation of office,[41] the regime ruled through the regional aristocracy. However, it neutralized that aristocracy's power by requiring its leaders to spend much time in court rituals—carrying out an elaborate etiquette that accompanied the hereditary ranks—and by making education compulsory. The central government required the regional lords to establish schools for the *samurai* (the hereditary warrior class). Attendance requirements were proportionate to rank: lower-ranking samurai were drilled in literacy, the Confucian classics, etiquette, and a highly stylized military art until age twenty-four; higher-ranking nobles were required to attend until the age of thirty or even thirty-six. Although the government assigned positions predominantly on the basis of hereditary rank, it did impose bureaucratic controls on its officials. All administrative action involved an elaborate system of written requests, orders, and reports, and these documents were accepted only if they followed precise stylistic conventions. Thus, potential political struggle and military revolt were controlled through a constant focus on formalities. The school system operated as a control device both by keeping the warrior class under custody for a considerable portion of their lives while drilling them in formalities, and by preparing them for the bureaucratic routine that made up the substance of government.

[40] Chang, p. 173.
[41] Dore, *Education in Tokugawa Japan*.

Weak and Partial Bureaucracies

I have suggested that bureaucratic government by either state or church produces a formal educational system oriented to rank and examination. The relationship can also be tested negatively: where government is not bureaucratic or is only weakly bureaucratic, formal educational hierarchies should be missing. The history of education in societies that have seldom been centralized under bureaucratic regimes supports this negative hypothesis. It also provides some positive examples of the partial formalization of education in those unusual times when bureaucratic government did develop a degree of strength.

India's history is illustrative. With relatively few strong, stable governments, the subcontinent was ruled by a shifting set of local regimes that were fairly weak in relation to the landowners, merchants, and priests. Education seems to have been relatively unimportant in government and, instead, tended to support the aspirations of private status groups. However, a few strong, bureaucratizing regimes did attempt to reinforce their authority through the educational system. For example, the Maurya regime (circa 300–200 B.C.), which briefly conquered most of India, tried to displace the caste system by favoring Buddhism and, seemingly, by using literate Buddhist monks as administrators.[42] We know that the government began to endow monasteries with property, thus changing the situation of the formerly itinerant monks. We also know that monasteries during this time trained their young monks in literacy, codified the sacred texts of Buddhism, and established advanced training in philosophical argument. The government apparently hoped that the strengthened monasteries would provide a working base for administering property and collecting taxes for the king.

This program failed in India. An anti-Buddhist reaction was accompanied by the resurgence of the caste system and the disintegration of the Maurya regime. What a Buddhist-based bureaucracy might have looked like, though, is illustrated by Tibet. Here the kings adopted Buddhism in the seventh century A.D. and founded their power on the monasteries, which held most of the property, engaged in most of the commerce, and even supplied military forces.[43] Through an amalgamation of nobility and monks, Tibet became a theocracy. Although the highest ranks were not determined by educational attainment, the direct hereditary principle was eliminated: the high lamas, such as the Dalai Lama, were selected by the age of six on the basis of certain spiritual signs, and before taking office as adults, they went through an extensive education in the monasteries.

The Greco-Roman world throughout most of its history provides another negative illustration of the relationship between bureaucracy and formalized education. During the earlier, more democratic periods of the city-states, the emphasis was on widespread citizen participation, rapid turnover in office, and, hence, government by "amateurs"; bureaucratic selection devices were explicitly ruled out. Even under the early Roman Empire, the administration of most local affairs was still in the hands of the wealthiest citizens of the subject cities, and public works

---

[42] Weber, *Religion of India*, pp. 233–56; and Thapar, *History of India*, pp. 70–91.
[43] Weber, *Religion of India*, pp. 282–90; McNiell, *Rise of the West*, pp. 522–23, 704; and Alexandra David-Neel, *Magic and Mystery in Tibet* (Baltimore: Penguin Books, 1971), pp. 94–110.

Educational Stratification
RANDALL COLLINS

and other civic projects were largely funded through their ostentatious contributions.[44] As we have seen, the educational systems fostered by such governmental arrangements have typically emphasized the aesthetic qualities of status-group membership.

Only during the late empire (in the fourth through sixth centuries A.D.), with the decline of the conquest and tribute economy, did the Roman state become more bureaucratic, begin to intervene in local affairs, and build up an extensive apparatus of officials. The officials adopted first Stoicism and then Christianity, both of which emphasized abstract moral rules and loyalty to principles above loyalty to individuals. The state began to oversee the schools. It promulgated rules on the payment of teachers and the number of teachers per town; required all teaching appointments to be confirmed by the government; in a few cases, established salaried professorships (at Rome as early as about A.D. 70, Athens about 170, and Constantinople in 425); and abolished rival forms of schooling (notably the Platonic and Neo-Platonic schools in Athens, which the western Roman emperor suppressed in 529). In fourth-century Rome, the emperor ordered students to register their enrollment with the government and required secondary schoolmasters to report the names of students finishing their studies. Thus began a practice of selecting officials by educational credentials.[45] The destruction of the empire by the German tribes cut short this process, although a form of education-based bureaucracy, combined with the influence of landed aristocrats, ruled the Byzantine Empire in the east for another thousand years.

The Islamic world was more clearly disposed toward bureaucratic government. The Islamic state was inseparable from a religious movement whose tenets were codified in the holy Koran and the commentaries on its laws.[46] But during and after Islam's rapid military expansion (circa A.D. 630–720), religion and state grew apart. There was a great deal of warfare among pretenders to the succession of Mohammed and recurrent disagreement between the more religiously learned *ulema* and the more secular warriors and politicians. By the ninth century, when the lands conquered by Islam began to fragment into separate states, religious authority was increasingly disassociated from government office, although many rulers still claimed the title of *caliph*, supreme representative and defender of Islam. Still, strictly speaking, there never arose a separate church organization. Rulers and wealthy citizens endowed individual mosques as displays of their piety, and leadership in religious matters was taken by the *ulema*, who taught the scriptures in the mosques and also acted as independent judges to settle disputes.

In the more powerful centralized states, such as that of the Abassids (who ruled most of the Middle East from Baghdad after 750, with gradually dwindling authority after 830), the Egyptian Mameluke state (circa 1200–1400), and the Ottoman state in Turkey (circa 1450–1800), government was relatively bureaucratic. Salaried officials collected taxes and administered laws; they rotated in office, kept records, and conducted extensive written correspondence. The Abassid and Mame-

---

[44] MacMullen, *Roman Social Relations;* and Marrou, *History of Education*, pp. 406–7.
[45] Marrou, *History of Education*, pp. 400–418.
[46] Bernard Lewis, *The Arabs in History* (New York: Harper & Row, 1966), pp. 80–98, 131–43.

luke officials were often *ulema* or their pupils. The Ottoman rulers founded schools of higher study, called *madrasas,* for the explicit purpose of training administrators as part of the Ottoman effort to reduce the aristocracy's independence. The *madrasas* gave the government more direct control over religion by removing the teaching and interpretation of religious laws from the community-centered mosques. In the *madrasas,* Moslem intellectual innovativeness was replaced by a rigid formalization of tradition. The bureaucratic administration thus followed a typical pattern of emphasizing formality precisely as a means of eliminating tendencies to independence.

Medieval Europe and the Bureaucratic Church

In medieval Europe, the greatest centralizing power was the papacy. Between 1050 and 1300, it made a bid for theocratic control, based on possession of the only large-scale literate organization in Europe. The church began to bureaucratize internally through the growth of the papal chancery, which became steadily more important in settling property matters among the many wealthy monasteries and cathedrals; the chancery then moved to regain control of church appointments from the feudal lords.[47] The universities, which proliferated from the early twelfth century onwards, arose in response to employment opportunities in the church bureaucracy. Though there were no formal examinations for church offices, the tendency arose for the pope to appoint bishops from the ranks of those holding doctorates in theology and canon law. Clerics seeking appointment to lower-ranking parish positions had their names submitted on lists prepared by their university officials; it appears that it was not necessary for candidates to have a degree but only to have been in attendance.

These schools were the first in world history to be bureaucratized internally. While schooling preparatory to the university consisted of informal literacy training by monks or local parish priests, the universities developed an elaborate internal structure. They had a series of courses, examinations, and degrees. Specialized courses (canon law, secular law, medicine, theology) branched off from the study of the lower arts. Specific periods of attendance were required for various degrees: two years for the Bachelor of Arts, four more for the Master of Arts, and up to eight more for higher degrees in theology. Although grades do not seem to have been assigned and students varied in age from the early teens through the thirties, in other respects the schools involved considerable standardization, hierarchy, and specialization—especially in comparison to the schools of the Orient or the schools of Mediterranean antiquity. This internal bureaucratization seems to have evolved in response partly to the increasing bureaucratization of the papacy, partly to increasing competition for recommendations for church appointments, and partly to the increasing competition of teachers for students. The teach-

---

[47] Richard W. Southern, *Western Society and the Church in the Middle Ages* (Baltimore: Penguin Books, 1970); Nathan Schachner, *Mediaeval Universities* (New York: A. S. Barnes, 1962); Hastings Rashdall, *The Universities of Europe in the Middle Ages,* rev. ed. (London: Oxford Univ. Press, 1936); and Philippe Ariès, *Centuries of Childhood: A Social History of Family Life* (New York: Knopf, 1962), pp. 137–75.

ers took the unprecedented step of organizing themselves into a guild—*universitas* meant "guild" in medieval Latin. The guild seems to have designed the university structure of internal specialization and required hierarchies of courses as a means of sharing students and extending the period of paid instruction. (Students paid their professors individually for their instruction.) Thus, during the twelfth and thirteenth centuries, the number of years required to attain the valuable doctorate in theology gradually extended to sixteen, as the competition for high church positions increased.[48]

As various principalities, kingdoms, and cities consolidated their power, however, the papacy's bid for domination of Europe failed, and the church again became the captive of contending states. From the fourteenth century onwards, student enrollment dropped sharply, and the structure of the university began to change. In England, where this process went furthest, the higher faculties disappeared, and the universities became collections of colleges or private residential halls in which students were instructed by tutors rather than university professors. Thus, the failure of the bureaucratic church-state led to the decline of bureaucratic education.

The development of modern school systems resulted from the consolidation of strong European bureaucratic states that were independent of the Catholic church. These secular school systems taught in the national language rather than the pan-European language of church Latin.[49] The militarily expansive and rigidly bureaucratized Prussian state led the way in the seventeenth and eighteenth centuries in building a public school system at the elementary and university levels and in drawing state officials from among holders of university degrees. During this same period, the French state created military and engineering schools so as to draw its administrators from a source independent of the aristocracy and the powerful church-controlled schools. The Russian state, in its efforts to centralize control, went to the extreme of making aristocratic status dependent on government service, which in turn was tied to state-defined school qualifications. England, virtually up until the end of the nineteenth century, maintained a relatively patrimonial form of government administration—including the purchase of military commands, widespread patronage politics, and local administration by amateur gentry—and placed the least emphasis on publicly supported education. Only with the civil-service reforms beginning in 1870 did the English government begin to build a public school system, to revive the ancient but long moribund universities, and to create new universities.[50]

---

[48] Schachner, p. 135.

[49] Ariès, p. 167; Lawrence Stone, *The Crisis of the Aristocracy* (New York: Oxford Univ. Press, 1967), pp. 303–31; Reinhard Bendix, *Nation-Building and Citizenship* (New York: Wiley, 1964), pp. 89–92; and Walter H. Bruford, *Germany in the Eighteenth Century* (Cambridge, Eng.: Cambridge Univ. Press, 1935), pp. 122–24.

[50] Joseph R. Gusfield, "Equalitarianism and Bureaucratic Recruitment," *Administrative Science Quarterly*, 2 (1958), 521–41. A detailed Weberian account is given in Hans-Eberhard Mueller, "Bureaucracy and Education: Civil Service Reforms in Prussia and England as Strategies of Monopolization," unpublished paper, Swarthmore College, Swarthmore, Pa., 1974.

In general, any strong, centralized state or church tends to be bureaucratically organized; the bureaucratic control devices themselves are the prime basis of its centralized authority. Such a state or church provides a demand for education, but the relationship between the state or church and the educational system may take several forms. In the weakest form, the state or church simply provides a market for schools that spring up independently, as in many Islamic states, the medieval papacy, and the Chinese Empire. The Ottoman and late Roman empires represent an intermediate form, in which the state oversees and offers some financial support for existing educational institutions. State influence on education is fairly strong where examinations are required for entrance to government office, as in Imperial China, Germany after 1800, and Britain after 1870. The state is most deeply involved in education where it requires school attendance. Attendance was compulsory for aristocrats in Tokugawa Japan and in Russia, but only in the last few centuries has it been required of the general population, beginning with Germany in the eighteenth century, followed by the United States, France, Japan, Italy, and Russia in the nineteenth and by England and other countries in the twentieth.

It is here that the recent Marxist argument—that schooling is used as a device for ensuring labor discipline and, hence, is developed by the dominant class in its own interest—takes on great relevance.[51] Clearly, this argument applies only to modern mass education, not to the elite education that characterized most premodern educational systems and that continues to comprise the elite stratum of modern educational systems. With this specification, the labor-discipline argument does find empirical support. Consider, for example, the conservative and conformist values expressed in school texts throughout the period of mass education, and the efficacy of primary schools in inculcating unreflective political loyalty.[52] Yet although modern education does discipline the lower social classes, the demand for labor discipline per se does not explain why some industrial societies have large mass-education systems and why some have small ones. For example, the educational system is huge in the United States, relatively large in Russia and Japan, and tiny in Britain, France, and Germany, even though the need for labor discipline is presumably the same in all industrial societies. (Compare the figures from the early 1960s shown in table 1.) Nor does the demand for labor discipline explain the existence of segregated class systems in some societies but not in others.

Historical evidence indicates that mass, compulsory education was first created not for industrial, but for military and political, discipline. The first compulsory, state-supported elementary schools were established in the early eighteenth century by Denmark and Prussia, and later by Japan, to accompany the creation of mass conscript armies.[53] In England, where a highly traditional military organiza-

---

[51] Bowles and Gintis, *Schooling in Capitalist America*.

[52] Richard de Charms and George H. Moeller, "Values Expressed in American Children's Readers," *Journal of Abnormal and Social Psychology*, 64 (1962), 36–142; and Robert D. Hess and Judith V. Torney, *The Development of Political Attitudes in Children* (Chicago: Aldine, 1967).

[53] Bendix, *Nation Building and Citizenship*, pp. 88–93. Japan created a universal, compulsory elementary-school system as part of its program of military reform, as it moved from relying on exclusively samurai armies to mass-conscript ones, according to Dore, *Education in Tokugawa Japan*, pp. 222, 250–51, 297–98.

Educational Stratification
RANDALL COLLINS

TABLE 1

	Percent completing secondary school	Percent attending university	Percent graduating from university
USA	75	39	18
USSR	47	19	9
Japan	57	11	11
France	30	11	—
England	12	6	5
West Germany	11	6	—

Sources: Tovsten Husen, "Social Structure and the Utilization of Talent," in *Essays on World Education*, ed. George Z. F. Bereday (New York: Oxford Univ. Press, 1969), p. 80; Philip J. Idenberg, "Europe: In Search of New Forms of Education," in *Essays*, ed. Bereday, p. 281; Nicholas De Witt, "Basic Comparative Data on Soviet and American Education," *Comparative Perspectives on Education*, ed. Robert J. Havighurst (Boston: Little, Brown, 1968), pp. 55-56; John E. Blewett, trans. and ed., *Higher Education in Postwar Japan: The Ministry of Education's 1964 White Paper* (Tokyo: Sophia Univ. Press, 1965), pp. 113, 118, 122, 158-9.

tion and the aristocracy's near deadlock on political power survived until the late nineteenth century, it was only with military and political reforms and the concomitant organization of a powerful working-class party that a compulsory school system was envisioned.

Capitalists' interest in using education to ensure labor discipline may have been a force behind the development of mass, compulsory education in some of these countries, but it was not the central motive: Prussia and Japan established compulsory schooling well before extensive industrialization, and England long after. The safer generalization is that bureaucratic states impose compulsory education on populations which are seen as potential threats to state control, and that those economic classes which are influential in the state will help define the nature of the "threat."

Finally, it seems clear that the initial impetus behind the development of bureaucratized schooling did not come from the bureaucratization of business enterprises. Bureaucracy within private business organizations developed quite late. There are few examples of it before the late nineteenth century in the United States.[54] The industrial organizations of England, France, and Germany in the early and middle nineteenth century did make considerable use of record keeping, and some of these organizations were large enough to have a degree of specialization and of administrative career hierarchy, but educational requirements and examinations were not part of this structure. Most nineteenth-century British or German clerks were trained through work "apprenticeship" after elementary schooling in literacy. Even in the twentieth century, managers in Britain and Germany have tended to have had little formal education, because the higher schools have been connected with careers in government and the elite profes-

---

[54] Alfred D. Chandler, "The Coming of Big Business," in *The Comparative Approach to American History*, ed. C. Vann Woodward (New York: Basic Books, 1968), pp. 220-37; and Reinhard Bendix, *Work and Authority in Industry* (New York: Wiley, 1956), pp. 198-253.

sions.⁵⁵ The civil-service exams for which students prepare have reflected the culture of the elite status group, exemplified in England by knowledge of the Greek and Latin classics and in Germany by knowledge of philosophy and law. Where industrial and commercial bureaucracies have emphasized educational requirements for employees—above all in the United States, Japan, and Russia and to a lesser degree in France—the educational system has taken the lead and business has responded.⁵⁶ This has resulted in a tendency for formal requirements to increase in both spheres.

Conclusion: Towards a Theory of Cultural Markets

We have seen that there are different types of education, each with its own determining conditions. Several of these conditions may operate simultaneously, resulting in a variety of types of education that coexist or even combine into a single, complex system. This is especially the case in the modern industrial world, where a great many interests in education have been mobilized. Sometimes these interests have conflicted, but they have nevertheless collectively resulted in a larger system of educational stratification. This system, I would suggest, is a market for cultural goods in which various sources of demand mesh with sources of supply. The effects of this market are usually not foreseen by the individual parties involved. Among these effects are changes in the rates of growth of educational systems, in the price and purchasing power of educational credentials, and in the structure of educational systems. Finally, crises may arise as the parties react to the unforeseen outcomes of the cultural market.

We have examined three types of education. Training in practical skills exists in any economy but is usually built informally into the work process. The practical skills of literacy and numeracy have been especially demanded, and sometimes provided by special teachers, wherever there has been literate administration or the development of commerce. Education in the leisure culture of a status group has prospered in relatively peaceful periods during which there is decentralized competition within a wealthy aristocracy, within a prosperous bourgeoisie, or within a rising working class; the nature of the status culture has varied with the groups involved. Highly formal educational systems with specified time sequences, examinations, and elements of compulsion have developed as bureaucratic devices are used, especially by centralized states, to control officials, feudal aristocracies, or, in modern periods of mass political mobilization, the general population.

Historically, these types of education have sometimes combined. To be sure, some of them are theoretically incompatible; for example, aristocratic status education has emphasized aesthetic and leisure themes that are explicitly intended to

---

⁵⁵ David Granick, *The European Executive* (New York: Doubleday, 1960), pp. 240-300; and Roy Lewis and Rosemary Stewart, *The Managers: A New Examination of the English, German, and American Executive* (New York: New American Library, 1961), pp. 58-75.

⁵⁶ Collins, "Functional and Conflict Theories," pp. 1003-4, 1014-16; Koza Azumi, *Higher Education and Business Recruitment in Japan* (New York: Teachers College Press, 1969); and Pierre Bourdieu, Luc Boltanski, and Monique de Saint Martin, "Les Stratégies de Reconversion: Les Classes Sociales et le Système d'Enseignement," *Social Science Information*, 12 (1974), 61-113.

Educational Stratification
RANDALL COLLINS

oppose both practical training and the narrower specializations of thoroughly bureaucratic education. But in practice, these seemingly incompatible types of education have appeared in combination. For example, familiarity with the status culture of the aristocracy has often been used as a criterion for selection of government officials in bureaucratic systems. The Chinese examination system tested the genteel skills of poetic composition and use of literary allusions, just as the British civil-service examinations tested knowledge of the literary classics. In modern times, bureaucratic and compulsory mass education has incorporated elements of practical education by training students in literacy and arithmetic. Similarly, secondary schooling, which developed in post-Renaissance Europe as a support for the status cultures of the prosperous classes, has been incorporated into a standard sequence of educational levels leading up to the university.

Bureaucratization has been the principal means for combining different types of education. The essence of bureaucratic controls is a stress on the keeping of formal regulations and records; any content, whether it be originally aesthetic, religious, legal, scientific, or practical, may be fitted into this system. Thus we find strong bureaucratic states and churches emphasizing various kinds of educational contents: the Chinese classics and the martial arts of Tokugawa Japan, the rhetoric of the late Roman Empire, the dialectics of the medieval university, the inflexible legal canons of Islamic culture, the Greek and Latin classics of British and German elite education, and the sciences of the elite schools in France and the Soviet Union. What all these educational programs have in common is structural formality: grades, examinations, required sequences, and set time periods for instruction that are absent from the pure forms of practical and status-group education. In bureaucratic structures, however, students know that the content of education is arbitrary: even if education is ostensibly aimed at cultivating practical skills, relatively few of these skills, at least in the modern world, seem to stay with students once they have passed through the system and received their credentials.

The various kinds of demand for education—practical, status-group, and bureaucratic—may be viewed more broadly as part of a *cultural market* in which social actors simultaneously attempt to attain certain goals. The interest of government in bureaucratic control over particular classes may mesh with the interest of these very classes in improving their cultural attainments for the sake of status. Thus, we find a symbiosis between the control interest of the Chinese emperors and the status interest of the gentry and, more ironically, between government concern for compulsory educational indoctrination of the modern masses and some interest in status mobility on the part of those masses. The interest of capitalists in ensuring labor discipline adds yet another demand to this market,[57] as does the interest of a particular ethnic group in maintaining its opportunities vis-à-vis other ethnic groups.

The extent to which education develops in different societies and historical periods varies according to the nature of their cultural markets. Abstractly, we may

[57] Bowles and Gintis, in *Schooling in Capitalist America,* similarly suggest that an impersonal market mechanism can bring about the creation of a school system in response to the predominant demands in the class structure.

see that cultural markets require a common currency and independent sources of supply and demand for cultural goods.

A *common cultural currency* derives from an elite culture, which has undisputed dominance because it legitimates a wealthy and powerful group.

The *supply of cultural goods* (or cultural capital, in Pierre Bourdieu's term[58]) is determined by the availability of teachers, of material resources for schools, of sufficient economic productivity or stratification to permit leisure for cultural activities, and of methods for producing (and especially mass-producing) books and writing materials.

The *demand for cultural goods* is determined by the number of individuals or groups who feel there is a potential payoff from education and by the economic and political resources they have to make their demands effective. The interests motivating these demands can be of all three types discussed above—practical training, status-group training, and bureaucratic control. Since, in principle, the demand for training in practical skills can be satisfied on the job, such training has been demanded in the form of schooling only where occupations and professions have been monopolistically organized through a formal credential system. The desire for training in the culture of a status group has been a stronger source of demand for formal education. Competition over status-group membership or group prestige has been strong during periods of political decentralization or political instability under a unified market economy. It has been even stronger when many culturally distinct ethnic groups live within a common system of economic or political stratification. Situations of ethnic competition have tended to increase the salience of the cultural sphere, first, because the basis of ethnic differences has been cultural and, second, because particular ethnic groups have attempted to use devices for cultural inclusion and prestige as crucial weapons for controlling top economic and political positions. Thus we find in India that the market for status-group education was largest during prosperous, politically decentralized periods when the extraordinary range of ethnic groups was channeled into the occupational monopolies of the caste system. Similarly, status-group education was particularly important in the Hellenistic empires built by Greek conquest of the culturally distinct Middle Eastern and Mediterranean states; in the ethnically diverse Islamic empire; in medieval Europe when an ethnically heterogeneous people were united by the papacy; and in the United States since the immigrations of the mid-nineteenth century.

The demand for cultural goods has also depended on the extent of political opposition to the dominant classes. Where governments have faced only a small politically mobilized class in the population, their demand for education as a bureaucratic control has been quite limited. Where a large population has been mobilized, however, the control interest of bureaucratic elites has been correspondingly large.

The development of a complex school system may itself create an additional demand for employees socialized by its own procedures. Furthermore, due to in-

[58] Pierre Bourdieu and Jean-Claude Passeron, *La Réproduction* (Paris: Les Éditions de Minuit, 1970).

ternal struggles for control, a school system may bureaucratize the careers of its own teachers.

Finally, a source of increases in demand has been population growth, if it has been connected with an existing interest in education. For example, as the Chinese population grew from the sixteenth century onward and as economic changes mobilized an increasing proportion of that population, the number of aspirants for government positions increased steadily. Similarly, population growth played into a mobilized interest in education to create the college-attendance boom of the United States in the 1960s.

What may this market model explain? The ramifications, I believe, are numerous; here it is possible to mention only a few. The varying rates of growth of educational systems (including negative rates) are, in principle, calculable from such a model. And the rate of growth relative to the availability of payoffs in the surrounding society will determine the purchasing power of education for those who acquire it. For example, the demand for education in China increased from the sixteenth through the nineteenth centuries, but the number of government positions was kept virtually constant. Thus, the cultural price of education increased: the examination system was gradually elaborated, resulting in a series of examinations that might take a scholar thirty years to complete.[59] In all educational systems there have been similar processes in which the demand for educational credentials has increased without a commensurate increase in payoffs. Oversupply of graduates may result in upper-level unemployment where job requirements remain constant, as occurred in Germany in the 1920s and in many Third World nations in the 1960s.[60] Where credential seekers are mobilized and able to put pressure on the government to expand the educational system, as in modern democracies, the cultural market adjusts by increasing the formal-training requirements for any given position and, sometimes, by increasing the number of positions for which such formal credentials are required.[61] The situation is analogous to inflation of a monetary currency, which results in a decrease in purchasing power.

[59] Chang, *The Chinese Gentry;* Franke, *Reform and Abolition.*
[60] Walter M. Kotschnig, *Unemployment in the Learned Professions* (London: Oxford Univ. Press, 1937); and Bert F. Hoselitz, "Investment in Education and Its Political Impact," in *Education and Political Development,* ed. James S. Coleman (Princeton, N.J.: Princeton Univ. Press, 1965), pp. 541–65.
[61] Weber noted this inflationary tendency in bureaucratic employment requirements in Europe in his day. Weber, *Economy and Society.* Another period of credential inflation occurred in Germany around 1800, when a mass of applicants for government positions crowded the universities, producing a reform which consisted of an extension of educational requirements to more positions. See Bruford, *Germany in the Eighteenth Century,* pp. 248–68; Henri Brunschwig, *La Crise de l'Etat Prussien* (Paris: Presses Universitaires de France, 1947); Hans Rosenberg, *Bureaucracy, Aristocracy, and Autocracy* (Cambridge, Mass.: Harvard Univ. Press, 1958); Franz Schnabel, *Deutsche Geschichte im Neunzehnten Jahrhundert* (Freiburg, Germany: Verlag Herder, 1959), I, 408–57. Inflationary phenomena have been especially noticeable in the expansion of American education since the late nineteenth century, as well as in France since World War II. See fn. 56. William G. Spady shows that the relative gaps in education among American social classes have remained constant throughout the twentieth century despite mass increases in the *absolute* level of schooling. "Educational Mobility and Access: Growth and Paradoxes," *American Journal of Sociology,* 72 (1967), 273–86. Similar results for France are reported by Pierre Bourdieu and Jean-Claude Passeron in *Les Héritiers* (Paris: Les Éditions de Minuit, 1964) and in *La Réproduction.*

The parties that enter the cultural marketplace usually are involved in social conflicts of some sort—whether struggles by economic classes for domination, revolution, or self-improvement, or the more complex conflicts that result when class struggle meshes with the prestige struggle of ethnic or other status groups. The differences among the main types of educational structures in the modern world can be explained by differences among lineups of contending interests.

The most prominent difference is between "sponsored-mobility" systems, such as those of Britain and most other Western European countries, and "contest-mobility" systems, such as those of the United States and the Soviet Union.[62] In the former type, children's careers are determined early, usually at the end of primary school. Some children proceed into elite university-preparatory schools stressing traditional high culture; others enter terminal vocational schools; and still others end their education at the elementary level. The group that enters the elite track is virtually guaranteed admission into and graduation from each succeeding level. For this group, mobility is said to be sponsored. In a contest-mobility system, there is no single decision point. Nearly all students are channeled into comprehensive secondary schools, and there is continuous attrition and competition for admission to each higher level.

Class-segregated, sponsored-mobility systems have emerged where there has been a radical mobilization of the middle or working class that has resulted in cultural polarization around distinctively commercial and technical educational ideals, but the upper class has nevertheless managed to maintain power. When such a social division occurs, educational systems have split, too: the middle and working classes are given distinctive educational enclaves while careers in the dominant occupations and political institutions remain monopolized by those who have moved through an elite educational system that maintains the traditional high culture. Contest-mobility systems, on the other hand, have emerged in industrial societies where class conflict has been submerged within a single market for cultural respectability. This may occur, as in the United States, where class differences are subordinate to divisions among many competing ethnic groups, or, as in the Soviet Union (which is also a multi-ethnic society dominated by a particular ethnic elite), where organized class conflict was eliminated, leaving only a single cultural standard for competition.

Conflict over economic interests is not eliminated in multi-ethnic situations, but it is fragmented among a much larger number of contending groups. This leads to greater competition for cultural credentials. Economic outcomes are not necessarily affected by whether class conflict is fragmented in this way; rates of mobility seem to be quite similar in societies with both sponsored and contest structures of education and seem to be quite stable over time when either type of system expands. The differences lie, rather, in the political and cultural spheres: the spon-

---

[62] The distinction is originated by Ralph H. Turner in "Sponsored and Contest Mobility and the School System," *American Sociological Review*, 25 (1960), 855–67. Turner bases his distinction on the supposed primacy of the value of ascription or achievement. In my view, however, such values (if in fact they exist outside the mind of the analyst) result from social structure rather than vice versa.

Educational Stratification
RANDALL COLLINS

sored-mobility structure keeps class cultures quite distinct and fosters class-based ideological parties, while the contest-mobility structure seems to blur class identification in politics. In sponsored-mobility systems, a sharp split is maintained between elite culture and low culture, while mass, popular cultural movements seem more prevalent in contest-mobility systems.

Inflation of educational credentials is especially likely in contest-mobility systems. For example, the United States has experienced this kind of educational inflation since at least the middle of the nineteenth century. From 1870 to 1970, school-attendance rates rose dramatically at every level, and higher levels were created and expanded as the lower ones filled up. At the same time, educational requirements for employment at all levels increased correspondingly, adjusting to the inflated supply of cultural currency. Such an inflationary process does not necessarily go on indefinitely; the downturn in educational attendance since approximately 1970 and the cultural revolution of student-protest movements and dropout culture of the 1960s are instances of reactions that may occur when a culture-producing system has been expanding in an inflationary way for some time.

An inflationary system, even if it merely expands the supply of currency while leaving the rest of the stratification system in a state of dynamic equilibrium, nevertheless affects cultural consciousness by mobilizing increasing proportions of the population in struggles for control of the stratification system. Such mobilization can become politically dangerous to an authoritarian government, which may react by cutting down the educational system. There are a number of instances of this in Chinese history (most recently in the 1960s) and in nineteenth-century Russian history. Or disillusionment may set in among the purchasers of cultural credentials. This was behind the precipitous drop in European university enrollments in the period after the Reformation, and something similar seems to be developing in America today. Finally, the currency itself can break down. The prestige of a particular elite culture and that culture's accompanying political and organizational domination may give way to independent currencies, as when the separate national cultures of early modern Europe replaced the old international culture of the medieval church. Although it would be hazardous to predict a future change of this magnitude for the United States, we certainly see a trend in this direction in the recent attacks on Anglo-Protestant cultural domination and the efforts towards a new cultural pluralism.

Our understanding of such possibilities depends on the construction of a workable theory of cultural markets. As yet, we are only beginning to see what such a theory would include and what it might explain. Its prospects are extensive. If we have come to see education as basic to our current system of stratification, an exploration of this phenomenon which moves beyond a naive, functionalist view suggests a major reformulation of all stratification analyses. For the interaction of cultural organization with the material economy is the key to all structures of domination, and the concept of the cultural market may provide a means of encompassing multifaceted interests and conflicts within a single explanatory structure.

Nonformal Education and Occupational Stratification: Implications for Latin America

THOMAS J. LA BELLE
ROBERT E. VERHINE
University of California, Los Angeles

La Belle and Verhine trace the development of nonformal education and question whether it can bring significant income and status benefits to the economically disadvantaged in developing countries. They review research on the relationship between education and occupation and examine two theories which purport to explain this relationship. The authors conclude that as long as the credentials of formal schools continue to be the most salient factor in the job market, nonformal education—education without traditional credentials—will do little to increase social and economic equality.

In many parts of the world a combination of social pressures and financial constraints has made it necessary to look beyond the formal school as the only widely accepted means of organized education. Discussions of educational alternatives are now commonplace and nonformal education has emerged as a popular al-

---

This article is based, in part, on La Belle, T. J., & Verhine, R. E. Education, social change and social stratification. In T. J. La Belle (Ed.), *Educational alternatives in Latin America*. Los Angeles: Latin American Center, University of California, 1975. We wish to thank the Latin American Center at UCLA for financial assistance in the preparation of this article. Portions of this article were written while Professor La Belle was on sabbatical leave from UCLA and receiving fellowship support from the Inter-American Foundation.

ternative. Defined as "... any organized, systematic, educational activity carried on outside the framework of the formal system to provide selected types of learning to particular subgroups in the population, adults as well as children" (Coombs & Ahmed, 1974, p. 8), nonformal education can include out-of-school programs in such areas as agricultural extension, community development, family planning, technical or vocational training, literacy and basic education and so on. In the Third World, these programs are primarily directed toward youth and adults for whom formal education has been either inappropriate or unavailable.

It is widely assumed that nonformal education can transmit new skills and values effectively and inexpensively, thereby contributing to national development and enhancing the status and income levels of marginal groups. Yet our contention is that these groups are disadvantaged not so much because of their lack of skills but, in part, because they lack the formal school credentials which are necessary for advancement. If this is true, can nonformal education—education without formal credentials—change occupational levels and raise standards of living? We believe not. Our hypothesis is that unless there are concomitant changes in the values and institutions associated with a society's occupational stratification process, nonformal education cannot achieve its long-term goal of greater social and economic equality. Since nonformal education is recommended largely for developing countries, we will examine our hypothesis in relation to these developing societies, particularly those in Latin America.

The article begins by tracing some of the issues which led to a concern for educational alternatives, especially nonformal education, and proceeds to a brief overview of contemporary thought in this area. The relationship between education and occupational stratification will then be examined with regard to the technical-function and the status-conflict theories, each of which has widely divergent implications for the success of nonformal education. Finally, our conclusions will discuss the potential contribution of nonformal education to occupational mobility in both urban and rural areas of Latin America.

The Attack on Formal Schooling
The emphasis in education throughout most of the world during the 1950's and most of the 1960's was on expanding school services to keep pace with the growth in population. This was especially apparent in developing countries where many educational decisionmakers assumed that schooling was an important vehicle for social change and national development. In the belief that building new schools and reducing dropout and repeater rates would result in an in-

creasing percentage of individuals educated for occupations and citizenship, schools often were held up as the panacea for social and individual development. In recent years, however, educators and social scientists have become increasingly disenchanted with the potential of formal schooling to achieve such goals. Despite their specific disillusionment with formal schools, the general belief in education for development persists. Thus, both disillusionment and optimism became the major reasons for the interest in educational alternatives—especially nonformal education—in developing areas.

Part of the growing disenchantment with the ability of formal schooling to alter society can be traced to educators in developed countries who studied the nature and function of the school as it related to the particular socioeconomic background characteristics of students. Basically, the empirical evidence which they analyzed called into question the viability of the school as an integral part of the developmental process by suggesting that educational achievement was more dependent upon conditions outside the schools than inside.[1] For example, in England two-thirds of the variance in achievement differences among eleven-year-olds was explained by family background factors (Central Advisory Council on Education, 1966). A similar study in the United States confirmed these findings (Coleman et al., 1966), as did the International Association for the Evaluation of Educational Achievement in its survey of mathematics achievement among thirteen-year-olds in a dozen relatively developed countries (Husén, 1972). Additional confirmation for this thesis came from a Rand review of the research on the determinants of educational effectiveness. The investigators concluded that available evidence fails to "show that school resources *do* affect student outcomes," while the "socioeconomic status of a student's family—his parent's income, education, and occupation—invariably prove to be significant predictors of his educational outcome" (Averch et al., 1972, p. 148). Furthermore, the report found that educational research does not indicate which school variables show consistent effects on student achievement. For example, neither distinct teaching methods, teacher differences, nor class size produced any sustained or consistent outcomes in student achievement. Given all of these research results, it is not surprising that considerable criticism was directed at the schools.

While dissatisfaction increased in developed countries, similar criticisms were

[1] Although the majority of the available research supports the strong positive relationship between socioeconomic status and school achievement, one recent study indicates that in-school factors rather than personal characteristics of students account for the majority of the explained variance in achievement (Farrell, 1973).

mounting in developing countries. One of the first individuals to articulate the inadequate school situation in Latin America and to point out the need for educational alternatives was Ivan Illich (1968, 1970). He argued that although universal schooling is beyond the means of developing countries, education is still recognized as the only legitimate avenue to participation in society. Thus, schools are destined to continue to provide privileges for the few at the expense of the many, producing a caste system by dividing society into two distinct classes: one with educational credentials, the other without. According to Illich, these credentials do not necessarily reflect an individual's ability to function in a particular capacity, but serve more to denote membership in a society's elite group.

Everett Reimer (1971), a colleague of Illich, believes that schools reinforce a "closed technological society" by functioning in four distinct but interrelated ways: first, they act as babysitters and thus prolong childhood roles; second, they sort youth into the social structure on the basis of educational attainment; third, they indoctrinate the young to accept conformity, social hierarchy and traditional political and economic ideology; and fourth, they develop skills and knowledge for success in accord with technological criteria. Both Illich and Reimer hold that these four functions are often in conflict, thereby making schools amorphous and inefficient. The solution, they maintain, is a change in the ideology of society which in turn would create new educational modes quite different from traditional schooling. In short, Illich and Reimer call for a more egalitarian society sustained by alternative educational processes.

In addition to such radical critiques, the more traditional scholars analyzed Latin American schools in the development context; that is, by measuring the increase in numbers of students educated, and predicting whether sufficient economic resources could be tapped to sustain and expand the school system to meet increasing individual and social demands. Reflecting practical and more widely held concerns, this latter group provided the major impetus for the search for alternatives (see, for example, Coombs, 1968).

Although educational systems in Latin America and elsewhere in the Third World had made great strides in school enrollment (an increase of approximately two-thirds at the primary level and double at the secondary and higher levels between 1960 and 1969), less than half of the school-age population of Latin America was enrolled in 1969 (Inter-American Development Bank, 1969). Given current population growth rates, there will be 41 million more school-age children in Latin America in 1980 than there were in 1970. Even at current enrollment rates, the effect of such growth at the primary school level means that by 1980 an additional 30 million students will need to be accommodated. Therefore, efforts to expand the school systems of Latin America in the 1970's must nearly double that of the 1960's.

Furthermore, population growth has also checked the progress made in reducing the numbers of adult illiterates. Although the percentage of adult illiterates in Latin America over the age of 15 has been reduced from 32.5 percent in 1960 to 23.6 percent in 1970, the actual number of illiterates continues to rise (Inter-American Development Bank, 1971).

One of the major constraints on the obvious need for school expansion in Latin America and elsewhere was and still is the lack of available funding. Recent calculations projecting school costs for Latin America suggest that by 1980, three times the amount of money spent in 1965 will be needed. This amount is expected to be 5.5 percent of the region's projected Gross Domestic Product, a level higher than that expended in most economically advanced countries (United Nations Economic Commission for Latin America, 1968; Ford Foundation, 1972).

Moreover, in almost all Latin American nations for the period 1960-1968, the growth of formal educational expenditures exceeded the growth of the Gross National Product (World Bank, 1971). Whereas enrollments during this period increased at an annual rate of 6.2 percent, expenditures for formal education increased 11.3 percent annually (Faure, 1972). Given the rising costs of salaries, supplies and facilities, and the increasing demand for education, along with competition for funds from other public service sectors, a growing number of educators and social scientists have recognized that Latin American governments must discover alternative mechanisms for the delivery of educational services.

An Emphasis on Nonformal Programs

By now, these criticisms and analyses of formal schooling have become part of the rationale for the increasing attention given to nonformal education in developing countries. While nonformal education retains the traditional goal of formal schooling—greater socioeconomic development—proponents assert that it can succeed where formal education has failed in part because it provides greater and more flexible educational choices for individuals (Adams, 1972). Further reasons for the attractiveness of nonformal education include: (1) decreasing resources and expanding school-age populations; (2) equal opportunity and access to education and the resources of society; (3) the need for educational innovation; (4) the need to supplement and complement the benefits of formal education; (5) the need to meet human needs in specific contexts; and (6) the possibility of shifting attention from school certificates to performance as the criterion of achievement (Brembeck, 1973). Coombs and Ahmed claim that in its versatility, adaptability and diversity, nonformal has greater benefits than formal education, especially in developing rural areas. In short, nonformal education is "totally pragmatic" (Coombs & Ahmed, 1974, p. 233).

Nonformal programs are seldom designed to replace formal schools. Instead, they are usually conceived as a supplement or complement to formal schooling or as a programmatic way of reaching a particular population for which schools have been ineffective or inappropriate (Callaway, 1973). Much of the literature on out-of-school education advocates an integrated approach to the delivery of educational services; that is, the coordination of efforts among formal, nonformal and informal programs.[2] For example, Harbison argues that poorer countries should approach skill development through both formal and nonformal training. He suggests that governments must select the appropriate educational method for the appropriate context. For example, nonformal methods may be more effective than formal schooling in adult contexts and rural areas in particular.

Coombs also advocated the integrated approach. His study, sponsored by UNICEF (1973), on the role and function of education for rural children and adolescents, states that nonformal education must be seen in the context of multiple learning systems. It clearly emphasizes the blend of formal, nonformal and informal learning. In a recent study sponsored by the World Bank, Coombs and Ahmed (1974) concluded that nonformal education can be effective in generating employment, productivity and income among adult farmers, artisans, craftsmen and small entrepreneurs when coordinated with other efforts at rural development.

Education and Occupational Stratification
Proponents of nonformal education believe that it, either alone or in consort with other educational efforts, can transmit the skills and values necessary for raising status and income levels. Moreover, it is claimed that nonformal education can be particularly successful in accomplishing this for economically marginal groups formerly denied educational opportunities. All of this assumes a relationship between educational and occupational attainment, regardless of

---

[2] Informal education is "... the lifelong process by which every person acquires and accumulates knowledge, skills, attitudes and insights from daily experiences and exposure to the environment..." (Coombs & Ahmed, 1974, p. 8).

whether the education is formal or nonformal. While empirical data on the effectiveness of nonformal education are scanty,[3] because of this assumption, we can look at the general relationship between education and occupational stratification.

A great many sociological studies have attempted to determine the relative importance of ascribed and achieved personal attributes to occupational position (measured by income and/or status) and mobility (measured intergenerationally and/or intragenerationally). Although these studies differ in methodologies, variables and sample populations, they consistently have found that formal educational attainment strongly influences occupational attainment, with a much greater influence on initial employment level than on subsequent promotions (Berg, 1970; Blau & Duncan, 1967; Blum, 1972; Coleman et al., 1972; Duncan et al., 1972; Duncan & Hodge, 1963; Eckland, 1965; Elder, 1968; Haller, 1968; Perrucci & Perrucci, 1970; Sewell et al., 1970). Numerous economic studies also show that education is a major determinant of income growth and differentiation for both individuals and nations (see summaries in Bowen, 1964; Bowman, 1966). Although most of these studies were done in the United States, recent sociological and economic studies conducted in various Latin American countries have produced similar results. Research by Jacobsen and Kendrick (1973) in Puerto Rico, La Belle (1975) in Venezuela, Carnoy (1964, 1972b) in Mexico and Puerto Rico, Holsinger (1974b) in Brazil, and Roberts (1973) in Costa Rica has indicated that formal education—at least in the urban areas of Latin America—has a significant impact on income and status.

Despite the consistency of these results across national boundaries, there is evidence suggesting that the impact of schooling on occupational attainment is positively related to an area's level of socioeconomic development (Duncan & Hodge, 1963; Boudon, 1973). Studies of labor market demand and supply show that modernizing economies tend to witness rising educational requirements at all levels of the job hierarchy.[4] Thus, despite the growth of popular demand for formal educational opportunities and an increasingly better educated work force, educational expansion has failed to produce any significant decline in social inequality (Boudon, 1973). As individuals in modern society attain higher levels of schooling, the value of that education is deflated by rising job requirements. Consequently, people must acquire more schooling simply to attain the same levels of social reward. Boudon's argument implies that increasing educa-

---

[3] See, for example, Sheffield & Diejomaoh, 1972; Wood, 1974.
[4] For a discussion of rising educational requirements, see, for example, Berg, 1970; Boudon, 1973; Faure, 1972.

tional attainment in areas with high levels of socioeconomic development does not necessarily change the social and occupational stratification system.

Presumably, there would be a greater correlation between schooling and occupational level if one could distinguish the aspects and kinds of training which are job or income related (Anderson, 1961). Research conducted in the United States by Blum (1972) and Coleman (1972) took an important step in this direction by considering as two separate variables the education acquired before and after entering the job market. Both studies found that education acquired after job-entry has a greater impact on status and income than does any other post-job-entry variable tested. However, it has significantly less influence than pre-employment educational attainment. Unfortunately, Blum and Coleman did not distinguish between formal and nonformal education in the post-employment education variable.

Two recent contributions to the literature on education and occupational stratification focus directly on the relative influence of formal and nonformal education in Latin America. In a study of industrial workers in Venezuela, an attempt was made to identify the relationships among family background, employment experience, formal schooling, on-the-job training, nonformal education and income. Regression analyses of monthly income on selected independent measures for *obreros* (workers) and *empleados* (employees) showed that higher salaries are associated with formal rather than nonformal education (La Belle, 1975). Therefore, the study concludes that it is unrealistic to encourage wage earners to pursue nonformal education for income benefits. Riske and Rust (1975), in a somewhat broader study in Port-of-Spain, Trinidad, analyzed the relationships among nonformal educational programs, occupational achievement and selected independent background measures. Again, formal schooling was found to be the principal route to higher job attainment. Furthermore, nonformal education program participants had already received much formal schooling. Hence, under current societal conditions, nonformal education may offer little status or income mobility to wage earners from lower socioeconomic positions.

One major reason for the failure of nonformal education to increase job attainment may be that employers do not value such credentials when compared with those offered by formal schools. Indeed, the important role of academic credentials in the stratification process is well documented in developed countries. Studies show that degrees and diplomas alone, independent of years in school or cognitive achievement, command additional income and status in the job market (Berg, 1970; Eckland, 1965; Hansen, 1963).

Perhaps the strongest empirical support for the validity of the hypothesis regarding the role of credentials in Latin America comes from a recent investigation by Bruno and Van Zeyl (1975). This study examined the ideology of credentialism through an attitude profile of a sample of Venezuelan personnel officers. These commercial and industrial managers emerged as strongly committed to formal education as an essential component of national progress. In hiring, they matched available jobs and salary levels with an applicant's educational background. Bruno and Van Zeyl asserted that the ideology of credentialism is based upon the belief that continued educational expansion and the establishment of educational requirements for skilled work are essential to modernization. They contended that individuals with alternative educational experiences will compete unsuccessfully for jobs with those who present conventional educational credentials.

Why are formal school credentials more influential in the job market than those offered by nonformal education programs if they both transmit the same skills and values? Two theories have been advanced to explain this. The technical-function theory asserts that education provides the specific skills and/or general capabilities that are required for employment. Educational requirements for jobs tend to rise as technological change steadily creates a need for more highly skilled workers. Thus, school credentials constitute proof that an individual possesses the skills and knowledge necessary for economic production. The status-conflict theory, on the other hand, proposes that formal education socializes individuals and confers elite status or respect for elite status. According to this theory, rising educational requirements for employment are a result of the competition among status groups who use education to dominate the job market by imposing their cultural standards on the occupational selection process. This theory suggests that credentials are more a mark of membership in a particular status group than proof of technical skill or achievement.

Before continuing our discussion of education and stratification, it should be stated that these theories allow us to place the diversity of research cited here in a framework. Many of the relevant sociological and economic studies mentioned here are context-specific and thus may not always be applicable to Latin America. Though these studies have found that apparently most people receive some status and income benefits from formal education, it is clear that the magnitude of these benefits differs substantially between race and sex groups (Blair, 1970; Blau & Duncan, 1967; Coleman et al., 1966; Hanoch, 1967; Hines et al., 1970; Welch, 1967), between regions (Blau & Duncan, 1967; Hines et al., 1970), and between countries (Anderson, 1961; Psacharopoulos, 1972). Moreover, in concentrating on employee attributes and/or income flows, these studies fail to focus on the total occupational selection process. Many do not consider, for example, the structure and requirements of the job market, the quantity and nature of schooling opportunities, and the attitudes, perceptions and behavior of employers. Thus, an additional problem with these studies is that while they posit that people benefit from formal education, they fail to account for such interrelated factors as the dominant cultural values, the rigidity of class and status lines and the linkage of occupational hierarchies to social stratification. However, if they are placed within a theoretical framework which explains in general how educational attainment is related to occupational attainment, these studies can be applied to Latin America. The technical-function and status-conflict theories allow us to do that.

The Technical-Function Theory
The first assertion of the technical-function theory is that skill requirements in an industrial society steadily increase because of technological change. This notion is supported by manpower studies conducted in numerous countries. The early stages of development appear to create a particularly strong demand for middle-level technicians and managers (Harbison & Myers, 1964). In Brazil, for example, despite the rapid increase in enrollment, the demand for middle-school graduates is nearly one and one-half times the supply (Havighurst & Gouveia, 1969). However, studies conducted in the United States suggest that the upgrading of job skill requirements as a result of technological change cannot account fully for the increasing impact of educational attainment on occupational attainment. Folger and Nam (1964) report that only 15 percent of the increase in educational levels in the United States in the twentieth century can be attributed to shifts in the occupational structure—a decrease in the proportion of low skill jobs and an increase in the proportion of high skill jobs. Moreover, investigations of the links between schooling and job skills by Berg (1970), Eckhaus (1964), Horowitz and Hernstadt (1966), and Jaffe and Froomkin (1968) have established that educational requirements for jobs have risen at a faster rate than the actual skill requirements for these jobs. Hence, more and more Americans are and will be in jobs which require less education than they have. Although these findings may not be applicable to Latin America, where the level and accessibility of schooling are relatively limited and the processes of industrialization are relatively new, they nevertheless indicate that the first assertion of the technical-function theory may not be universal.

The second assertion of this theory is that formal schooling transmits the specific skills and/or general knowledge necessary for more highly skilled jobs. This presupposes a type of schooling which teaches and selects for skills and qualities leading to occupational success in an industrial economy. However, such schooling may not be prevalent in Latin America. For the most part, Latin American formal education continues to reflect the values of a traditional, aristocratic society. Most schools are academic and emphasize preparation for fields which offer high status but are not directly productive in an economic sense (Lipset, 1967). Indeed, they often foster a disdain for manual work and for those who perform it (Fernandes, 1963). Of course, many educational systems in Latin America are in the process of altering their goals and operations in accordance with the economic and social demands of modernization. But even when schools are geared specifically to an industrial economy, it is not clear that they successfully transmit the necessary skills and knowledge, at least if one assumes that people with these skills are readily employable. For example, in several developing countries, economic studies of the returns derived from vocational/technical secondary schools demonstrate that with the existing labor market setting, these schools are poor private and public investments (Al Bukhari, 1968a, 1968b; Bowles, 1965; Callaway, 1963; Foster, 1966, 1971). In addition, investigations in the United States have determined that graduates of vocational programs are no more likely to be employed than are high school dropouts (Plunkett, 1960; Duncan, 1964).

In contrast, economic cost-benefit analyses indicate that on-the-job training is a relatively sound investment. Mincer (1962) found that the rate of return on selected investments in on-the-job training, such as apprenticeships and medical specializations, is indistinguishable from the rate of return on total college education costs. Machlup (1970) examined the demand and cost considerations of formal education in relation to schooling alternatives and concluded that both on-the-job training and adult education programs have greater short-term economic returns than formal schooling, despite the latter's far greater rate of return over a lifetime. These results support the report by Clark and Sloan (1966) that most manual workers in the United States acquire their skills on the job or casually. The evidence attesting to the higher short-term returns for on-the-job training, coupled with the research showing low economic yields from vocational secondary schools, casts some doubt on the assertion that schools contribute to occupational stratification through the transmission of necessary job skills.

The importance of formal education to nonmanual job skills is also questionable. Soderberg (1963) notes that approximately 40 percent of the engineers in the United States during the early 1950's lacked college degrees. Hargens and Hagstrom (1967) report that educational quality has little effect on the subsequent productivity of research scientists. Studies conducted in São Paulo, Brazil, show that 40 percent of the technical or professional employees over age 35 have had no more than a primary school education (Havighurst & Gouveia, 1969).

Although it is debatable whether or not formal education is necessary to transmit manual and nonmanual job skills, proponents of the technical-function theory might argue that schooling is important because it provides the basic knowledge necessary for workers to benefit from further training. This contention is supported by time-lag correlations between education and economic growth suggesting that the main contribution of education to economic development occurs at the level of mass literacy (Peaslee, 1969). Thurow (1970) emphasizes the complementary nature of formal education and specific skills training and asserts that the benefits from training and education taken together will be larger than the benefits from formal education and experience taken separately. On the other hand, Berg (1970) questions the assumption that formal education contributes to worker trainability. His careful evaluation of training programs conducted by the United States Armed Forces indicates that discrete measures of aptitude are generally much better predictors of trainee performance than educational attainment.

Proponents of the technical-function theory could also argue that schooling is important because it fosters attitudes conducive to economic production. Indeed, Myrdal (1968) suggests that schools may play an important role in the creation of more modern attitudes toward life and work (for example, punctuality, ambition, readiness for change). This contention receives support from a large body of empirical research, including Holsinger's longitudinal study of primary schools in Brazil (Armer & Youtz, 1971; Holsinger, 1974a, 1974b; Inkeles, 1969). However, the results of modernization studies must be judged in light of other investigations, including many conducted in Latin America which indicate that schools tend to reflect and perpetuate rather than change the sociocultural milieu in which they function (Henry, 1963; Comitas, 1967; Stimson & La Belle, 1971). For example, Nash (1965, p. 143) concludes from his study of schooling in Central America that "[l]ocal schools tend to be conservative agents, transmitting by means that reinforce local tendencies toward stability. Education becomes a force for social change only when the process of social change is well underway." Thus it is possible that schools do not so much initiate attitude change as they support and accelerate changes emerging from modernization.

David O'Shea (1974) persuasively argues this point, reasoning that students probably acquire attitudes favorable to modernization from their parents prior to entering school. Ironically, it should also be noted that insofar as schools do succeed in fostering attitudes conducive to modernization, they may be raising expectations and aspirations to a level beyond fulfillment and thus serve to retard economic output. Studies conducted in the United States (Berg, 1970) and Africa (Cash, 1969; Adams & Bjork, 1969) have demonstrated that educational achievement is associated with the frustration, alienation and oppositionism of workers.

An evaluation of the technical-function theory should also consider the relationship between mental ability and occupational attainment.[5] This relationship would be positive if rising educational requirements for jobs reflect employers' desire to hire more mentally able workers. While older studies appeared to confirm this expectation (Anderson, 1952; Boalt, 1954), more recent research challenges this contention. In his analysis of the economics of education, Becker (1964) reveals that although there is a positive association between mental ability and educational attainment, the latter accounts for much more of the variance in earnings. Using a complex recursive model, Sewell et al. (1970) find that job status, while strongly associated with years of schooling, is correlated only weakly and indirectly with mental ability.

While these studies cast doubt on the validity of the second component of the technical-function theory, economic research seems to offer strong evidence that formal education provides the capabilities needed in an industrial society. Macro- and micro-economic studies uniformly have shown that investment in education, whether made by individuals or by nations, yields substantial returns in income (see summaries in Bowen, 1964; Bowman, 1966). As a result, many economists now view human resources as a form of capital, a means of production, and the product of investment in education. However, a careful look at these economic analyses suggests that their findings are not as convincing as they appear at first glance.

The much touted residual studies (Denison, 1962; Schultz, 1963), for example, are arbitrary in attributing the observed difference between the rate of growth of GNP and the rate of increase in measurable inputs to the effects of education. In fact, the residual may result from the improved quality of capital assets rather than from education. Moreover, these studies fail to account prop-

---

[5] Ability here refers to mental intelligence as measured by scores on a standardized aptitude test. Conclusions from these studies must be viewed with caution since they consider only one component of ability.

erly for on-the-job learning, nonformal training and the effects of worker attitudes and motivation (Harbison & Myers, 1964). Inter-country correlations (Harbison & Myers, 1964; Galenson & Pyatt, 1964), a second group of economic studies, are similarly limited because they do not consider causality. Though high correlations are reported between enrollment ratios at all levels of education and GNP per capita, it is unclear whether investments in education contribute to economic growth or vice versa. The issue is confused further by the fact that educational expansion is often the product of political demand, resulting in the overproduction of educated personnel in many countries (Callaway, 1973, p. 15).

Micro cost-benefit studies also suffer from severe limitations. When taken together they offer strong support for the notion that education is an economically productive endeavor in most every region of the world (see summaries in Carnoy, 1967; Psacharopoulos, 1972). However, when examined individually each is deficient in some aspect of its research design (Berg, 1970). Moreover, these studies are suspect because of their reliance on the neo-classical marginal wage theory which assumes an economically rational world in which employers allocate human resources for maximum production and pay workers in accordance with their real output. The questionable basis of this theory, especially in the Latin American context, will become clear later in this paper.

Therefore, the various economic studies do not necessarily prove that formal education provides the capabilities required to augment economic production. In fact, there is some evidence that educational attainment, though associated with income levels, does not correspond closely to worker productivity. Berg (1970), in his summary of research dealing with the direct influence of education on individual productivity, concludes that in general, better-educated employees were often less productive than the blue- and white-collar workers, managers and professionals in the sample. He suggests that schooling corresponds to wage differentials, not because education contributes to productivity, but because it helps a person to obtain a better paying job in the first place.

One might argue that the technical-function theory fails to account adequately for the evidence because employers are misinformed; they erroneously believe that in demanding higher levels of education for employment, they are hiring more capable, trainable, and productive workers. At the same time, however, one might argue that employers are not as concerned with the economic productivity of their workers as is generally believed. For example, it appears that employers have imprecise conceptions of skill requirements for jobs, and that they rarely collect or analyze data pertaining to worker productivity or the contribution of education to such productivity (Berg, 1970). Furthermore, organizations generally do not force employees to work at maximum efficiency. Procedures or personnel are changed only when performance falls noticeably below the minimum levels set for workers (Dill et al., 1962; March & Simon, 1958). Research shows that employers in Latin America may be even less likely than their North American counterparts to base decisions on rational economic criteria. Studies of the attitudes and behavior of Latin American entrepreneurs confirm that they place little emphasis on bureaucratic and competitive norms; personal characteristics and family origins are valued more than technical or organizational abilities (Cardoso, 1967; Lauterbach, 1962; Lipset, 1967).

The Status-Conflict Theory

An alternative explanation for the role of formal education in social and occupational stratification is provided by the status-conflict theory, largely derived from Max Weber (1968). It has been examined carefully in North America by Randall Collins (1968, 1971), and in Latin America by Martin Carnoy (1972a). According to this theory, society is characterized by a continual struggle among cultural groups for wealth, power and prestige. Membership in these groups gives individuals a fundamental sense of identity; they generally accept one another as status equals. The theory further maintains that status groups use the schools to preserve and strengthen their relative positions in society, and that the primary function of schools is to teach and select for particular status groups by imparting the values, manners, interests, tastes and experiences associated with the group in control of the educational system. Educational requirements for employment, rather than flowing from functional economic demands, enable the particular status group controlling schooling to control the work place as well. By basing occupational attainment on educational attainment, the elite status group assures the selection of higher level employees from its own membership and lower level workers who at least have been indoctrinated to respect its cultural superiority. The status-conflict theory suggests that educational requirements for employment tend to rise over time in response to the increasing supply of educated persons. As other status groups, particularly the middle class, demand the education that will enable them to compete with elites, more and more people will want to become educated. Thus, employers raise educational requirements to maintain both the relative prestige of their own managerial ranks and the relative respectability of the middle ranks (Bowles, 1971; Collins, 1971).

Lending support to the status-conflict theory are a number of historical and descriptive studies which indicate that schools are founded by powerful and autonomous groups either to provide exclusive education for their children or to promote respect for their cultural attributes. In the United States, for example, historical research shows that a major reason for the rapid proliferation of schools during the colonial period was the competition among communities and religious groups for power and prestige (Bailyn, 1960). Moreover, it appears that the impetus for the public school system in the nineteenth century came from a white, Anglo-Saxon elite who wished to propagate Protestant, middle-class standards (Cremin, 1961; Curti, 1935; Katz, 1971). Studies in Latin America have pointed to the historic role of formal schooling in the formation of elites (Carnoy, 1974; Havighurst & Moreira, 1964; Thut & Adams, 1964). As education evolved from being a function of the church to a function of national governments, it continued to serve two basic functions: to prepare elites for high status and leadership positions and to incorporate non-elites into the lower strata of the social system. Although the highest social classes reserved the upper levels of education for themselves, "schooling was expanded to socialize marginal groups into the portion of the economic structure controlled by the liberal elite and under a set of rules developed by the ruling group and transmitted through the school" (Carnoy, 1974, p. 160). Education in Latin America today, especially on the secondary level, still bears the mark of centuries of domination by a landed elite. It continues to place emphasis on the borrowed European aristocratic tradition of academic, humanistic learning that is deemed appropriate for preparing a select few for leadership roles.

Additional support for the notion that schools provide training and respect for the elite culture comes from anthropological studies of schools in both developed and underdeveloped regions of the world (Gay & Cole, 1967; King, 1967; Rosenfeld, 1971). They show that the language, values and cognitive styles promoted and reinforced in the school are those associated with the cultural group controlling the school. Thus, it is implied that when the referent culture of students differs from that of the school, their chances of success in school are seriously jeopardized. This implication is particularly relevant to rural Latin America where the school has been described as "an exotic and sickly import from the cities, deriving from national policy rather than local demands" (United Nations, 1968, pp. 67-68). Moreover, case studies of formal education in rural Latin America suggest that high dropout and nonattendance rates are consequences of a type of schooling that has little meaning in the rural milieu (Norst & McClelland, 1968; Nash, 1965; Reichel-Dolmatoff, 1961). The match between the culture of the schools and the culture of the status group may explain why sociologists and economists find that social origins tend to act as a strong predictor of both years of schooling completed and achievement scores (Averch et al., 1972; Coleman et al., 1966; Jencks et al., 1972; Sewell, 1971).

Hence, those who succeed in formal schools and thereby gain access to high status and income appear to come from families already enjoying these benefits. This suggests that the democratization of schooling opportunities accompanying modernization in Latin America has not given everybody an equal chance to acquire elite status. Schools continue to function on the basis of culturally determined merit which favors the ruling group, whether that group is traditional or modern. As in the case of the occupational marketplace, schools tend to reward individuals who come from middle- and upper-socioeconomic class backgrounds and to constrain those individuals who do not (Economic Commission for Latin America, 1968).

Carnoy (1972) has used these conclusions to develop a dynamic model which explains the role of education in developing economies and which supports the status-conflict theory. The model attributes two distinct functions to formal schooling: socialization and elite formation. In the lower grades, the school's primary purpose is socialization. The students in these grades are from heterogeneous socioeconomic backgrounds. But at a certain level, the school's role changes from socialization to selection and elite formation. For the most part, students in the upper grades are either those born into the upper strata of society or those who have acquired elite characteristics. Carnoy's model also proposes that as enrollments in the lower levels of schooling increase in response to the popular demand for more educational opportunities and the economic need for highly skilled labor, the point at which rigorous selection takes place moves to higher and higher grade levels. Using economic rate of return data, Carnoy posits that those levels of schooling to which elites maintain exclusive access are those which yield the highest economic returns. Therefore, elites are able to satisfy the popular demand and economic need for more schooling in developing economies without giving up their own economic and policy-making power. Carnoy's reasoning is similar to Boudon's argument suggesting that the expansion of formal educational opportunities will not be accompanied by significant change in the structure of the stratification system.

Whereas Carnoy has focused on the selection process, others have stressed the importance of the types of schools attended. Evidence suggests that democratization of educational opportunities is generally accompanied by the segregation of social classes into separate schools of disparate quality and status. Vaizey (1967) has written that even if a wholly egalitarian ethic were to prevail in the public sector, private facilities would always tend to restore the inequality prevailing in the economy as a whole. In the United States, differences in occupational attainment exist between graduates of prominent and less prestigious secondary schools, colleges, graduate and law schools (Hargens & Hagstrom, 1967; Havemann & West, 1952; Landinsky, 1967; Smigel, 1964). Research also shows that private schools for children of the white, Anglo-Saxon Protestant upper class were founded in the United States in the 1880's when the mass indoctrination function of public schools made them unsuitable as a means of maintaining the cohesion of the elite culture (Baltzell, 1958). In Latin America a similar phenomenon has taken place. Solari (1967) notes, for example, that with the expansion of secondary education in response to demands of industrialization, middle- and upper-class groups have retained exclusive access to traditional academic institutions while members of the lower classes have been relegated to less prestigious vocational or technical schools. In the same vein, Sussman (1968) offers empirical evidence showing that when opportunities to attend secondary public schools were expanded in Puerto Rico between 1944 and 1960, the middle classes began to withdraw to prestigious private schools.

It can now be asked whether employers actually use education as a means of selection for cultural attributes. The preceding analysis of the technical-function theory has suggested that they do; for example, educational requirements for jobs tend to rise faster than the skill demands of those jobs, and employers do not seem to be as concerned with the economic productivity of their workers as is commonly believed. More direct support for the status-conflict theory concerning the United States comes from a large body of sociological literature showing that background factors have a major impact on job selection and attainment.[6] For example, 60 to 70 percent of American business leaders come from upper- and upper-middle-class families,[7] and such factors as religion, race, ethnic heritage, sex, accent, name and manners have a significant impact on an individual's employment opportunities.[8] Job market research conducted by Collins (1968, 1971) is particularly relevant in determining the validity of the status-conflict theory. For example, those organizations which are clearly dominated by the white, Anglo-Saxon Protestant upper class also tend to be those organizations which set the highest educational requirements for employment. In addition, Collins finds that educational requirements for white-collar workers are highest in organizations which place the strongest emphasis on normative control of

---

[6] See, for example, Blum, 1972; Blau & Duncan, 1967; Blum, 1972; Coleman et al., 1972.
[7] See, for example, Bendix, 1956; Mills, 1963; Newcomer, 1955; Warner & Abegglen, 1955.
[8] See, for example, Blair, 1970; Blau & Duncan, 1967; Hines et al., 1970; Landinsky, 1967; Noland & Bakke, 1949; Nosow, 1956; Taeuber et al., 1966; Turner, 1952; Welch, 1967.

their employees. In testing the relative impact of technical change and normative control of employees on educational requirements for employment, Collins' findings show that although both conditions affect educational requirements, those associated with the status-conflict theory are more significant than those associated with technical change.

If the status-conflict theory has any relevance for an industrial society like the United States, where the dominant values emphasize economic rationality and technical efficiency, it can be expected to have even greater validity in Latin America. The elite orientation of Latin American society has received much attention in the literature. A heritage of political centralization, the dominance of an authoritative religious institution and the prevalence of an agrarian plantation economy have helped to perpetuate control by an elite, whose values, often referred to as particularistic and ascriptive, tend to be those associated with traditional, pre-industrial societies (Parsons, 1961). In fact, these values even characterize urban industrial leaders. Cardoso (1967), for instance, contended that new industrial elites in Latin America have adopted the value patterns of the old aristocratic elite in order to assimilate into these dominant groups. Hence, family particularism appears to be much more common among Latin American businessmen than among their counterparts in more developed nations. Lauterbach (1962) noted that in Latin America entire managerial groups often come from one family, and that the great majority of managers interviewed either considered this to be appropriate or had not considered alternatives. In Brazil, even the growth of large industries and corporate forms of ownership has not drastically changed these patterns. Many companies have made adjustments between family control and the demands of running a big business either by giving technical training to the children or in-laws of the owner or by having family members work closely with technically-educated, non-family administrators (Lipset, 1967).

Given the adherence to particularistic and ascriptive values by the Latin American elite, and given that formal schools select for elite cultural characteristics, the status-conflict theory provides an especially powerful explanation for occupational stratification. The fact that the status-conflict theory is also applicable to an industrialized society such as the United States suggests that as Latin America continues to move from an agrarian to an industrial economic base, the significance of the status-conflict theory is not likely to diminish greatly.

Implications for Nonformal Education

The foregoing analysis of the technical-function and status-conflict theories makes it possible to speculate on the probable role of nonformal education in developing societies. The technical-function theory suggests that industrialization leads to an upgrading of job skill requirements and that formal schools do not appear to be efficient transmitters of job-related skills and knowledge. This suggests that nonformal education can make a significant contribution to economic growth. Such nonformal programs are likely to be successful at skill training because they can be: (a) skill specific and based on practical learning, (b) adaptable to the needs and problems of particular groups, and (c) relatively inexpensive because of their short duration and informal setting.

The analysis of the status-conflict theory, however, indicates that skill attainment is not the central ingredient in the occupational stratification process. Employers are concerned as much with the social and cultural attributes of their employees as with their level of technical skills or knowledge. Therefore, formal academic credentials are important in occupational selection because they are symbols of an elite-oriented and dominated socialization process. Especially in Latin America, with its industrial and agrarian elites, it is unlikely that nonformal education can provide significant status or income benefits. As nonsanctioned efforts directed at non-elite groups, nonformal education programs are incapable of validating or legitimatizing their experiences. As demands for attainment through the formal system escalate, such programs appear destined to remain at the bottom of the educational status hierarchy.

Hence, it appears that those who propose the use of nonformal education to meet demands for equality of opportunity have failed to give adequate consideration to the acceptable normative indices of success. Our analysis indicates that as long as employers look to formal school credentials as indices of the attainment of elite cultural attributes, it is likely that nonformal education will do little more than prepare non-elites to be more productive workers while relegating them to relatively inferior status positions. This conclusion, based on a broad sampling of the literature, supports the primary hypothesis stated at the outset of this paper: Nonformal education is unlikely to have a significant impact on socioeconomic status without concomitant changes in the values and institutions which support the stratification process. The reader will note that this conclusion is similar to Ivan Illich's notion of viewing alternative educational processes in conjunction with alternative future societies. It receives additional support in Latin America from Raúl Prebisch:

The acceleration of development demands sweeping changes in structures and in mental attitudes. They are essential if technical progress is to be assimilated, its advantages turned to account, its contradictions resolved, and its adverse effects counteracted; and essential also for the promotion of the social mobility both for its own sake and because it too is one of the indispensable requirements of technological progress. Social mobility is not merely a matter of general education and technical training; it is a basic question of structures. (1971, p. 12)

For many, the assertion that the efficacy of nonformal education depends on altering existing value and institutional configurations will appear too visionary or too vague. Indeed, based on our review of the literature, a reasonable argument can be made that there are at least two situations in which nonformal education conceivably could enhance status and income positions without radical changes in the sociocultural milieu: when nonformal programs are tied closely either to job openings or to formal schooling structures, and when nonformal programs are directed at entrepreneurs, especially urban craftsmen and rural farmers, whose station in life is not based on a position in the hierarchy of a large-scale economic enterprise.

The idea of linking nonformal programs with either the job market or the formal school is not new. As we have demonstrated, it forms the basis of what others have called the "integrated approach." A number of nonformal education programs currently operating in Latin America have been designed along such lines. A good example is the manpower training program in Brazil known as PIPMO, which applies national and state funds to locally organized, short-term, skill-oriented training programs designed to prepare participants for awaiting jobs. Hence, PIPMO purports to guarantee employment to all those who complete its courses. The apprenticeship training programs throughout Latin America, such as SENA in Colombia and SENAC and SENAI in Brazil, are other examples of vocational/technical training closely related to the job market. Brazil's national adult literacy campaign, MOBRAL, consists of several stages intended to parallel the formal schooling hierarchy. Upon completion of this four-year program, the student can move directly into higher levels of the formal school. Furthermore, many vocational/technical programs in Latin America are designed to enable graduates to move into more traditional and prestigious forms of education. Havighurst and Gouveia (1969) report that some vocational schools in São Paulo have achieved legitimacy in the eyes of the middle class because they are structured to qualify graduates to pass the rigorous university admissions test.

However, despite some obvious advantages of the integrated approach, it remains no better than a weak and partial solution to the problem of nonformal education with respect to occupational stratification. Merely guaranteeing a student a job, as is the case with PIPMO, will not necessarily lead to significant long-term status and income gains. Indeed, it may serve to lock graduates into the lower strata of the occupational hierarchy and ultimately widen the separation between social classes. An approach which links nonformal education to formal schooling appears attractive because it would enable individuals to acquire both the productive skills and the legitimate credentials required for upward status and income mobility. It is likely that the successful person is one who has had both formal and nonformal educational experiences. However, this approach ignores the problems associated with formal schooling which were outlined earlier in this paper.

These conclusions are drawn almost exclusively from the research literature which has examined these phenomena in urban areas, an environment most reliant on and constrained by formal school requirements. However, the literature does not indicate the effects of nonformal education on the entrepreneur, especially the independent craftsman or farmer who is less dependent on the formal educational hierarchy. This brings us to the second instance where nonformal education might provide status and income benefits to participants without dramatic alterations in the occupational structure. One might argue, for example, that the entrepreneur who does not have to rely on the commercial and industrial reward structure, but instead draws his rewards from production which he himself controls, may be the most viable target for nonformal education. It is possible that such individuals could use new skills or information for an almost immediate enhancement of their living standard and would not be dependent upon convincing others of their competence in terms other than the product produced. However, we are pessimistic about the impact of nonformal education on the entrepreneur. Our pessimism has to do with more than education *per se,* since the success of the entrepreneur is ultimately dependent on the availability of supportive mechanisms and other institutions in the wider environment.

One example upon which we base our view comes from Whetten's (1948) description of the community development work of a Mexican Cultural Mission team in the rural village of San Pablo del Monte. One of the first activities undertaken by the team was the organization of local tortilla makers into a large cooperative. Mills would be purchased cooperatively for grinding corn, machines secured for making tortillas mechanically, a station wagon would haul the tortillas to the nearby city of Puebla and bring back corn, and small stands would be erected in Puebla for selling the tortillas. These steps were planned to increase economic returns to the people and to produce and market tortillas more efficiently. It had been customary for up to 1,500 women from San Pablo del Monte and adjoining villages to carry their corn daily to one of the 15 or 20 small mills, return home to prepare the tortillas, and then walk or ride a bus 6 miles to Puebla with 25 to 50 pounds of tortillas to sell in the market where each had to pay a fee for the privilege of selling. Whetten describes the results of the project:

This scheme would obviate the necessity for all the fifteen hundred women to make the trip and sell the product individually. The director of the mission talked the proposition over with responsible state authorities who, in turn, advised him to consult the cacique, since such a scheme might interfere with the latter's established business. Vested interests prevented the formation of the cooperative. The cacique threatened to fight the proposal to the bitter end. It is said that he has a monopoly on transportation and owns the buses which run between San Pablo and Puebla and which now carry full loads. He charges a fee for each person and each basket each way. Obviously, any proposal to substitute other forms of transportation or even to curtail the number of passengers would seriously interfere with his business. The owners of the corn grinders also objected strenuously, since their grinding fees would be curtailed; the city of Puebla objected because, instead of collecting marketing fees from fifteen hundred people, they would be able to collect from only a limited number. Even the consumers objected that machine-made tortillas might not taste so good as hand-made ones. (pp. 445-446)

It should be clear that nonformal education programs, whether or not they are integrated with other forms of education, have an extremely limited impact in such projects. The major forces at work are political and economic, and these require equally powerful incentives for social change. Such obstacles are common in many micro-social change programs throughout Latin America. Even the highly praised Cornell-Peru project in Vicos encountered major political and economic obstacles. Briefly, the Cornell-owned hacienda in Peru was the site of a major social change effort on behalf of the highland Indians. The original plan was to turn the hacienda over to the Indians five years after the project began. Allan Holmberg, the director of the project, remarked:

It was inconceivable in the local area that such a property might be sold back to its indigenous inhabitants. Consequently, local power elites immediately threw every possible legal block in the way of the title reverting to the Indian community. They set a price on the property that would have been impossible for the Indian community ever to pay; members of the project were charged with being agents of the Communist world; the

Vicosinos were accused of being pawns of American capitalism; Peruvian workers in the field were regarded as spies of the American government. (1965, p. 7)

Settlement was delayed for almost five years when North American political persuasion finally aided the community's movement toward independence.

Thus, nonformal education programs designed to encourage social mobility —whether they are in the context of community development, agricultural extension, vocational/technical training, or motivation and consciousness raising— inevitably confront obstacles resistant to the power of education. At times, such barriers can be overcome through the creation of new markets, improved transportation systems and the availability of credit or technology. Often, however, such obstacles cannot be easily overcome because they are entangled in larger social issues, such as the opportunity structure, agrarian reform and world-wide pricing policies, which pose even greater economic and political controls. Thus, in order for nonformal education to continue addressing even micro-level problems, it must take a more systemic stance. From the outset, it must be recognized that educational inputs constitute only one rather minor component in what should be an overall strategy of change which integrates several diverse, yet functionally interdependent sectors.

To the optimist, our assessment of the potential impact of nonformal education on occupational stratification, whether it concerns wage earners or entrepreneurs, provides a rather sobering and perhaps unacceptable view. Irrespective of one's orientation, it can be assumed that for many years nonformal education will continue to function in a similar manner: occasionally providing significant socioeconomic mobility for participants when the prevailing socioeconomic system permits, and generally fostering short-term gains for the unemployed, the unskilled and the semi-skilled. Although the nonformal education movement has many limitations, it may still provide experiences leading to social awareness, self-management and some increase in income. These, in turn, eventually may forge a cumulative force capable of provoking more basic structural social transformations. But as long as nonformal education is regarded as a panacea for developing countries, such change is unlikely to occur.

References

Adams, D. Foreword. In R. G. Paulston (Ed.), *Non-formal education: An annotated international bibliography.* New York: Praeger, 1972.

Adams, D., & Bjork, R. M. *Education in developing areas.* New York: McKay, 1969.

Al Bukhari, N. *Issues in occupational education and training: A case study in Jordan.* Stanford, Calif.: School of Education, Stanford University, 1968. (a)

Al Bukhari, N. *Issues in occupational education and training: A case study in Tunisia.* Stanford, Calif.: School of Education, Stanford University, 1968. (b)

Anderson, C. A. A skeptical note on the relation between vertical mobility and education. *American Journal of Sociology,* 1961, **66,** 560-570.

Anderson, C. A., Brown, J. C., & Bowman, M. J. Intelligence and occupational mobility. *Journal of Political Economy,* 1952, **60,** 218-239.

Armer, M., & Youtz, R. Formal education and individual modernity in an African society. *American Journal of Sociology,* 1971, **76,** 604-626.

Averch, H. A., Carroll, S. J., Donaldson, T. S., Kiesling, H. J., & Pincus, J. *How effective is schooling?: A critical review and synthesis of research findings.* Santa Monica, Calif.: Rand, 1972.

Bailyn, B. *Education in the forming of American society.* Chapel Hill: University of North Carolina Press, 1960.

Baltzell, E. D. *An American business aristocracy.* New York: Macmillan, 1958.

Becker, G. S. *Human capital.* New York: Columbia University Press, 1964.

Becker, G. S. Investment in human capital: A theoretical analysis. *Journal of Political Economy,* 1962, **70** (5, Part 2), 9-49.

Bendix, R. *Work and authority in industry.* New York: Wiley, 1956.

Berg, I. *Education and jobs.* New York: Praeger, 1970.

Blair, P. Rates of return to schooling of majority and minority groups in Santa Clara County. Unpublished doctoral dissertation, Stanford University, 1970.

Blau, P. M., & Duncan, O. D. *The American occupational structure.* New York: Wiley, 1967.

Blum, D. White and black careers during the first decade of labor force experience. Part II: Income differences. *Social Science Research,* 1972, **1** (3), 271-292.

Boalt, G. Social mobility in Stockholm: A pilot investigation. *Transactions of the Second World Congress of Sociology.* Vol. 2. London: International Sociological Association, 1954.

Boudon, R. *Education, opportunity, and social inequality: Changing prospects in Western society.* New York: Wiley, 1973.

Bowen, W. *Economic aspects of education: Three essays.* Princeton, N.J.: Industrial Relations Section, Department of Economics, Princeton University, 1964.

Bowles, S. Cuban education and the revolutionary ideology. *Harvard Educational Review,* 1971, **41,** 472-500.

Bowles, S. Efficiency in the allocation of resources in education: A planning model with application to Northern Nigeria. Unpublished doctoral dissertation, Harvard University, 1965.

Bowman, M. J. Human investment revolution. *Sociology of Education,* 1966, **39,** 111-137.

Brembeck, C. Introduction. In C. Brembeck & T. J. Thompson (Eds.), *New strategies for educational development.* Lexington, Mass.: Lexington Books, 1973.

Bruno, J., & Van Zeyl, C. Educational ideology in Venezuela: A counterforce to innovation. In T. J. La Belle (Ed.), *Educational alternatives in Latin America: Social change and social stratification.* Los Angeles: Latin American Center, University of California, 1975.

Callaway, A. Frontiers of out-of-school education. In C. Brembeck & T. J. Thompson (Eds.), *New strategies for educational development.* Lexington, Mass.: Lexington Books, 1973.

Callaway, A. Unemployment among African school leavers. *Journal of Modern African Studies,* 1963, **1,** 351-357.

Cardoso, F. H. The industrial elite. In S. M. Lipset & A. Solari (Eds.), *Elites in Latin America.* New York: Oxford University Press, 1967.

Carnoy, M. The cost and return to schooling in Mexico: A case study. Unpublished doctoral dissertation, University of Chicago, 1964.

Carnoy, M. Rates of return to schooling in Latin America. *Journal of Human Resources,* 1967, **2** (3), 359-374.

Carnoy, M. The political economy of education. In T. J. La Belle (Ed.), *Education and development: Latin America and the Caribbean.* Los Angeles: Latin American Center, University of California, 1972. (a)

Carnoy, M. The rate of return to schooling and the increase in human resources in Puerto Rico. *Comparative Education Review,* 1972, **16** (1), 68-84. (b)

Carnoy, M. *Education and cultural imperialism.* New York: McKay, 1974.

Cash, W. C. A critique of manpower planning in Africa. In M. Blaug (Ed.), *Economics and education.* Baltimore: Penguin Books, 1969.

Central Advisory Council on Education. *Children and their primary schools.* London: Her Majesty's Stationery Office, 1966.

Clark, H. F., & Sloan, H. S. *Classrooms on Main Street.* New York: Teachers College Press, 1966.

Coleman, J. S., Campbell, E. Q., Hobson, C. J., McPartland, J., Mood, A., Weinfeld, F. D., & York, R. L. *Equality of educational opportunity.* Washington, D.C.: U.S. Government Printing Office, 1966.

Coleman, J. S., Blum, Z. D., Sorenson, A. B., & Rossi, P. White and black careers during the first decade of labor force status. *Social Science Research,* 1972, **1** (3), 243-270.

Collins, R. A comparative approach to political sociology. In R. Bendix et al. (Eds.), *State and society.* Boston: Little, Brown, 1968.

Collins, R. Functional and conflict theories of educational stratification. *American Sociological Review,* 1971, **36,** 1002-1019.

Comitas, L. Education and social stratification in contemporary Bolivia. *New York Academy of Sciences, Transactions, Series II,* 1967, **29** (7), 935-948.

Coombs, P. H. *The world educational crisis: A systems analysis.* New York: Oxford University Press, 1968.

Coombs, P. H., & Ahmed, M. *Attacking rural poverty: How nonformal education can help.* Baltimore: Johns Hopkins University Press, 1974.

Coombs, P. H., with Prosser, R. C., & Ahmed, M. *New paths to learning for rural children and youth.* New York: International Council for Educational Development, 1973.

Cremin, L. A. *The transformation of the school.* New York: Knopf, 1961.

Curti, M. *The social ideas of American educators.* New York: Scribners, 1935.

Denison, E. F. *The sources of economic growth in the United States and the alternatives before us.* New York: Committee on Economic Development, 1962.

Dill, W. R., Hilton, T. L., & Reitman, W. R. *The new managers.* Englewood Cliffs, N.J.: Prentice-Hall, 1962.

Duncan, B. Dropouts and the unemployed. *Journal of Political Economy,* 1964, **73,** 121-134.

Duncan, O. D., Featherman, D. L., & Duncan, B. *Socioeconomic background and occupational achievement: Extension of a basic model.* New York: Seminar Press, 1972.

Duncan, O. D., & Hodge, R. Education and occupational mobility: A regression analysis. *American Journal of Sociology,* 1963, **68,** 629-644.

Eckhaus, R. S. Economic criteria for education and training. *Review of Economics and Statistics,* 1964, **46,** 181-190.

Eckland, B. K. Academic ability, higher education, and occupational mobility. *American Sociological Review,* 1965, **30,** 735-746.

Elder, G. H., Jr. Achievement motivation and intelligence in occupational mobility: A longitudinal analysis. *Sociometry,* 1968, **31,** 327-354.

Farrell, J. P. Factors influencing academic performance among Chilean primary students. Paper presented at the American Educational Research Association annual convention, New Orleans, March 1973.

Faure, E. (Ed.). *Learning to be.* Paris: UNESCO, 1972.

Fernandes, F. Pattern and rate of development in Latin America. In E. de Vries & J. M. Echevarria (Eds.), *Social aspects of economic development.* Paris: UNESCO, 1963.

Folger, J. K., & Nam, C. B. Trends in education in relation to the occupational structure. *Sociology of Education,* 1964, **38,** 19-33.

Ford Foundation. *Ford Foundation assistance to Latin American education in the seventies.* New York: Author, 1972.

Foster, P. J. *Education and social change in Ghana.* Chicago: University of Chicago Press, 1966.

Foster, P. J. Presidential address: The revolt against the schools. *Comparative Education Review,* 1971, **15** (3), 263-275.

Galenson, W., & Pyatt, G. *The quality of labor and economic development in certain countries.* Geneva: International Labor Office, 1964.

Gay, J., & Cole, M. *The new mathematics and an old culture: A study of learning among the Kpelle of Liberia.* New York: Holt, Rinehart & Winston, 1967.

Haller, A. O. Education and the occupational achievement process. In U.S. National Advisory Commission on Rural Poverty, *Rural Poverty in the United States.* Washington, D.C.: U.S. Government Printing Office, 1968.

Hanoch, G. An economic analysis of earnings and schooling. *Journal of Human Resources,* 1967, **2** (3), 310-329.

Hansen, W. L. Total and private rates of return to investment in schooling. *Journal of Political Economy,* 1963, **71** (2), 128-141.

Harbison, F. H. *Human resources as the wealth of nations.* New York: Oxford University Press, 1973.
Harbison, F. H., & Myers, C. A. *Education, manpower, and economic growth.* New York: McGraw-Hill, 1964.
Hargens, L., & Hagstrom, W. O. Sponsored and contest mobility of American academic scientists. *Sociology of Education,* 1967, **40,** 24-38.
Havemann, E., & West, P. S. *They went to college.* New York: Harcourt Brace, 1952.
Havighurst, R. J. Educational leadership for the seventies. *Phi Delta Kappan,* 1972, **53** (7), 403-406.
Havighurst, R. J., & Gouveia, A. J. *Brazilian secondary education and socio-economic development.* New York: Praeger, 1969.
Havighurst, R. J., & Moreira, J. R. *Society and education in Brazil.* Pittsburgh: University of Pittsburgh Press, 1964.
Henry, J. *Culture against man.* New York: Vintage, 1963.
Hines, F., Tweeten, L., & Redfern, M. Social and private rates of return to investment in schooling by race, sex groups and regions. *Journal of Human Resources,* 1970, **3,** 318-340.
Holmberg, A. R. The changing values and institutions of Vicos in the context of national development. *American Behavioral Scientist,* 1965, **8** (7), 3-8.
Holsinger, D. B. The schooling environment as a context for individual modernization. Chicago: Comparative Education Center, University of Chicago, 1974. (Mimeograph) (a)
Holsinger, D. B. Education and the occupational attainment process in Brazil. Chicago: Comparative Education Center, University of Chicago, 1974. (Mimeograph) (b)
Horowitz, M. A., & Hernstadt, I. L. Changes in the skill requirements of occupations in selected industries. In National Commission on Technology, Automation, and Economic Progress (Ed.), *Technology and the American economy: Employment impact of technological change.* Appendix. Vol. II. Washington, D.C.: U.S. Government Printing Office, 1966, 225-287.
Horst, O. H., & McClelland, A. The development of an educational system in a rural Guatemalan community. *Journal of Inter-American Studies,* 1968, **10,** 474-497.
Husén, T. Does more time in school make a difference? *Saturday Review,* 1972, **55** (18), 32-35.
Illich, I. *Deschooling society.* New York: Harper & Row, 1970.
Illich, I. The futility of schooling in Latin America. *Saturday Review,* 1968, **51** (16), 57-59, 74-75.
Inkeles, A. Making men modern: On the causes and consequences of individual change in six developing countries. *American Journal of Sociology,* 1969, **75** (2), 208-225.
Inter-American Development Bank. *Socio-economic progress in Latin America.* Ninth annual report. Washington, D.C.: Social Progress Trust Fund, 1969.
Inter-American Development Bank. *Evaluation report on IDB operations in the education sector.* Washington, D.C., September 1971.
Jacobsen, B., & Kendrick, J. M. Education and mobility: From achievement to ascription. *American Sociological Review,* 1973, **38,** 439-460.

Jaffe, A. J., & Froomkin, J. *Technology and jobs: Automation in perspective.* New York: Praeger, 1968.
Jencks, C., Smith, M., Acland, H., Bane, M. J., Cohen, D. K., Gintis, H., Heyns, B., & Michelson, S. *Inequality: A reassessment of the effect of family and schooling in America.* New York: Basic Books, 1972.
Katz, M. B. *Class, bureaucracy, and schools.* New York: Praeger, 1971.
King, A. R. *The school at Mopass: A problem of identity.* New York: Holt, Rinehart & Winston, 1967.
La Belle, T. J. The impact of nonformal education on income in industry: Ciudad Guayana, Venezuela. In T. J. La Belle (Ed.), *Educational alternatives in Latin America: Social change and social stratification.* Los Angeles: Latin American Center, University of California, 1975.
Landinsky, J. Higher education and work achievement among lawyers. *Sociological Quarterly,* 1967, **8,** 222-232.
Lauterbach, A. Managerial attitudes and economic growth. *Kyklos,* 1962, **15,** 374-400.
Lipset, S. M. Values, education, and entrepreneurship. In S. M. Lipset & A. Solari (Eds.), *Elites in Latin America.* New York: Oxford University Press, 1967.
Machlup, F. *Education and economic growth.* Lincoln: University of Nebraska Press, 1970.
March, J. G., & Simon, H. A. *Organizations.* New York: Wiley, 1958.
Mills, C. W. *Power, politics and people.* New York: Oxford University Press, 1963.
Mincer, J. On-the-job training: Costs, returns, and implications. *Journal of Political Economy,* 1962, **70** (5, Part 2), 50-79.
Myrdal, G. *Asian drama: An inquiry into the poverty of nations.* New York: Twentieth Century Fund, 1968.
Nash, M. The role of village schools in the process of cultural and economic modernization. *Social and Economic Studies,* 1965, **14** (1), 131-143.
Newcomer, M. *The big business executive.* New York: Columbia University Press, 1955.
Noland, E. W., & Bakke, E. W. *Workers wanted.* New York: Harper, 1949.
Nosow, S. Labor distribution and the normative system. *Social Forces,* 1956, **35,** 25-33.
O'Shea, D. *Education, the social system and development.* Denver, Colo.: Social Science Foundation and Graduate School of International Studies Monograph Series in World Affairs, University of Denver, 1974.
Parsons, T. *Structure and process in modern studies.* Glencoe, Ill.: Free Press, 1961.
Paulston, R. *Non-formal education: An annotated international bibliography.* New York: Praeger, 1972.
Peaslee, A. Education's role in development. *Economic Development and Cultural Change,* 1969, **17,** 293-318.
Perrucci, C. C., & Perrucci, R. Social origins, educational contexts, and career mobility. *American Sociological Review,* 1970, **35,** 451-463.
Plunkett, M. School and early work experience of youth. *Occupational Outlook Quarterly,* 1960, **4** (1), 22-27.
Prebisch, R. *Change and development: Latin America's great task.* New York: Praeger, 1971.
Psacharopoulos, G. Rates of return to investment around the world. *Comparative Education*

Review, 1972, **16** (1) 54-57.
Reichel-Dolmatoff, G., & Reichel-Dolmatoff, A. *The people of Aritama: The cultural personality of a Colombian Mestizo village.* Chicago: University of Chicago Press, 1961.
Reimer, E. *School is dead: Alternatives in education.* New York: Doubleday, 1971.
Riske, R., & Rust, V. Nonformal education and the labor sector in Trinidad. In T. J. La Belle (Ed.), *Educational alternatives in Latin America: Social change and social stratification.* Los Angeles: Latin American Center, University of California, 1975.
Roberts, C. P. The economics of education in Costa Rica: Effects on earnings of family background, school performance and occupation. Unpublished doctoral dissertation, University of California, Los Angeles, 1973.
Rosenfeld, G. *Shut those thick lips! A study of slum school failure.* New York: Holt, Rinehart & Winston, 1971.
Schultz, T. W. *The economic value of education.* New York: Columbia University Press, 1963.
Sewell, W. H. Inequality of opportunity for higher education. *American Sociological Review,* 1971, **35,** 698-809.
Sewell, W. H., Haller, A. O., & Ohlendorf, G. W. The educational and early occupational status attainment process: Replication and revision. *American Sociological Review,* 1970, **35,** 1014-1027.
Sheffield, J. R., & Diejomaoh, V. P. *Non-formal education in African development.* New York: African American Institute, 1972.
Smigel, E. O. *The Wall Street lawyer.* New York: Free Press of Glencoe, 1964.
Soderberg, R. C. The American engineer. In K. S. Lynn (Ed.), *The professions in America.* Boston: Beacon Press, 1963.
Solari, A. Secondary education and the development of elites. In S. M. Lipset & A. Solari (Eds.), *Elites in Latin America.* New York: Oxford University Press, 1967.
Stimson, J., & La Belle, T. J. The organizational climate of Paraguayan elementary schools: Rural-urban differentiation. *Education and Urban Society,* 1971, **3** (3), 333-349.
Sussman, L. Democratization and class segregation in Puerto Rican schooling: The U.S. model transplanted. *Sociology of Education,* 1968, **41,** 321-341.
Taeuber, A. F., Taeuber, K. E., & Cain, G. G. Occupational assimilation and the competitive process: A reanalysis. *American Journal of Sociology,* 1966, **72,** 278-285.
Thurow, L. *Investment in human capital.* Belmont, Calif.: Wadsworth, 1970.
Thut, I. N., & Adams, D. *Educational patterns in contemporary societies.* New York: McGraw-Hill, 1964.
Turner, R. H. Foci of discrimination in the employment of nonwhites. *American Journal of Sociology,* 1952, **58,** 247-256.
United Nations Economic Commission for Latin America. *Education, human resources and development in Latin America.* New York: Author, 1968.
Vaizey, J. Some dynamic aspects of inequality. In *Social Objectives in Educational Planning.* Paris: Organization for Economic Cooperation and Development, 1967.
Warner, W. L., & Abegglen, J. C. *Occupational mobility in American business and industry: 1928-1952.* Minneapolis: University of Minnesota Press, 1955.
Weber, M. *Economy and society.* New York: Bedminster Press, 1968.

Welch, F. Labor market discrimination: An interpretation of income differences in the Rural South. *Journal of Political Economy,* 1967, **75** (3), 225-240.

Whetten, N. L. *Rural Mexico.* Chicago: University of Chicago Press, 1948.

Wood, A. W. *Informal education and development in Africa.* The Hague, Netherlands: Institute of Social Studies, 1974.

World Bank. *Education sector working paper.* Washington, D.C.: International Bank for Reconstruction and Development, 1971.

Rally 'Round the Workplace: Continuities and Fallacies in Career Education

W. NORTON GRUBB
University of California, Berkeley

MARVIN LAZERSON
University of British Columbia

Career education has become an extraordinarily prominent educational reform movement in the last few years. It takes, as its basic premise, the contention that education does a poor job of preparing students to enter the labor force. Career educators propose to change this situation by integrating work skills into curricula and improving job and educational counseling curricula. In this article, Norton Grubb and Marvin Lazerson question whether career education is an appropriate response to the problems it addresses. First, they argue that career education is basically a reconstitution of vocational education, an earlier reform with a similar purpose, and that career education is likely to replicate vocational education's failures. Second, they argue that the assumptions career educators make about education, work, and the labor market are erroneous, and present a variety of evidence to support their argument. Grubb and Lazerson conclude that the ills career education proposes to solve—unemployment, underemployment, and worker dissatisfaction—are intrinsic to our economic system, and consequently that career education is a hollow, if not an invidious, reform.

Few educational reform movements have achieved prominence as quickly as career education. Since first receiving public exposure in 1971—almost entirely through the efforts of the United States Office of Education and its Commissioner, Sidney Marland—career education has received the endorsement of almost every major educational organization as well as the United States Chamber of Commerce.[1] What began as a $9 million allocation of discretionary funds from the Office of Education mushroomed to $61 million by 1974 in federal Office of Education and National Institute of Education funds alone. N.I.E. contributed almost 20 percent of its own budget. Almost every state department of education has appointed career education coordinators; many states have passed or are considering career education mandates in their educational legislation, and have developed comprehensive career education development models. In 1974, 30 percent of the country's 17,000 school districts had formally brought career education into their schools. In Los Angeles, a Community Alliance for Career Education has been established as a consortium of eighty-five corporations and companies to "deliver comprehensive career education" to all students, while the Los Angeles school district has joined with nine others to develop models for implementation throughout California. In Dallas, the $25.1 million Skyline Career Development Center opened in 1972 on an eighty-acre campus with an enrollment of 4,000 students. Jumping on the bandwagon, publishers of educational materials are distributing increasing numbers of curriculum guides, testing materials, and books on the philosophy and implementation of career education.[2]

But the impact of career education cannot be measured simply in terms of numbers or money specifically earmarked for "career education." The movement's importance lies in its participation in and stimulus to vocationalism in education more generally. In government circles, state departments of education, and local communities, claims are being made that students are not learning how

---

[1] The educational organizations supporting career education include the National Eduction Association, the National Association of Chief State School Officers, the American Vocational Association, the National Advisory Council on Vocational Education, the Association of Secondary School Principals, the American Association of Junior Colleges, the College Entrance Examination Board, and the National Institute of Education.

[2] The literature on career education is already vast. Because of his influence, we have relied heavily on the writing of Sidney P. Marland, particularly *Career Education: A Proposal for Reform* (New York: McGraw-Hill, 1974). See also Kenneth Hoyt, Rupert Evans, Edward Mackin, and Garth Mangum, *Career Education: What It Is and How To Do It* (Salt Lake City: Olympus, 1972); Kenneth Hoyt, Nancy Pinson, Darryl Laramore, and Garth Mangum, *Career Education and the Elementary School Teacher* (Salt Lake City: Olympus, 1973); and Sidney P. Marland, Harold Lichtenwald, and Ralph Burke, "Career Education, Texas Style," *Phi Delta Kappan,* 56 (1975), 616–20, 635.

to work, that they are spending too much time in school, and that they should be trained explicitly for jobs. Vocationalism is becoming rampant. In 1972, 24 percent of all high-school youth were in vocational education programs; the projection for 1977 is more than 50 percent. Increasingly, the assumption is that the educational system has raised expectations that the social and economic structure cannot meet, and that a readjustment of schools to occupational realities will resolve tensions between school and work. As the executive director of the American Vocational Association put it, this is the "best of times for vocational education."[3]

Career education is a major factor in these developments, although an exact model of what career education actually is has yet to emerge. Indeed, career educators have been aggressive in refusing to define career education precisely. One definition, for example, views career education as "preparation for all meaningful and productive activity, at work or at leisure, whether paid or volunteer, as employee or employer, in private business or in the public sector, or in the family."[4] Since this covers every activity that can be labeled education, it is necessary to ask more specific questions. What particular activities do career educators emphasize? What basic changes would they make in schools? What assumptions underlie these reforms?

At its most grandiose, career education calls for a dramatic reorientation of the entire educational system toward the world of work so that all phases of the curriculum would be job-oriented. It would require that students leaving the educational system at any level be knowledgeable about available jobs and the skills they demand and, more important, that students possess immediately marketable skills. In the elementary school this requirement would involve exposing children to the kinds of work available to adults and inculcating in them an appreciation of work. Elementary teachers would emphasize the career implications of all phases of the curriculum. The teachers would introduce practical problems such as understanding recipes or estimating product costs in arithmetic. They would simulate work experiences even more dramatically by actually producing a product. These changes would inculcate a recognition of "the social significance of work, the interdependence of workers on one another, the necessity for workers to co-

---

[3] Lowell Burkett, "Latest Word from Washington," *American Vocational Journal*, 50 (1975), 9; James O'Toole, "The Reserve Army of the Underemployed: I—The World of Work," *Change*, May 1975, 26–33, 63 and O'Toole, "The Reserve Army of the Underemployed: II—The Role of Education," *Change*, June 1975, 26–33, 60–63.

[4] Hoyt et al., *Career Education and the Elementary School Teacher*, p. 2.

operate with one another, the importance of completing assignments on time, the principle of worker responsibility for carrying out assignments, and the way in which each worker contributes to some broader objective than can be seen from viewing only the specific work tasks assigned to him."[5]

In junior and secondary high schools, activities would be more clearly directed towards choosing future work roles and acquiring specific skills. Although all students would participate in career education, it is primarily designed for those in the "general" curriculum, currently a dumping ground for students in neither academic nor vocational programs. Typically, grades seven through ten would be reserved for "career exploration," through which students would become familiar with groups of occupations—"career clusters"—and begin to make tentative choices about the cluster to specialize in.[6] The last two grades of high school would then be given over to specialized training in the cluster chosen earlier. The goal is to give every high-school graduate a set of marketable skills in a particular cluster. Thus the high-school diploma would become a terminal degree, rather than a license for further schooling. The clusters themselves might consist of careers within one industrial sector. The Office of Career Education has developed fifteen suggested clusters which follow such industry divisions as agriculture, manufacturing, construction, and personal services. Alternatively, clusters could consist of specialized occupations found in all sectors or could focus on subject areas such as science or mathematics. But it is clear that career education programs would offer clusters very similar to traditional vocational skill-training programs and to college preparatory programs.[7]

While the concepts of career education might be valuable for two-year and four-year colleges, career educators stress that too many pupils unnecessarily go on to college. Therefore, they have concentrated on reforming elementary and secondary education and on preparing high-school graduates for the world of work. In part, the efforts of career educators at the college level would be redundant: two-year colleges are already occupational in emphasis and four-year colleges, under the pressure of the recent recession and the credentialing crisis, have increasingly become pre-professional schools. The proportion of pupils in two-year colleges enrolled in vocational courses is apparently approaching 50 percent, and

---

[5] Hoyt et al., *Career Education and the Elementary School Teacher*, pp. 29 (quotation) and 111–12 (examples).
[6] On the development and implementation of clusters, see Marland, *Career Education*, chs. 8–11 and ch. 16.
[7] See, for example, the description of the Dallas program in ch. 11 of Marland.

increasing, while many of the changes in four-year colleges consist simply of integrating undergraduate and graduate education in such fields as law and medicine, an integration often underway before the advent of career education.[8]

In addition, career educators call for opening the schools to adults, so that those who wish to advance or change their careers and those who lose their jobs because of technical change can be retrained for other work. Here the recommendations are particularly fuzzy, but career education for those already in the work force seems to involve continuing education, on-the-job courses, and programs similar to manpower training. Yet, while career educators acknowledge that retraining adult workers is important, particularly in a rapidly changing economy, they see such retraining as distinctly subordinate to the reform of elementary and secondary education.

In the high school, career education thus seeks to meet basic requirements of secondary education: a high-school diploma, preparation for advanced schooling, and an immediately marketable skill. It seeks to reproduce actual work settings, orient academic work toward vocational ends, and establish close ties to local industry; career education advisory councils draw heavily on business support and representation. Career educators believe that "students will enjoy career education because of its realism, educators will advocate [it] because of its relevance, communities and school patrons will approve [it] because of its congruence with societal needs, and business and employers will aggressively support [it] because of its practicality and efficiency."[9]

Describing the important elements of career education does not explain why career educators feel their reform movement is so critical. To understand this, one must look at the assumptions career educators have about work and the relationship of schooling to work. Career educators argue that, by isolating the young from work, schools make work into an abstract concept, something difficult for students to understand. Rather romantically, they point out that the youth of earlier generations were directly involved in the daily work experience of their community, whereas today's youth rarely see the world of work and cannot readily understand what bankers, insurance men, or accountants do:

As a child I could dust boxes and burn rubbish in my father's store. As I took

[8] Jerome Karabel, "Community Colleges and Social Stratification," *Harvard Educational Review*, 42 (1972), 521–62, estimated that 30 percent of community-college students were in vocational courses. There is a consensus, but no particularly reliable information on which to base it, that this figure has increased to about 50 percent since 1971.

[9] Marland, p. 185.

on higher rank, I got to wash the windows and sweep the sidewalk. The day I waited on my first customer, at about age fifteen, I knew a lot about that store and a lot about my father as I watched him work. . . . And down the street I could marvel as a ten-year-old at the magic of Mr. Peche's bottling company operations, and sometimes wash bottles with the spinning brush when he would let me. Later I could ride with the veterinarian on his calls to attend sick cows and horses. . . . But these vistas of work and friendship with a variety of workers are largely denied our young people today. . . . They have never had a chance to be close to it [the economic system] or close to people whom they love and respect and who are a part of it.[10]

Young people thus neither appreciate the value of work nor the need to prepare for it and lack the motivation commonly associated with the "work ethic."

Career educators place great faith in the moral benefits of work. They argue that work builds individual character and confers a sense of competence and responsibility that carries over into familial and civic responsibilities.[11] On a social level, working permits individuals to see the interrelationships within society, and to find and understand their own social positions. Work is therefore a powerful force for social cohesion. Because of its intrinsic importance, career educators claim that all work can have equal dignity and meaning, although they acknowledge that this is not now the case. Work is exciting, and once students recognize this, their present disenchantment and alienation will give way to motivation for work.

Career educators also assume, in a less romantic vein, that jobs are both increasing in technical sophistication and requiring less education than most people have. Since jobs frequently are made obsolete by technical advances, recurrent specialized training is necessary for the labor force to keep up with ever-increasing skill requirements and for individual workers to obtain job security. Thus career education will reduce the likelihood of individuals being prepared for dead-end jobs. It will also correct the higher unemployment rates among minorities and lower-class youth who are thought to lack useful skills.

The problem of "over-educated" youth differs from the problem of ill-trained youth in that most available jobs require less formal schooling than has generally been assumed. Many students are in college not because they need college skills to get a job but because they and their parents see college education as a measure

---

[10] Marland, pp. 19–20.
[11] For a similar argument see Panel on Youth of the President's Science Advisory Committee, *Youth: Transition to Adulthood* (Chicago: Univ. of Chicago Press, 1974).

of social and economic worth. These "over-educated" youth are unable to obtain jobs that use the skills college gives them; instead, relatively simple jobs come to have high educational requirements. Career educators assume that when students are aware of alternatives to college and can establish "realistic" goals through career-awareness programs, unnecessary college attendance will decrease.

In sum, because career education provides job-relevant training for specific careers and is therefore economically relevant, it eliminates the mismatch between training and jobs at every point in the educational system. Potential dropouts who view conventional schooling as irrelevant to their needs will be motivated to stay in school and learn the skills they need for employment. College-bound youth will revise their occupational goals so that continuation in school is clearly related to occupational aims. Finally, the problem of over-credentialing will disappear. Career educators claim that all of these changes will decrease unemployment.

Historical Continuities in Career Education

Career educators have gone to great lengths to dissociate career education from traditional vocational education. But the development of career education cannot be understood except in a historical context. Career education is in fact a continuation of older movements which were designed to emphasize the vocational aspects of schooling.[12] These movements, which date from the 1880's, resulted from pressures from outside and within the educational system.

Concern about economic productivity and social disorganization were paramount among the external pressures upon schools a hundred years ago. Beginning in the 1880's schools were attacked for being irrelevant to the economy, failing to teach the skills necessary for success in the new industrial order, and inhibiting national economic growth. Businessmen claimed that skilled labor was scarce, that workers were insufficiently flexible, efficient, and committed, and that America's future economic expansion depended on the development of its human rather than its natural resources. Simultaneously, the educational system was criticized for being unresponsive to the social consequences of rapid industrializa-

[12] For a fuller discussion of the issues presented here, see *American Education and Vocationalism: A Documentary History, 1870–1970*, ed. Marvin Lazerson and W. Norton Grubb (New York: Teachers College Press, 1974). See also Sol Cohen, "The Industrial Education Movement, 1906–1917," *American Quarterly*, 20 (1968), 95–110; Marvin Lazerson, *Origins of the Urban School* (Cambridge: Harvard Univ. Press, 1971); and David B. Tyack, *The One Best System* (Cambridge: Harvard Univ. Press, 1974).

tion and urbanization. Small workshops and the apprenticeship system were replaced by large factories and the specialization of labor. Workers were unable to comprehend the production process as a whole, since they were only exposed to a small part of it. Manual labor was devalued. Because of these changes, the argument went, a generally shiftless attitude toward work had set in. The other social institutions—family, church, and community—that had earlier been counted on to inculcate moral values had weakened as well. Finally, the influx into the cities of vast numbers of southern and eastern Europeans and rural southern Blacks exacerbated urban problems and ethnic, racial, and class conflict.

While calls for educational reform to increase economic productivity and to limit social decay came from outside the educational system, educators faced a different set of problems within the school system. Faced with an increasingly heterogeneous student body in the high schools, educators felt the need to reorganize schools in accordance with industrial efficiency models and to adapt the curriculum to fit the student. To many, the educational system seemed to be failing. The problem was most clearly indicated by high dropout rates, which critics viewed as evidence of the economic irrelevance of existing schools and as a threat to the ideal of equality of opportunity through education.

Within this context, the vocational education movement gathered support from businessmen, educators, social reformers, and labor. Its advocates argued that vocational education would produce a skilled labor force, contribute to further economic development, elevate manual labor to a higher status, and restore relevance to the schools. By teaching industry, discipline, submission to authority, respect for property rights, and acceptance of one's place in the industrial order, vocational education would combat social decay, industrial unrest, and alienation from work. Pupils would cease to drop out of school because vocational training would give them the skills they would need as adults in the labor market. Moreover, poverty would be eradicated. Finally, vocational education would provide a greater recognition of individual and group differences by reshaping the curriculum and pedagogy to fit the socioeconomic backgrounds, abilities, aspirations, and the "probable future of the child."[13]

Viewed in a broader social context, the introduction of vocationalism into the schools was part of a movement by the educational system to embrace the goals, structure, and methods of corporate capitalism. Increasingly, schools adopted the

---

[13] The quotation is from David Snedden, "Differences Among Varying Groups of Children Should Be Recognized," *Manual Training Magazine*, 10 (1908), 1–8. See also Edward A. Krug, *The Shaping of the American High School, 1880–1920* (New York: Harper, 1964), ch. 8.

structure of corporate firms: the division of labor and bureaucratization, the stress on greater efficiency and "production" through testing, ability grouping, and cost-effectiveness studies. The major impact of vocational education was therefore not the shift in curriculum; enrollment in vocational courses remained under 7 percent until the 1960's.[14] Rather, the impact was the transformation of the purposes and structure of the educational system, the reorientation of schooling toward vocational ends, and the reinforcement of racial, class, and sex biases in public education.

The structure of vocational education has remained largely unchanged since the passage of the 1917 Smith-Hughes Act, which provided federal funds for vocational training. Intervening legislation has increased the amount of funds available and introduced greater flexibility in the use of those funds. The Vocational Education Act of 1963 and subsequent amendments in 1968 have broadened the scope of vocationalism and have focused vocational training on the educationally and economically disadvantaged, as a means both to reduce technological unemployment and to integrate these groups into the occupational structure.[15]

These changes emerged in the wake of a general assessment that vocational education since the early part of the century had failed. Students never flocked to vocational education courses; they rarely found jobs in the area for which they had been trained, and many did not even stay in school long enough to complete their training. In terms of status, income, job mobility, unemployment, and job satisfaction, vocationally trained students did no better and often did worse than students in academic programs. Moreover, funds had been inflexibly allocated to areas of questionable need. In 1965, home economics and agriculture accounted for 55 percent of the vocational enrollment. Both fields had dubious futures: the former depended on a view that woman's place was in the home, the latter was an area that offered declining work opportunities.[16] The stigma of second-class status remained strong, although the addition of "general curriculum" programs in high schools added a stratum below vocational education.[17]

[14] See the data in Lazerson and Grubb, *American Education and Vocationalism*.

[15] On changes in the 1960's, see the Panel of Consultants on Vocational Education, *Education for a Changing World of Work* (Washington, D.C.: U.S. Government Printing Office, 1963), and the Advisory Council on Vocational Education, *Vocational Education: The Bridge Between Man and His Work* (Washington, D.C.: U.S. Government Printing Office, 1968).

[16] As late as 1972, 3.1 million of the 11.6 million students in vocational education were in consumer and homemaking programs. See Shirley McCune, "Vocational Education: A Dual System," *Inequality in Education*, 16 (1974), 26–34.

[17] See, for example, Advisory Council on Vocational Education, *Vocational Education;* David

The 1960's reforms, as well as today's career education proposals, were designed to correct these flaws, and some have interpreted the changes as significant redirections of vocational education. More striking than the changes, however, have been the continuities between the past and the present. First, the advocates of vocationalism have consistently attacked schools for separating the home from the world of work, the growing child from adults in work settings. From this view—which, though broadly correct, is overly romanticized—these advocates argue that children are unprepared to work when they reach adulthood, and that schools must put work back into the daily experience of the young.

A second theme tying traditional vocational education to career education is the assertion that schools have exacerbated the separation of manual skills from mental skills, reinforcing academic snobbery and creating feelings of inferiority among the "manually motivated." Social values that stress the superiority of one group over another are thus seen as rooted in the imbalance between academic and vocational learning that creates an oversupply of highly educated individuals. To correct these evils, schools must integrate manual work with academic learning.

A third continuity has been the belief that career education or vocationalism will solve economic crises. Early in this century the crises were the perceived shortage of skilled labor, the necessity for breaking the strength of unions, and the need to develop the country's human resources for economic expansion. During the 1960's and 1970's vocationalism and career education have each been seen as a way of combating technology-caused unemployment and underemployment. We will consider each of these themes below.

Advocates have also argued that both vocational training and career education will contribute to the resolution of America's social and moral problems, particularly by integrating groups threatening the tranquillity of society and the schools. Initially, the principal threats were European immigrants and rural Blacks who lacked "industrial discipline," the work habits and attitudes necessary for functioning in capitalist workplaces.[18] In the 1960's, the threatening groups were city-dwelling racial minorities. Career education had added as a target group those

---

Rogers, "Vocational and Career Education: A Critique and Some New Directions," *Teachers College Record,* 74 (1973), 471–511; and Beatrice Reubens, "Vocational Education for *All* in High School?" in *Work and the Quality of Life,* ed. James O'Toole (Cambridge: M.I.T. Press, 1975).

[18] On the integration of diverse groups historically into the industrial economy, see Herbert Gutman, "Work, Culture, and Society in Industrializing America, 1815–1919," *American Historical Review,* 78 (1973), 531–88.

"overeducated youth" who, because of their inability to find jobs commensurate with the skills and expectations they have acquired in college, threaten to be inept and disruptive workers.

There are, we should point out, some differences between the vocational education of the past and career education. The concern with middle class "overeducated" youth is new. Moreover, career education is considerably more ambiguous about the requirements of the workplace than the earlier vocational movement was. There also appears to be some movement within career education to enlarge available work roles for women. On balance, however, the assumptions of vocationalism have been consistent for more than half a century.

Criticisms directed against vocationalism have also been consistent. First, major evaluations of vocational programs have invariably noted their failures to resolve economic and educational problems, their lack of contact with labor market conditions, their preparation of students for jobs that do not exist, and their use of antiquated methods and equipment.[19] Testimony that employers prefer not to hire graduates from vocational programs and that such students are unable to obtain jobs in the areas for which they have been trained has consistently cast doubt on the economic value of vocational education. More recently, studies of the economic returns to vocational education have not found any economic advantages to vocational as opposed to non-vocational preparation at the high-school level.[20] Even in the narrowest economic terms, which have been its prime *raison d'être*, vocational education appears to have failed.

Second, vocational education has been charged with fostering a dual system of education, with lower-class and minority boys tracked into low-status vocational programs, lower-class and minority girls tracked into traditionally female occupations, and middle- and upper-middle-class students of both sexes placed in aca-

[19] The major evaluations of vocational education have been John Russell and Associates, *Vocational Education* (Washington, D.C.: U.S. Government Printing Office, 1935), the Panel of Consultants on Vocational Education (see note 15), and the Advisory Council on Vocational Education (see note 17). Curiously, all three of these reports, after criticizing vocational education for persistent failures, go on to reaffirm the importance of vocational education in solving economic and educational problems. See also General Accounting Office, *What is the Role of Federal Assistance for Vocational Education?* (Washington, D.C.: U.S. Government Printing Office, 1974).

[20] The most thorough review of this literature is that of Beatrice Reubens. Other useful reviews can be found in Jacob Kaufman, "The Role of Vocational Education in the Transition from School to Work," in *Public-Private Manpower Policies*, ed. Arnold Weber, Frank Cassell, and Woodrow Ginsberg (Madison: Industrial Relations Research Association, 1969); Kenneth J. Little, *Review and Synthesis of Research on the Placement and Follow-Up of Vocational Education Students* (Columbus: Center for Vocational and Technical Education, 1970); and Garth Mangum, *Reorienting Vocational Education* (Ann Arbor: Institute of Labor and Industrial Relations, 1968).

demic programs. The charge is even broader, since vocationalism fostered a form of curriculum differentiation that led to ability grouping, testing, and guidance counseling. These practices have fostered class and racial segregation within the schools that is unrelated to the vocational/academic split. Despite pleas by career educators that such segregation will be overcome, there is little evidence that those most discriminated against because of racial and class background will not still be channeled into career programs of relatively low status which offer dismal prospects for the future.

Finally, the problems that vocationalism has claimed to be able to solve—school dropouts, the lower status accorded "manual" as opposed to "mental" work, unemployment and underemployment, poverty, alienation—remain as troublesome as ever.

It seems unlikely that career education will be more effective in resolving these issues today than vocational education has been in the past, especially since career education has little to say about the actual roots of current social problems. The persistent failures of vocational education, in light of the continuities between the "new" and "old" vocational education movements, are sufficient to cast doubt on the claims made for career education.

Current Sources of Support for Career Education

The historical continuities reveal the roots of career education in the recurrent drive toward vocationalism during the twentieth century. It is also necessary, however, to look at the specific context of the late 1960's and early 1970's, because the immediate sources of support for career education are the trends and frustrations that have emerged in the last decade. In particular, the failure of liberal social and educational reform policies, the dilemmas posed by large numbers of youth whose economic and political roles have become a source of controversy, and the growing sense of crisis about work in America have stimulated support for career education and for a number of closely related educational reform proposals.

Attempts to reform the schools have always been prominent during periods of social stress.[21] But rarely have the attacks on schooling been as vitriolic as they were in the Sixties, and never before had criticism from the Left received so much attention. Critics complained that schools deadened the spirit, lacked creativity,

---

[21] See Michael B. Katz, *The Irony of Early School Reform* (Cambridge: Harvard Univ. Press, 1968), and Tyack, *The One Best System*.

and left students illiterate.[22] These conditions touched everyone, but the worst served were the poor and nonwhite, who were segregated and systematically deprived of dignity as well as chances for future success.[23] The swell of criticism led to a series of proposals that promised to redistribute power and resources within the existing school system, such as community control or compensatory education, or that promised to shift control over schooling from school systems to students and parents, such as alternative schools or deschooling.[24]

The desire to reform schooling was partly motivated by the same concerns that stimulated the manpower and community action programs of the Great Society. But the actual reforms became less credible as the Sixties wore on. The manpower programs were increasingly criticized as ineffective and then abandoned.[25] Moreover, a succession of studies argued that school resources were ineffective in producing cognitive skills and could not be used to equalize the life chances of the poor and the prosperous.[26] Others argued that schooling had become a credential with little relevance to individual or national productivity.[27]

---

[22] See, for example, Paul Goodman, *Compulsory Mis-education and the Community of Scholars* (New York: Vintage, 1964); Edgar Friedenberg, *Coming of Age in America* (New York: Vintage, 1963); and Charles E. Silberman, *Crisis in the Classroom* (New York: Vintage, 1971).

[23] See, for example, Herbert Kohl, *36 Children* (New York: New American Library, 1967), and Jonathan Kozol, *Death at an Early Age* (Boston: Houghton Mifflin, 1967). See also the reports cited above on the failure of vocational education to reach disadvantaged children.

[24] The literature on this subject is vast; see, for example, Marilyn Gittel, *Participants and Participation* (New York: Praeger, 1967); Leonard Fein, *The Ecology of the Public Schools* (New York: Pegasus, 1971); Allen Graubard, *Free the Children* (New York: Pantheon, 1972); John Bremer and Michael von Moschzisker, *The School Without Walls* (New York: Holt, Rinehart, 1971); and Center for the Study of Public Policy, *Education Vouchers* (Cambridge, Mass.: Center for the Study of Public Policy, 1970).

[25] Sar Levitan, *The Great Society's Poor Law* (Baltimore: Johns Hopkins Univ. Press, 1969); Peter Marris and Martin Rein, *Dilemmas of Social Reform* (Chicago: Aldine, 1967).

[26] This line of argument was begun by James S. Coleman, Ernest Q. Campbell, Carol J. Hobson, James McPartland, Alexander M. Mood, Frederic D. Weinfeld and Robert L. York, *Equality of Educational Opportunity* (Washington: D.C.: Office of Education, U.S. Dept. of Health, Education and Welfare, 1966). For a summary of the literature, see Harvey A. Averch, Stephen J. Carroll, Theodore S. Donaldson, Herbert J. Kiesling, and John Pincus, *How Effective is Schooling? A Critical Review and Synthesis of Research Findings* (Englewood Cliffs, N.J.: Educational Technology Publications, 1974). See also the controversial work of Christopher Jencks, Marshall Smith, Henry Acland, Mary Jo Bane, David Cohen, Herbert Gintis, Barbara Heyns, and Stephen Michelson, *Inequality: A Reassessment of the Effects of Family and Schooling in America* (New York: Basic Books, 1972). Radical commentators have pointed out that the educational reforms of the Sixties were at best liberal palliatives and served to divert attention from more radical reforms of the underlying economic system. See especially Samuel Bowles and Herbert Gintis, *Schooling in Capitalist America: Educational Reform and the Contradictions of Economic Life* (New York: Basic Books, 1976).

[27] The interest in credentialing was started by Ivar Berg in *Education and Jobs* (New York:

This reevaluation of schools' efficacy undercut the possibility of further liberal reforms. Since more radical proposals have been politically untenable, the only avenues for reform efforts—at a time when schools continue to be under attack from many quarters—have been essentially conservative ones.

The crises of the schools have been exacerbated by a demographic peculiarity. The baby boom after World War II inflated the numbers of youth during the 1960's. In response to demand for more schooling by an increasingly competitive labor market, and perhaps in response to the Vietnam draft, young people stayed in school rather than start work.[28] Their average increase in educational attainment led to a number of other problems. First, an exacerbation of credentialing made higher levels of education necessary to get decreasingly interesting jobs. Second, with the prolongation of their dependent status, young people found the transition to adult responsibility more and more problematic.[29] Finally, as increased schooling generated students' expectations of more independent, intrinsically interesting work than could be provided by the available jobs, dissatisfaction grew.[30]

However, dissatisfaction with work extended beyond the over-educated and under-motivated. The "discovery" of widespread and increasing worker discontent in the early 1970's indicated a problem that was critical not only in itself, but also in its economic effect. A decline in productivity worsened the United States' international competitiveness and the inflation-unemployment trade-off. Moreover, there was fear of labor unrest, caused this time not by wage demands, but by conflict over the nature of work and control over the work process.

While career education represents a continuation of earlier vocational movements, it arose partly as a response to these specific complaints. The proposals of career educators also resemble several proposals from a variety of other sources. The National Commission on the Reform of Secondary Education, the Panel on Youth of the President's Science Advisory Committee, and such radical critics of the schools as Ivan Illich have all concluded that direct work experiences are necessary to integrate school and work and have reaffirmed vocationalism as a central goal of the educational system.[31] Even the authors of *Work in America*, having

---

Praeger, 1970). See also the essays in Margaret Gordon, ed., *Higher Education and the Labor Market* (New York: McGraw-Hill, 1974).

[28] Norman Ryder, "The Demography of Youth," in *Youth: Transition to Adulthood*, Panel on Youth (Chicago: Univ. of Chicago Press, 1974).

[29] This is the main point of the Panel on Youth's *Youth: Transition to Adulthood*.

[30] Samuel Bowles, "Contradictions in U.S. Higher Education," in *Modern Political Economy: Radical v. Orthodox Approaches,* ed. James H. Weaver (Boston: Allyn and Bacon, 1972).

[31] National Commission on the Reform of Secondary Education, *The Reform of Secondary Educa-*

documented the adverse effects of work as it is currently structured, recommend that schools simulate work environments and expand continuing education programs so as to draw work and education closer together.[32] Simmering just below the surface of these proposals, as well as those of career educators, are fears that the United States is prone to racial, student, and worker unrest and that, if more effective socialization measures are not undertaken, dissatisfaction with school and work may lead to a recurrence of the conflicts of the 1960's. Career education is thus not an isolated response; its assumptions about work and school have been widely accepted, and its proposals have been independently corroborated.

The Nature of Work Under Advanced Capitalism

Career education is not directed toward changing the occupational and economic structure. Instead, it takes that structure and the nature of jobs as given, and tries to match potential workers to jobs. For career education to achieve its goals, its assumptions about the nature of work must be accurate. To the extent that these assumptions are inaccurate, we can expect career education to replicate the historical weaknesses of vocational education.

Career educators are right in assuming that work is a critical activity, in the sense that it is central to individual self-definition; we are not yet such an affluent society that leisure has become our primary occupation.[33] But while most people value work in the abstract, career educators have ignored mounting evidence that the particular jobs available in advanced capitalist economies lack the moral qualities attributed to work generally.[34] In fact, most work is boring. Its

---

tion (New York: McGraw-Hill, 1973); Panel on Youth, *Youth: Transition to Adulthood;* Ivan Illich, *Deschooling Society* (New York: Harper, 1971). For a more complete analysis of the Panel on Youth report, critical as we are of its assumptions about work, see William H. Behn, Martin Carnoy, Michael A. Carter, Joyce C. Crain, and Henry M. Levin, "School is Bad; Work is Worse," *School Review*, 83 (1974), 49–68. For an analysis of why Illich is not the radical reformer he appears to some to be, see Herbert Gintis, "Towards a Political Economy of Education," *Harvard Educational Review*, 42 (1972), 70–97.

32 *Work in America* (Cambridge: M.I.T. Press, 1973), ch. 5. See also James O'Toole, "The Reserve Army of the Underemployed."

33 For a summary of the importance of work, see *Work in America*, ch. 1. Some career educators recognize the possibility that work may become less important relative to leisure activities. In this case, the purpose of career education would be to prepare individuals to spend their leisure time creatively; see Marland, pp. 41–42. This, however, conflicts with the thrust toward job preparation, and illustrates the general uncertainty over the adult roles career education should anticipate.

34 For the most thorough documentation on this point, see *Work in America* and some of the papers prepared for that volume, collected in O'Toole, *Work and the Quality of Life*. See also Harold L. Sheppard and Neal Q. Herrick, *Where Have All the Robots Gone?* (New York: Free

unvaried routine, the simplicity of most tasks, and the constant supervision characteristic of hierarchical settings all deny workers a sense of competence and a feeling of responsibility. Because their roles in the production process are so small and the products they produce are so often superfluous and trivial, workers have little sense of accomplishment. They are denied a sense of connectedness with their fellow workers and the rest of the economy because they are systematically isolated from one another and because personal relations are mediated by impersonal market relationships. Hence, the faith that the moral benefits of work can counteract a sense of individual aimlessness or a lack of attachment to social institutions is seriously misplaced.[35] In fact, given the negative aspects of most jobs, the introduction of "real work" in the schools might have just the opposite effect from that intended: feelings of alienation, anomie, and disconnectedness, or physical manifestations such as hypertension, high blood pressure, and poor mental health might begin earlier.

There is, in addition no reason to suspect that working conditions are improving or that levels of job dissatisfaction will decrease. The central drive in capitalist development is the accumulation and concentration of capital, which under corporate capitalism comes to be held and managed by corporate firms rather than by individual entrepreneurs. The production process is carried out by workers who have little stake in production other than their wages. In fact, contrary to the desires of capitalists and managers, workers have every incentive to work as little as possible.[36] Production managers are largely concerned with the pace of work and the introduction of new procedures and technical processes, all in the interests of profits and capital accumulation. Following principles of "scientific management," managers break jobs down into their smallest components, assigning each component to a different worker. This fragmentation of tasks has two effects from the standpoint of management: since workers no longer have knowledge of the whole production process, they are increasingly dependent on managers to be told what to do, and since workers trained in all aspects of production are paid more highly than those who are not, replacement of the former by the latter reduces labor costs.

Press, 1972); Judson Gooding, *The Job Revolution* (New York: Walker, 1972); Studs Terkel, *Working* (New York: Random House, 1972); and Richard Sennett and Jonathan Cobb, *The Hidden Injuries of Class* (New York: Knopf, 1972).

[35] For evidence that even advancement in the occupational structure often fails to eliminate these feelings, see Sennett and Cobb.

[36] For a graphic description of the constant battle between workers and managers over the amount of work performed, see William Foote Whyte and Melville Dalton, *Money and Motivation* (New York: Harper, 1955).

While this practice may be efficient by capitalist criteria—that is, it may result in the greatest profit because of increased control and lower labor costs—the implications for workers themselves are devastating. Jobs become increasingly repetitious, and require little competence. As a consequence, they become uninteresting, unfulfilling, wasteful of human capacities, and conducive to physical and mental health problems.[37]

The degradation of work has been continuous. In the middle and late nineteenth century, the use of machinery led to the replacement of skilled craftsmen by semi-skilled operatives and a small number of skilled machinists and mechanics. Early in this century, the introduction of scientific management and the assembly line further divided and routinized jobs. A similar division of labor has affected white-collar work.[38] There is no indication that this process has stopped. While the conventional wisdom holds that automation increases the skill levels required by the mass of workers, in fact it either decreases the skills required by most workers, by concentrating skill and expertise in the hands of a small number of employees and degrading other jobs, or replaces one set of low-skill jobs with others of equally low requirements.[39]

Recognizing these trends is important since they fly in the face of basic post-World War II economic and social policies that presumed the United States was moving from a production-of-goods economy based on physical labor to a distribu-

[37] For an expanded analysis, see Harry Braverman, *Labor and Monopoly Capital* (New York: Monthly Review Press, 1974); see also Stephen Marglin, "What Do Bosses Do? The Origins and Functions of Hierarchy in Capitalist Production," *Review of Radical Political Economics*, 6 (1974), 60–112. For a general discussion of underemployment see O'Toole, "The Reserve Army of the Underemployed." There are, of course, a small number of jobs with high skill levels and greater worker discretion. But since the process of capitalist development is incessant in its search for ways to increase control and cut costs, even these jobs are themselves subject to division and degradation. For example, many jobs that have been performed by highly trained engineers are now being performed by computers, replacing engineers with unskilled technicians and a smaller number of high-level programmers (see Braverman, ch. 10).

[38] Braverman, ch. 15.

[39] James Bright, "The Relationship of Increasing Automation and Skill Requirements," in *The Employment Impact of Technological Change*, National Commission on Technology, Automation, and Economic Progress (Washington, D.C.: U.S. Government Printing Office, 1966). He presents evidence that skills on the average decrease as automation increases. An example is the development of computer-aided machines (numerical control techniques) to eliminate machinists and other skilled workers; see Braverman, ch. 9. In another paper in the same volume, "Changes in Skill Requirements of Occupations in Selected Industries," Morris Horowitz and Irwin Herrnstadt conclude, on the basis of a literature review and an analysis of five industries, that overall skill levels have on the whole neither increased nor decreased over a period of fifteen years of automation. See also Charles E. Silberman, *The Myths of Automation* (New York: Harper, 1966) for anecdotal evidence on the lack of skill increases necessitated by automation.

tion-of-services economy based on mental abilities. Incorporated into that premise were the beliefs that white-collar jobs would replace blue-collar jobs, with a subsequent increase in worker satisfaction; that automation would soon reduce the number of unskilled and semiskilled jobs to insignificance; that economic productivity was most effectively enhanced by advanced schooling; and that leisure would soon become a major preoccupation of the American worker. Many of these beliefs have now been challenged. While there has been a decline in the proportion of unskilled workers, most jobs remain (and will remain) dull and uncreative. Complex jobs are frequently broken down into routine work requiring limited skills. Most white-collar workers shuffle papers in routine fashion. Service work, the area of most rapid growth, amounts to little more than cleaning up after others, often without the benefits of union protection, decent salaries, or security. Service workers account for over 20 percent of the work force; nearly 30 percent of them earn less than $4,000 annually. Finally, the expected "leisure revolution" has not occurred. Where time has become available, many workers have sought second jobs. In short, as Levitan and Johnston conclude, "the evolution of the postindustrial economy has clearly not resulted in a 'quality of work revolution.' . . . Millions of dull factory jobs remain, and millions of equally dull office jobs have been lately added to the job market."[40]

One of the major assumptions of career education is thus correct: Raising a person's level is not necessary for him or her to keep pace with automation and the increasing technical sophistication of work. Such training wastes time and resources, and gives students the false expectation that jobs will utilize their skills. But while acknowledging that extended education is unnecessary for most jobs, career educators paradoxically claim that the skills jobs require are too complicated to learn on the job without the intervention of schooling. Yet skills for most occupations are learned relatively easily and quickly.[41]

More disturbing is the false hope that career education will enhance worker mobility. The fragmentation of work roles under capitalism creates a large number of low-skill jobs and a small number of high-skill jobs. As increasing amounts of control and responsibility are vested in a small group of engineers, managers, and professionals, and as the formal requirements for entry into these occupa-

[40] Sar Levitan and William Johnston, *Work is Here to Stay, Alas* (Salt Lake City: Olympus, 1973), p. 109; see also O'Toole and Braverman.

[41] For schooling and training requirements by industry and by occupation, see Richard Echaus, "Economic Criteria for Education and Training," *Review of Economics and Statistics*, 46 (1964), 181–89; and James Scoville, "Education and Training Requirements for Occupations," *Review of Economics and Statistics*, 48 (1966), 387–94.

tions become more rigid, the ability of workers to move up a progression of jobs is reduced. Career ladders are, for most workers, rather short; most mobility is instead horizontal to different jobs that require about the same level of skill and responsibility.[42]

Whether career ladders are becoming even shorter is unclear, but the phenomenon of the secondary labor market reveals that many jobs do not have larger opportunities built into them. These jobs tend to be poorly paid, with bad working conditions, capricious supervision, and short or non-existent job ladders; as a consequence, turnover is high. Such jobs are found disproportionately in those occupations and sectors that are growing rapidly, especially clerical and sales occupations and the service sector. In addition, there is a widespread conversion of primary sector jobs into secondary jobs, and this further reduces the possibilities of job mobility.[43] Finally, as James O'Toole has noted, many new jobs or "new careers" that appear to have upward mobility possibilities—health paraprofessionals, teachers' aides, and technicians with two-year degrees are prime examples—in fact do not contain career ladders. It is also useful to note that the seven largest expanding occupational groups are secretaries, retail sales clerks, pre-college teachers, restaurant workers, drivers and deliverymen, bookkeepers and cashiers, and cleaning workers. These account for almost twenty million workers, most of whom are in rapidly changing occupations that are unchallenging and allow for little flexibility or creativity.[44]

It is foolish to make claims for the efficacy of schooling programs without acknowledging the structure of labor demand. Since relatively few jobs are arranged in career ladders of any length, the declaration that career education will prepare all individuals for careers rather than dead-end jobs is based on a misconception of the world of work. Rather than prepare an individual for the highest posi-

[42] On horizontal mobility in the automobile industry, see Ely Chinoy, *Automobile Workers and the American Dream* (Boston: Beacon, 1955). There are few longitudinal data on intra-occupational mobility. For a non-longitudinal study, see Peter Blau and Otis Duncan. *The American Occupational Structure* (New York: Wiley, 1967).

[43] On the secondary labor market generally, see Peter Doeringer and Michael Piore, *Internal Labor Markets and Manpower Analysis* (Lexington, Mass.: Heath, 1971); Michael Piore, "On-the-Job Training of Disadvantaged Workers," in *Public-Private Manpower Policies*, ed., Arnold Weber, Frank Cassell, and Woodrow Ginsberg (Madison: Industrial Relations Research Association, 1969); Michael Piore, "Notes for a Theory of Labor Market Stratification," Working Paper No. 95, Dept. of Economics, M.I.T, Oct. 1972; David Gordon, "From Steam Whistles to Coffee Breaks," *Dissent* (1972), 197–210; and David Gordon, *Theories of Poverty and Underemployment* (Lexington, Mass.; Heath, 1972).

[44] See O'Toole, "The Reserve Army of the Underemployed," and Levitan and Johnson, *Work is Here to Stay, Alas.*

tions on the occupational ladder, the kinds of courses and clusters offered in career education are designed explicitly to prepare students for entry-level jobs. As long as jobs themselves are arranged in short ladders and the route to occupations of greater responsibility and status lies only through increased formal schooling, the claim that career education will prepare individuals for a progression of jobs is hollow.

Career educators are prone to a similar misunderstanding of the economy. The notion that unemployment is due to the mismatch of workers and jobs, and can therefore be cured by training workers for those jobs which do exist, ignores the fact that the employment level is dependent on the overall health of the economy.[45] "Normal" unemployment—the level that is politically tolerable—was between 3 percent and 4 percent during the 1950's, and rose to about 5 or 6 percent in the late 1960's. At the present time, with unemployment hitting a nationwide high of 9.2 percent in June 1975, "normal" unemployment appears to be between 6 and 8 percent.[46] Here, as before, career educators have misunderstood the nature of the labor market, and as a result their claims that career education can reduce unemployment are seriously inflated.

The same misperception about the nature of the demand for labor underlies the views of career educators toward dropouts. For some groups within the population, notably minority and lower-class youth, leaving school is economically rational because the monetary returns to additional years of secondary school are low or non-existent.[47] Schools are in fact not meeting the economic needs of these

[45] See Rogers, "Vocational and Career Education." For a similar point with respect to manpower training see Garth Mangum, *MDTA: Foundation of Federal Manpower Policy* (Baltimore: Johns Hopkins Univ. Press, 1968). The ability of career educators to match workers to jobs is in any event doubtful; the ability of vocational educational graduates to find jobs in areas they have been trained in has been dismal, as Beatrice Reubens in "Vocational Education for *All* in High School?" has documented. Even in the $21.5 million school in Dallas that Marland describes as a model for career education, the planners seriously miscalculated the demand for different clusters.

[46] The rise in acceptable levels of unemployment bears no relation to the mix of skills available in the labor force for two reasons: education and training levels have continuously increased during this period, and the period of time is long enough so that imbalances between the composition of demand and supply for labor would have been corrected. There are, of course, cycles of shortages in specific occupations followed by surpluses due to over-reaction; these have occurred most spectacularly and visibly with engineers, teachers, and Ph.D.'s. But the contribution to the overall unemployment rate due to such surpluses is trivial and short-lived; adjustments to imbalances of supply and demand in most occupations are rather swift, even in occupations which require lengthy training cycles. See Richard Freeman, *The Market for College Trained Manpower* (Cambridge: Harvard Univ. Press, 1971).

[47] See, for example, Barbara Bergman and Gerolyn Lyle, "The Occupational Standing of Negroes by Area and Industry," *Journal of Human Resources*, 6 (1971), 44–55; Bennet Harrison, "Educa-

groups. However, the view that career education can lead to employment always assumes that the cause of unemployment is a mismatch between the skills that available jobs require and the skills that schools provide. But if the demand for labor is insufficient, discrimination is serious, and the worst jobs demand little skill—as is the case—then some groups will always be unemployed and underemployed, and additional skill training will serve no purpose.[48]

The surfeit of "over-educated" students is a separate but related problem. Career educators ascribe it to an erroneous but widespread "myth": that only a college education can prepare an individual for a satisfying future. Students thus plunge blindly on to college without plans or goals; the result is a surplus of college-educated youth that is likely to increase.[49] Career educators assume that bringing students into contact with the world of work and giving them "realistic" aspirations will blunt students' drives to college. Career educators presume that the crisis of credentialing is largely due to students' irrational perceptions of and competition for the rewards of college. But such a view fails to recognize that the conditions underlying over-credentialing may not be wholly irrational. Given an occupational structure with relatively few jobs at the top, and with all social goods—income, status, control over work, job satisfaction—allocated disproportionately to those top jobs, it is rational for individuals to do whatever they can to obtain those jobs. Of course, the rational attempts of individuals to increase their education levels result in an excess of years in school and a concomitant devaluation of credentials. Only three kinds of changes can reverse this trend: the reallocation of social goods to jobs with lower training requirements, which would necessitate a radical transformation of the economy; a willingness on the part of employers to ignore educational attainments in selecting employees; and a refusal on the part of educational institutions to accede to demands for increased schooling. The first two of these are beyond the power of the schools themselves. The

---

tion and Underemployment in the Urban Ghetto," *American Economic Review*, 62 (1972), 796–812; Stephan Michelson, "Incomes of Racial Minorities" (unpublished paper, Brookings Institution, 1968); Bradley Schiller, "Class Discrimination versus Racial Discrimination," *Review of Economics and Statistics*, 53 (1971), 263–69; Randall Weiss, "The Effect of Education on the Earnings of Blacks and Whites," *Review of Economics and Statistics*, 52 (1970), 150–59; and Geoffrey Carliner, *Returns to Education for Blacks, Anglos, and Five Spanish Groups*, Working Paper No. 250, Institute for Research on Poverty, Univ. of Wisconsin, 1975.

[48] For a theory of job competition see Lester Thurow, "Education and Economic Inequality," *The Public Interest*, 28 (1972), 66–81.

[49] The most frequently cited projection is that, by 1980, only 20 percent of jobs will require a college degree, but 52 percent of high-school graduates are continuing to college. See O'Toole, "The Reserve Army of the Underemployed."

third is within their power, but is unlikely in the face of the political and economic pressures students can bring to bear.

The assumptions of career educators about the nature of work and the demand for labor are largely a myth. The world they posit, in which career education can make all work satisfying and all training useful, is a world we would no doubt prefer to the one we inhabit. But in constructing this Utopia, career education simply reflects the more general dilemma of schooling. Capitalism is an economic system in which capital is central. As part of a drive for profits and the accumulation of capital, managers in an economic system like ours endlessly divide, simplify, and eliminate jobs. This results in an increase in unemployment and a constant status of underemployment for most workers. The economic system values capital resources at the expense of human resources. Yet the schooling system is charged with the development of human resources, and thus its central purpose is in sad contradiction to that of the economic system it serves.[50]

Conclusions

Many of career education's criticisms of school and work are well-taken. Schools are not especially pleasant places, and "general" education programs in particular are dumping grounds which should be abolished. The educational requirements for jobs have been artificially inflated, and access to jobs has become an increasingly rigid process. There is substantial dissatisfaction with work, though in an economic recession simply having a job becomes paramount.

But career education has little to offer in resolving these problems. Despite its assertions to the contrary, it is primarily a renewal and expansion of vocational

[50] It is possible to conceive of a system in which work and school are integrated. In China, for example, students produce goods that are sold in stores or used to produce other goods as part of their normal course of studies. But there is a logic to the integration that does not hold for the United States. The production of goods and food is meaningful in a society that has only recently emerged from widespread poverty. In contrast, while there are unmet needs in the United States, goods produced in the American private sector are often superfluous, trivial, or dangerous, and are produced for the profit of the few. In addition, worker participation in decision making appears widespread in China and the distribution of social goods relatively egalitarian. A strong sense of community and purpose also serves to animate work among the Chinese people. Few of these conditions hold for the United State where almost all jobs are motivated by external reward—primarily wages, and secondarily status and power. See Committee on Concerned Asian Scholars, *China! Inside the People's Republic* (New York: Bantam, 1972); Jan Myrdal, *Report from a Chinese Village* (New York: Pantheon, 1965); and a film made by Betty McAfee of a Peking elementary school during an American Federation of Teachers-sponsored visit to China in 1973.

education, a movement that has previously proven itself ineffective in reducing the gap between rich and poor, in enhancing school learning, in solving social and economic problems, and in improving the status of physical work. Career education's view of the moral benefits of work is incongruent with the nature of most jobs or the logic of corporate capitalism. Its presumption of training for career ladders with substantial upward mobility is largely fraudulent, given the present job structure. Finally, its argument that unemployment, underemployment, and worker dissatisfaction are largely due to a mismatch between job requirements and worker skills and expectations blames the victims for crimes committed by the economic structure.

Career education is not directed at resolving social problems, developing avenues of upward mobility, or making school and work more satisfying experiences. It is aimed instead at reducing expectations, limiting aspirations, and increasing commitments to the existing social structure. The replacement of hazy educational goals with "realistic" vocational goals, while appearing benevolent, actually strengthens the "cooling-out" function of schooling.[51] College graduates are less satisfied, less controllable, and less productive in menial jobs than workers without higher education,[52] and there are few non-menial jobs. Career education attempts to attenuate this dysfunction by bringing aspirations in line with the availability of high-skill jobs, by replacing high aspirations with lower ones, and by preparing students in ways that make continuation to higher education more difficult.

We thus conclude that career educators have a mistaken sense of priorities. We do not believe that the rebellions of the 1960's were largely due to overexpectations or to ineffective socialization. Rather, they were responses to substantive social issues: inequalities in the economic structure, racism, and a corrupt war. Career education ignores the substance of these issues. Accepting the economic system as just, it seeks to make people satisfied with their roles in a society that distributes social goods inequitably. It stresses the importance of increasing productivity without asking what is being produced and toward what ends. It claims that American society does not need all the "intellectual and developed

---

[51] For a description of the "cooling-out" function, see Burton R. Clark, "The 'Cooling-Out' Function in Higher Education," *American Journal of Sociology*, 45 (1960), 569–76; and Jerome Karabel, "Community Colleges and Social Stratification."

[52] For evidence that over-qualified workers are the worst in terms of output measures, see Lynn Rigby, *The Nature of Human Error* (Albuquerque: Sandia Laboratories, 1970) and Berg, *Education and Jobs*. On the general theme of the dysfunction of higher education for most jobs, see Bowles, "Contradictions in U.S. Higher Education."

capacities of its citizens in the work force"[53] without asking whether such a waste of capabilities makes sense. But Americans have a right to demand an equitable distribution of goods and a sharing of power and, if all jobs cannot be made interesting, to have compensatory monetary and social rewards. These alternatives belong to a very different world from the one career education proposes for us.

[53] Marland, *Career Education*, p. 41.

Notes on Contributors

MARSHA D. BROWN is Assistant Professor in the Graduate School of Public Affairs at the University of Washington, Seattle. She is a doctoral candidate at Harvard University, Graduate School of Education. Her current research interests include sex differences in family-background and high-school effects on educational outcomes and the effects of home background and college environment on women's career aspirations.

RANDALL COLLINS, formerly Associate Professor of Sociology at the University of California, San Diego, is now engaged in private research and writing. His present areas of interest are educational credentialism as a form of social stratification and sociology of science from an historical-comparative perspective. He authored *Conflict Sociology* (1975) and *The Discovery of Society* (2d ed. 1978).

PAUL J. DIMAGGIO is a tutor and a doctoral candidate in sociology at Harvard University and an associate project director at the Center for the Study of Public Policy, Cambridge. A former co-chairperson of the *Harvard Educational Review*, he was written on education, culture, and the arts for *Theory and Society, Social Forces, Working Papers for a New Society,* and other scholarly journals.

FREDERICK ERICKSON, Associate Professor of Education, Harvard University, is interested in the study of education from the perspective of anthropology. His research interests lie in developing methods of qualitative field research, especially for sociolinguistics and the ethnographic study of verbal and nonverbal communication. During 1976-77 he was president of the Council on Anthropology and Education. He is co-author of *Talking to the Man: The Social and Cultural Organization of Communication in School Counseling Interviews* (in press).

W. NORTON GRUBB is a research economist with the Childhood and Government Project at the University of California, Berkeley. His research concerns the past and current relations among the family, the state, and the economic system. He is principal author of a forthcoming book, tentatively titled *Wednesday's Child: Bearing the Costs of Post-War America,* on children and the various institutions of social reproduction including the family.

CHRISTOPHER S. JENCKS is Professor of Sociology at Harvard University and an editor of *Working Papers for a New Society*. Principal author of *Inequality* (1972), his current research concerns the educational and family determinants of economic success.

JEROME KARABEL is a Research Associate at the Huron Institute, Cambridge, and at the Center for European Studies, Harvard University. Co-editor of *Power and Ideology in Education* (1977), he is preparing a book on class and politics in American higher education.

THOMAS J. LABELLE is Assistant Dean and Associate Professor at the Graduate School of Education, University of California, Los Angeles. He has edited *Education and Development* (1972) and *Educational Alternatives in Latin America* (1975) and has authored *The New Professional in Venezuelan Secondary Education* (1973) and *Nonformal Education and Social Change in Latin America* (1976).

MARVIN LAZERSON is Professor of Education at the University of British Columbia. Author of *Origins of the Urban School* (1971), he has co-edited *American Education and Vocationalism* (1974) with W. Norton Grubb and co-authored "Government Financing, Child Care, and the Schools," *School Review*, November 1977. A consultant with the Childhood and Government Project at the University of California, Berkeley, he is working with Grubb on a study of the history of the family and its relationship to state institutions.

ROBERT E. VERHINE is a doctoral student in the School of Education, University of California, Los Angeles, and Visiting Professor at the Federal University of Bahia, Brazil. He is conducting dissertation research on the relationship between nonformal education and occupational attainment of industrial workers in Brazil. He is co-author with Thomas J. LaBelle of "Education, Social Change, and Social Stratification," in *Educational Alternatives in Latin America* (1975), ed. Thomas J. LaBelle.

EDUCATION, PARTICIPATION, AND POWER: ESSAYS IN THEORY AND PRACTICE

Fundamental to these essays is what Paulo Freire calls an "option for man" — a stance which calls for teachers and students alike to become conscious agents in a dynamic, mutual process of action and reflection. These articles represent practical experiences which demonstrate that men and women can choose a hopeful future.

ROBERT RIORDAN, Introduction

HERBERT GINTIS
Toward a Political Economy of Education: A Radical Critique of Ivan Illich's *Deschooling Society*

DENIS GOULET
An Ethical Model for the Study of Values

CENTER FOR NEW SCHOOLS
Strengthening Alternative High Schools

FRANK ADAMS
Highlander Folk School: Getting Information, Going Back and Teaching It

AN INTERVIEW WITH ARTHUR E. THOMAS
Community Power and Student Rights

Harvard Educational Review
Longfellow Hall, 13 Appian Way,
Cambridge, Massachusetts 02138

Reprint No. 10
$3.95

SCHOOL DESEGREGATION:
The Continuing Challenge

Including, together for the first time

— "School Desegregation in Large Cities: A Critique of the Coleman 'White Flight' Thesis" by Thomas F. Pettigrew and Robert L. Green

— "Response to Professors Pettigrew and Green" by James S. Coleman

— "Reply to Professor Coleman" by Thomas F. Pettigrew and Robert L. Green

— "Not One Judge's Opinion: *Morgan v. Hennigan* and the Boston Schools" by Roger I. Abrams

— "Winson and Dovie Hudson's Dream" by Marian Wright Edelman

— "Busing for Racial Balance," a statement by the Editors.

In the fall of 1974, as national guardsmen and tactical police lined the streets around Boston's high schools, the editorial board of the **Harvard Educational Review,** in an editors' statement, committed itself to consider carefully the issues surrounding the controversy over school desegregation and to publish articles on that topic.

This reprint documents the journal's efforts to fulfill that commitment. Containing some of the most informative and significant writing yet published on the complex subject of school desegregation, it will be useful to interested citizens, policy makers, journalists, and teachers of courses in race relations, the sociology of education, and educational politics.

HARVARD EDUCATIONAL REVIEW
Longfellow Hall, 13 Appian Way
Cambridge, Massachusetts 02138

Reprint No. 11
$3.50